THE WORKING CLASS IN AMERICAN HISTORY

Editorial Advisors

David Brody
Herbert G. Gutman
David Montgomery

THE MECHANICS OF BALTIMORE

THE MECHANICS
OF BALTIMORE

WORKERS AND POLITICS
IN THE AGE OF REVOLUTION
1763–1812

CHARLES G. STEFFEN

UNIVERSITY OF ILLINOIS PRESS
URBANA AND CHICAGO

Publication of this work was supported in part
by a grant from the Andrew W. Mellon Foundation.

Library of Congress Cataloging in Publication Data

Steffen, Charles G. 1952—
The mechanics of Baltimore.

(The Working class in American history)
Includes index.
1. Skilled labor—Maryland—Baltimore—Political
activity—History. 2. Labor and laboring classes—
Maryland—Baltimore—Political activity—History.
3. Baltimore (Md.)—Politics and government.
I. Title. II. Series.
HD8079.B2S73   1984   322'.2'097526   83-6891
ISBN 0-252-01088-4

to my parents

ACKNOWLEDGMENTS

Many people helped me to write this book. Craig Buettinger, Josef Barton, Henry C. Binford, Timothy Breen, and Frank R. Safford read all or parts of the manuscript at an early stage. Richard J. Cox, then of the Maryland Historical Society, and Dianne P. Frese and Phebe R. Jacobsen of the Hall of Records pointed me to many valuable sources I would otherwise have missed. I would also like to express my gratitude to Robert C. Ritchie and Harry N. Scheiber, who first encouraged my interest in American history as an undergraduate. Although neither one has read this book, they both contributed greatly to what went into it. To Alfred Young I cannot say thank you enough. He pored over each of what seemed to be endless drafts of the manuscript, challenging me to refine and broaden my analysis. Al is the best teacher I have ever had.

Finally, I owe my parents much more than this book, but I hope they will accept it with love.

CONTENTS

Contents

INTRODUCTION

This book treats the skilled workingmen of Baltimore—"mechanics," as they usually called themselves—from 1763 to 1812. During the Age of Revolution mechanics awakened to political consciousness. They fashioned their own radical vision of republicanism that clashed with the conservative republicanism of merchants and lawyers. They also laid the institutional foundation of a mechanic community in the militia, craft societies, and general associations of workingmen. In Baltimore the emergence of the mechanics as a self-conscious political force shaped the movement for a new national constitution, the development of the first party system, the fight for a republican city charter, and the breakdown of Republican party unity after 1800. At the turn of the century the institutional base of the mechanic community began to collapse, but the workingmen's special brand of republicanism endured.

For all these reasons I would argue that the politicization of the mechanic population represented perhaps the major change in Baltimore politics from the Revolution to the War of 1812.

This is not the prevailing view among historians. Most studies on early American politics imply that the workingmen were little more than bystanders deferring to the class on top, the merchants. Not until the Jacksonian era, with the emergence of workingmen's parties, city central trades' unions, and national trade associations, did mechanics shed their deferential outlook and become independent political actors in their own right. Alexander Hamilton, in his Federalist Paper No. 35, put this view best: he called merchants "the natural representatives" of the mechanics. Yet Hamilton's argument contained as much wishful thinking as dispassionate analysis. We know that in his own day urban workingmen exhibited far less deference than Hamilton would have us believe, as his own experience in New York City might have taught him.

The Hamiltonian view is still with us in part because historians have tended to carve up their fields and treat them in isolation. Since John R. Commons labor historians have devoted most of their energies to examining the origins, structure, and development of trade unions. Political historians have focused on formal party organizations and especially the elite leadership or, more recently, on the statistics of voting behavior. Social historians have pored over tax records, censuses, city directories, probate records, and other material inviting quantitative analysis. Intellectual historians have read erudite disquisitions and pamphlets addressed to a small audience. Thus we have fine individual studies on trade unions, political parties, social structure, and elite thinking. But we lack synthetic works that might tie them together. In this book I have tried to examine Baltimore's mechanics in all their multifaceted activities, which seems to me the chief distinction between the "new" and "old" labor, political, and social history. I hope my study will be placed alongside the works of other historians who are trying to wrestle their fields from narrow confines.

For all the changes it has undergone over the years, this book has retained its focus on class formation. At first I took a rather cookbook approach to the problem of class, treating it like a loaf of bread that contained certain ingredients. All I had to do was determine the right combination of "factors," the proper proportions of wealth, status, and power, and suddenly the class would stir to life. It took some time before I realized the obvious: a class is not a loaf of bread. It is a relationship created every day by people who live it. This impressed me as the key insight of E. P. Thompson's *The Making of the English Working Class*. The working class he examined was not made by the disembodied forces of history like dough for the kneading; it made itself through collective struggle. As I tried in subsequent revisions to fill in the missing dimension of class struggle and class consciousness, I found the study acquiring a heavily political cast. I seemed to be following the mechanics into every corner of Baltimore's political life.

The era 1763–1812 witnessed two great democratic revolutions that convulsed the entire western world. To Baltimore's mechanics, the enlightened age inaugurated by the American Revolution and continued by the French promised to sweep away tyranny and liberate oppressed peoples everywhere. This was a new world—anything seemed possible. In the 1790s mechanics knew few restraints in voicing their republican optimism and confidence, as is suggested by one of their Independence Day toasts: "All our Brethren of Mankind who wish well to the Cause of Liberty, may they speedily be eased of their oppressive Taxes, which they are obliged to pay to Support a Set of Despots and their Sycophants." If the rhetoric seems overblown, the vision was nonetheless inspired. During the Age of Revolution Baltimore's mechanics articulated a new collective identity. They fashioned it from their experiences in the workplace, not the marketplace—in the shops, yards, and manufactories. As they struggled for power and respectability, mechanics helped create a new republican order.

PART ONE

A CITY AND
ITS WORKERS,
1729–1812

1

THE RISE OF BALTIMORE

Baltimore was founded in 1729. For a generation it seemed no different from a dozen other small settlements springing up at the head of the Chesapeake Bay; its claim to distinction consisted of a blacksmith's shop, flour mill, and tobacco warehouse. Yet Baltimore was fated for a more dynamic future than its slow beginnings seemed to portend. Spurred by an agricultural revolution in the Maryland and Pennsylvania countrysides as well as dramatic disruptions in the Atlantic economy, Baltimore at mid-century began to boom. By 1790 it had risen to become the new republic's fourth largest city with aspirations to overtake the three still ahead: New York, Philadelphia, and Boston.

Although the Baltimore of the Jeffersonian era looked utterly unlike the colonial village from which it had emerged, the two shared more than might be apparent at first glance. Baltimore's economy had expanded tremendously, to be sure, but the same forces that sparked expansion around 1750 continued to sustain it fifty years later. Despite the establishment of new governments at the state level in 1776, national level in 1788, and municipal level in 1797, the same festering issues continued to convulse its politics. If Baltimore had become richer and bigger, its occupational structure, wealth distribution, and residential patterns withstood the pressures of growth and looked about the same in 1790 as in 1812. In other words, beneath the frenzied and seemingly chaotic pace of urbanization, Baltimore enjoyed a strong element of stability. For in 1812, no less than in 1729, Baltimore was a preindustrial town.

Baltimore's first decades were far from auspicious. To begin with, the town founders had picked an unpromising site for settlement. Not only did the terrain slope up from the Patapsco River, which hindered the townspeople from spreading out, but parts of the shoreline lay under mosquito-ridden marsh. The river off the settlement was too shallow for large-draft ships, clogged with silt that Jones' Falls dumped into the Patapsco. The Falls created other hazards as well, occasionally flooding its banks and endangering people and property. As late as 1752 Baltimore had only a few hundred inhabitants and they clustered in two dozen houses along the river. In the same year a townsman made a sketch of the village, a kind of crude photograph, which revealed just two small vessels riding in the harbor—tenuous links to the outside world of commerce. Although in 1747 the Maryland assembly ordered a tobacco inspection warehouse to be built, it had relatively little to inspect until after the Revolution when Baltimore's merchants moved into the Chesapeake tobacco trade. So little traffic ran along the town streets that Baltimore needed only one drayman, George Strebeck, who got by with a single team of horses. Since in this village setting most men were jacks-of-all-trades, no more than a handful of mechanics could earn full-time livings at their crafts. A 1752 list of thirty townspeople, probably household heads, identified just six artisans: two carpenters, a tailor, a cooper, a wagoner, and a barber. The only genuine manufacturing enterprise was a brewery built by two Germans in the 1740s. In short, Baltimore was a typical eighteenth-century hamlet whose social life alternated between one church, Anglican St. Paul's, and a pair of taverns.[1]

The 1750s marked a turning point, better yet, a taking-off point. New people began pouring into the Chesapeake port from the Middle Atlantic region and beyond, so that by 1776 Baltimore's population stood at 6,700. By 1790 it had reached 13,500, by 1800 26,500, and by 1810 46,600. On the eve of the Revolution Baltimore was the ninth largest American town, at the turn of the century the third. During most of the two or three decades after 1790 no other major city could match Baltimore's rate of growth, not Boston or Philadelphia, not even New York.[2]

The men and women crowding into Baltimore were a mixed lot. Perhaps the most striking characteristic of the city's population, compared with other seaboard ports, was its racial heterogeneity. Blacks rose from 12 percent of Baltimore's population in

Baltimore in 1792 (courtesy of the Maryland Historical Society).

1790 to 22 percent twenty years later; by the latter date New York and Philadelphia had half as many, Boston a fifth. Moreover, the black community underwent a revolution in legal status that also set Baltimore apart from its northern neighbors. From 1790 to 1810 Baltimore's free black population multiplied eighteen-fold to nearly 6,000, while New York's increased seven times, Philadelphia's four times, and Boston's two times.

The burgeoning population of Baltimore was mixed ethnically as well. It included a substantial number of Germans, who had commonly followed a migratory route through Philadelphia and southeastern Pennsylvania. Baltimore also had a conspicuous pocket of French inhabitants driven from St. Domingue during the Haitian Revolution, which lent an international and cosmopolitan flavor to street life. As Baltimore rose to become the center of Maryland's indentured servant trade, it acquired a population of Irish Catholics. Especially vocal were the Scotch-Irish, who began arriving in force after the 1760s and who provided a number of politically ambitious merchants. Religious diversity followed hand in hand with the ethnic mix, which contributed to Baltimore's well-deserved reputation as a sectarian battleground. Baltimore became the scene of one religious schism after another, fertile soil for the revivals that periodically swept through the country in the late eighteenth and early nineteenth centuries. Indeed, Baltimore was the informal headquarters of the Methodist church, an energetic proponent of the "Second Great Awakening."[3]

What brought these people to Baltimore? The answer is wheat. After the first decade of the eighteenth century German farmers started to settle southeastern Pennsylvania and they instinctively planted wheat, the crop they knew best from the Old World. Within little time these Germans were pushing south into western Maryland, filling up the fertile Monocacy valley and transforming it into the bread basket of the province. In 1748 the western settlers had grown so numerous that the Maryland assembly established a separate county for them, Frederick. By 1790 Germans constituted 12 percent of Maryland's population, according to one estimate based on the surnames in the federal population census for that year; only Pennsylvania and the youthful western populations of Kentucky and Tennessee had relatively more. At the same time tobacco planters along Maryland's Eastern Shore were converting to wheat, discouraged by the sluggish market for tobacco and the soil exhaustion resulting from continued cultivation.

Baltimore was ideally situated to tap the wheat trade around it. By the mid-eighteenth century a road had been constructed between Baltimore and Frederick, cutting through the heart of the wheat country, which one historian has called "the birth certificate of Baltimore City." Entrepreneurs continued to finance the building of roads, canals, bridges, and turnpikes to open the enormous agricultural backcountry. By 1810 three turnpikes fanned out from Baltimore, one of which met the National Road at Cumberland, Maryland, and crossed the Appalachian Mountains to Wheeling, Virginia. Baltimore's merchants soon cornered the wheat market in western Maryland, challenged their Philadelphia competitors in southeastern Pennsylvania east of the Susquehanna River, and started forging inroads into the Eastern Shore. The wheat trade in turn stimulated industry. The incomplete 1810 manufacturing census indicates that the per capita output of flour in Maryland's northern counties amounted to almost $20, compared to only $13 for the Eastern Shore and a mere $3 for the southern counties. Sixty-five flour mills were operating on the outskirts of Baltimore City, legally in Baltimore County. Only neighboring Frederick County, the center of the wheat trade, had more.[4]

The wagonloads of wheat, flour, and bread rolling into town caused Baltimore's export trade to climb sharply. Although the level of exports hinged delicately on events overseas over which Baltimore had no control, the structure of the trade changed little after taking shape in the 1760s. Four markets received Baltimore's exports: the West Indies, southern Europe, the Atlantic seaboard, and the British Isles. In the British and French West Indies, sugar planters recklessly threw all their resources into the production of the white gold while importing food and provisions from the outside. Because Baltimore was closer to the sugar islands than its major competitors, it succeeded in carving out a large share of the market. Baltimore imported sugar, molasses, rum, cotton, cocoa, and coffee from the Caribbean while exporting its three chief staples: wheat, lumber, and iron products. After 1750 devastating warfare and bad harvests combined to create a great demand for grain in the Mediterranean world, and once again Baltimore's flour merchants were anxious to accommodate. This trade was balanced heavily in Baltimore's favor, for the town imported little from southern Europe besides salt and wine. New England farmers could not produce enough from their rocky soil to feed the rising number of townspeople, so they too turned to Baltimore for help. Baltimore received oil, fish, rum, and molasses from Massachusetts while the other important coastal markets—Virginia and the Carolinas—supplied pork and naval stores. Successful merchants managed to accumulate sufficient profits in their dealings with the West Indies, the Atlantic seaboard, and southern Europe to finance their imports from the British Isles, especially cotton cloth and East Indian silk.

The Revolution upset these trading patterns but did not overturn them. After the 1780s Baltimore's merchants entered the Chesapeake tobacco trade, which had been traditionally dominated by English and Scotch factors. As they did so, they shifted their business activities from southern to northern Europe, where the demand for tobacco was greater. For a time it seemed that France might eclipse Britain as America's chief trading partner, but this dream of Jefferson and others never materialized. France could not supply the manufactured products to which Americans had grown accustomed, leading Baltimore's merchants to resume their imports from Great Britain.[5]

The 1790s propelled Baltimore's export trade to unprecedented heights. The French Revolution and the international upheaval it provoked after 1792 tore down commercial barriers throughout the Atlantic world. The Caribbean colonies needed provisions as much as ever, but their customary lines of supply became vulnerable to attack and unreliable. For Baltimore the prospects were attractive but dangerous, for all the warring nations at some time rejected America's claims as a "neutral" trader. In early 1794 the British navy underscored the hazards of neutral trading by seizing several hundred American ships in the French colonies. Four years later the American and French republics were harassing each other's shipping in an undeclared naval war. From a commercial standpoint these disruptions proved to be temporary inconveniences, for Baltimore's exports multiplied five-fold between 1792 and 1800. But the Embargo Act of 1807 brought the export boom to an abrupt end, and, except for a brief recovery in mid-1809, the town's trade continued to languish through the War of 1812.

During these years Baltimore experienced two economic changes that would gain greater importance after 1812. First, there was a business revolution. As the increasing magnitude of commercial transactions strained the old, informal ways of doing business and getting credit, merchants turned to banks as the solution, the first of which was established in 1791. Within another fifteen years Baltimore could count three more. Second, there was an industrial revolution, or rather the seeds of one. After the Embargo Act merchants channeled their investments from commerce into more lucrative areas like real estate and manufacturing. By the end of the War of 1812 a half-dozen textile factories were operating outside the city. Although the mills that produced woolen and cotton cloth employed no more than a few hundred operatives, not enough to threaten the old handicraft system of manufacturing, they presaged radical changes in the traditional productive process.[6]

The rise of Baltimore set the stage for a political struggle whose basic outlines remained unchanged despite the interruptions of the Revolution, the establishment of new state and national governments, and the emergence of the first party system. In the later eighteenth century a typical assemblyman could survey the Maryland political scene with confidence. He was probably a large landowner, a slaveholder, and a tobacco planter; Anglican in faith and Anglo in descent; from one of the colony's southern counties. Since the late seventeenth century his class had ruled the assembly. New faces had appeared and vanished among the governing elite, factions rose and fell with shifting political alliances in the mother country, but all had represented the interests of the planter gentry. The assemblyman could stroll through Annapolis, the provincial capital, and take heart. Here was the showcase of the gentry, whose growing number of elegant townhouses bore witness to what one historian has termed an Annapolitan "age of affluence." He could pass through the doors of the assembly hall expecting success. For generations he and his colleagues in the House of Delegates had been steadily reducing the powers and privileges of the governor and proprietary interest.

On the eve of the Revolution Maryland's planter gentry never seemed so united and self-assured, certain in their right to rule. But then a rival appeared. The new counties of northern and western Maryland, which were drawing thousands of settlers by the 1750s, represented a different kind of society from that which had produced the ruling class. There were fewer plantations, more farms; greater ethnic and religious diversity, less slaveholding. From the perspective of the assembly it must have seemed that the heterogeneous and volatile society of Pennsylvania was spilling over into Maryland. Nowhere did this threat appear more starkly than in Baltimore, which was fast developing into the economic, cultural, and political locus of northern Maryland.[7]

A clash was inevitable. From the 1760s through the early national period Baltimore fought its own small war for independence, not against the British but rather against a conservative assembly determined to preserve the dominance of the planter gentry. The assembly persisted in handling Baltimore like a backwater village long after it ceased being one. Each of Maryland's counties elected four representatives to the assembly and Annapolis two; Baltimore had none. The assembly refused Baltimore a city charter that would confer a measure of self-government, reserving that special privilege for Annapolis. During the colonial era Baltimore was governed by a board of commissioners which was handpicked by the assembly, not the townspeople. In fact, from 1729 until 1786 not a single local official was elective, the clearest indication of the assembly's effort to undermine autonomy in Baltimore. The fact that other towns enjoyed a more representative government must have rankled Baltimoreans. Bostonians elected their selectmen and a host of lesser officials. New Yorkers chose their aldermen. Philadelphians picked their sheriffs, tax assessors, coroners, and commissioners.[8]

Chafing under these restraints, Baltimoreans seized the opportunities presented by the Revolution to strike against them. To coordinate the local movement against imperial policy after the 1760s, the citizens of Baltimore chose committees of inspection, correspondence, and observation. These represented an embryonic municipal government and gave townspeople a heady taste of home rule. By 1776 the demands for local political independence had reached the point where Maryland's ruling elite, frightened at the prospect of losing control over the Revolution, could no longer resist them. In that year a state constitutional convention gave Baltimore two delegate seats in the assembly, the same as Annapolis. Four years later the assembly made Baltimore an official port of entry, a belated acknowledgment of its economic importance. In 1786 Baltimore received its first elective officials, street commissioner and port warden. Eleven years later it got a city charter. The document was too conservative for most townspeople, however, leading to nearly a decade of demands for reform. On this point, too, the assembly ultimately gave way. In 1805 it instituted ballot voting in city elections and three years later cut property qualifications for local office holding.[9]

Decades of struggle had imbued Baltimoreans with a siege mentality. Whatever their economic or social standing, however they might define their particular interests, almost all townspeople shared the desire to liberate Baltimore from the planter-dominated government at Annapolis. This common commitment provided the foundation for a powerful alliance between merchants and mechanics, the two major groups around which urban politics revolved. When issues arose that seemed to pit Baltimore's interests against those of Annapolis, merchants and mechanics joined forces.

As early as 1763 both groups cooperated in the formation of the Baltimore Mechanical Company, an early experiment in self-government and an implicit challenge to the policies of the assembly. In 1777 radical merchants and mechanics again united in the Baltimore Whig Club, an extralegal organization that expressed the town's dissatisfaction with the conservatism of the new state government and its unwillingness to harry tories from the land. The same political alliance buttressed the city's Republican party after 1793, which clashed with the predominantly Federalist counties of southern Maryland. In this sense the first party system grew out of long-standing political divisions in Maryland. For leadership as well as organization the Republicans depended on the Baltimore Mechanical Society, which represented the skilled workers, and the Baltimore Republican Society, which spoke for a radical faction of the merchant-lawyer elite. But this coalition was always fragile, forged as it was in opposition to a common antagonist. On an increasing number of questions merchants and mechanics clashed. Thus a paradox arose. Although mechanics could unite with merchants when the occasion demanded, they increasingly struck out along an independent course, often in defiance of their erstwhile allies. The mechanics were fast awakening to political consciousness, perhaps the main theme in Baltimore politics after the Revolution and one explored in this book.[10]

Maryland's political leaders, both at Baltimore and Annapolis, were not self-effacing. They believed they were doing something that posterity should remember and revere, so they wrote about it. Thus the political historian has no lack of material. Not so fortunate is the social historian. During the colonial and Revolutionary periods only a chance document survives to illuminate the nature of Baltimore society. Not until the 1790s can the historian attempt a quantitative examination of the city's social structure, for only then did the newly formed municipal and federal governments begin counting people and assessing their wealth systematically. The first Baltimore city directory was published in 1796 and new ones appeared every other year or so. They listed most adult white males, a few females, but no blacks, together with occupation and residence. The first federal population census was taken in 1790 and at ten-year intervals afterward. While the manuscript schedules do not possess the wealth of information of the post-1850 censuses, they do identify the household head, the age and sex of the household members, and the number of slaves and free blacks. City tax lists provide the wealth of individual townspeople along with the ward where their holdings were located. Nearly all of the biases contained in these sources—and there are many—came at the expense of people with no stable residence, no steady job, no taxable property. But compared to the earlier dearth, the records of the early national period are rich indeed.

Social historians look for change instinctively. They would be disappointed with early national Baltimore, whose social structure budged hardly at all. Consider the city's occupational distribution presented in Table 1. It is more or less the same in 1796 and 1815. In both years the largest occupational group consisted of mechanics, who accounted for nearly five out of every ten entries in the directories. Beneath them came the draymen, sailors, dock workers, and those identified in the directories as simply

TABLE 1
OCCUPATIONAL STRUCTURE OF
BALTIMORE: 1796, 1814

Occupation	1796 (N = 2,545)	1814 (N = 4,322)
Mechanic	46%	48%
Laborer	19	11
Merchant	16	15
Service	11	15
Trader	8	11
Total	100%	100%

SOURCES: *Baltimore Town and Fell's Point Directory* (Baltimore, n.d. [1796]); *Baltimore Directory and Register, for 1814–15* (Baltimore, 1814).

"laborer" who together made up the unskilled work force. In 1796 they represented the second largest group with two of every ten entries, but two decades later they had fallen to last place with just one of ten. We should not make too much of this shift, however, for it seems to have resulted from the unconscious racism built into the directories. In the two decades after 1790 free blacks, mostly unskilled laborers, advanced from 2 to 11 percent of the city's total population. According to the pioneering 1817 directory, which included a separate section on 353 free blacks for the first time, 70 percent of the entries were unskilled. We can plausibly infer that as free blacks multiplied in both absolute and relative terms, they came to constitute a swelling proportion of the unskilled work force. By excluding these laboring men, the directory compilers created the false impression that the relative number of unskilled workers was slipping. Merchants were the third ranking occupational group with one or two of every ten entries. In addition to the powerful wholesalers who called themselves either "dry goods merchant" or just "merchant" in the directories, this category encompassed the lesser retailers who identified with a specialized branch of commerce, like the "hardware merchant" or "china merchant." The service trades were about as numerous as the merchants, perhaps a bit less in 1796. They embraced an especially diverse assemblage of occupations, extending from the professional physicians and lawyers to the nonprofessional ship captains and school teachers. In both years

TABLE 2

OCCUPATIONAL STRUCTURE OF
MECHANIC POPULATION: 1796, 1814

Craft	1796 (N=1,069)	1814 (N=1,931)
Clothing	28%	28%
Construction	25	21
Shipbuilding	11	12
Food	10	8
Wood	9	9
Metal	7	8
Luxury	4	6
Leather	4	4
Stone/Clay	2	4
Total	100%	100%

SOURCES: See Table 1.

the smallest group, one entry out of ten, were the traders. Here were the small-time operators of grocery stores, inns and taverns, coffee shops, and boarding houses, who catered to local needs and fashions.[11]

The mechanics, who outnumbered all other groups, were by no means an undifferentiated mass of skilled laborers. They too were divided by wealth, craft, and their position in the apprentice-journeyman-master hierarchy. Table 2 displays the occupational structure of the mechanic population. Once more, it is virtually identical in the two years. The single noteworthy change was the falling percentage of construction workers, which may have reflected a building slowdown during the War of 1812. The clothing, construction, shipbuilding, and food trades held their positions at the top, accounting for between two-thirds and three-fourths of the mechanics. Those craftsmen who fashioned products from clay or stone and those who manufactured luxury items were at the bottom.

Baltimore's wealth distribution changed no more than its occupational structure did. In Table 3 the overall distributions for 1804 and 1815 are practically mirror images, and from Table 4 a similar picture emerges. In both years wholesale merchants were the richest group, unskilled workers the poorest, mechanics in between and toward the bottom. In both years the richest group had about eight or nine times more property than the poorest one. Nor did the share of the city's total property owned by each group change. Wholesale merchants consistently owned slightly over two-fifths of everything assessed, while mechanics, who as a group ranked second, had something above one-fifth. In spite of the opportunities Baltimore offered to newcomers hoping to make their mark, few new faces appeared among the patricians. In 1815 eighteen people constituted the wealthiest .5 percent of Baltimore's property holders. Sixteen of them appear on the 1804 list. All of them belonged to the top 10 percent, fourteen to the top 4 percent, and nine to the top 5 percent. So the richest individuals in 1815 had generally been among the richest eleven years earlier. Merchant William Patterson, the number one wealth holder in both years, personified how fortunes were made and conserved.

If we dissect the mechanics' property holdings, once again

TABLE 3
WEALTH DISTRIBUTION IN BALTIMORE: 1804, 1815

Decile	1804	1815
Bottom Tenth	1%	1%
2nd	1	1
3rd	2	2
4th	2	2
5th	3	3
6th	4	5
7th	7	7
8th	11	10
9th	19	18
Top Tenth	52	52
Total	100%	100%

SOURCES: Alphabetical Lists of Assessed Persons, 1804, Baltimore County Commissioners, MHR; Baltimore Assessment Record Book, MS. 55, MHS.

Notes: Property designated for assessment included land and improvements, slaves, horses and cattle, silver, furniture, and other household goods. The assembly exempted from taxation plantation tools, provisions that were to be consumed in a year, ready money, clothing, licensed vessels, and "working tools of mechanics and manufacturers actually and constantly employed in their respective occupations." See Chapter IV, "An Act to raise supplies," Laws of Maryland (Annapolis, 1782).

TABLE 4
WEALTH DISTRIBUTION BY OCCUPATION: 1804, 1815

| | 1804 | | | 1815 | | |
Occupation	Mean Wealth	Percentage of Total Wealth	N	Mean Wealth	Percentage of Total Wealth	N
Merchant						
Wholesale merchant	£770	45%	260	$2,223	43%	325
Retail merchant	444	7	76	1,379	7	86
Service Trade						
Public official	273	4	58	890	4	79
Professional	410	7	75	1,530	8	93
Nonprofessional	132	3	83	462	5	191
Trader						
Public house proprietor	272	4	116	548	2	45
Grocer	292	7	99	731	6	138
Mechanic	206	22	476	666	23	599
Laborer	91	1	44	278	2	91

SOURCES: Alphabetical Lists of Assessed Persons, 1804; Baltimore Assessment Record Book; *Baltimore Directory, for 1804* (Baltimore, n.d. [1804]); *Baltimore Directory and Register, for 1814–15.*

Notes: Of the 2,988 persons in the 1804 tax list, the occupations of 1,287 were identified in the city directory. Of the 3,656 individuals in the 1815 list, 1,647 were identified.

we find little change. The distributions for the mechanics, shown in Table 5, are the same. This pattern of continuity continues to hold true when we break down the mechanics' wealth by craft, as in Table 6. Admittedly, the crafts were not wholly stationary. Shipbuilders dropped a few notches, perhaps because several prominent shipwrights had assumed the title of merchant in the decade after 1804. On the other hand, clay workers catapulted from last into second place, perhaps because the 1815 tax list included several prominent brickmakers who owned kilns in the western "precincts" of town. Yet these changes did not disturb the general pattern of stability. Leather workers belonged to a group by themselves, as much businessmen as craftsmen, having invested extensively in tanyards and establishing commercial ties to the suppliers of hides and purchasers of leather. Consistently at the bottom were the wood workers, construction workers, and

TABLE 5
WEALTH DISTRIBUTION OF MECHANICS:
1804, 1815

Decile	1804	1815
Bottom Tenth	—	—
2nd	2%	2%
3rd	2	2
4th	3	3
5th	4	4
6th	7	7
7th	8	9
8th	12	12
9th	19	18
Top Tenth	43	43
Total	100%	100%

SOURCES: See Table 4.

TABLE 6
WEALTH DISTRIBUTION BY CRAFT: 1804, 1815

	1804		1815	
Craft	Mean Wealth Holding	N	Mean Wealth Holding	N
Leather	£307	29	$1,188	36
Shipbuilding	277	47	645	73
Metal	271	55	637	57
Food	234	49	727	70
Luxury	175	27	533	46
Clothing	174	93	687	105
Wood	173	48	715	56
Construction	159	108	471	133
Stone/Clay	157	20	1,064	37

SOURCES: See Table 4.

clothing workers—traditionally the indigent fringe of the mechanic community.

In residence as well as in occupation and wealth, Baltimore looked much the same in 1790 and 1812. Baltimore was no different from other urban sites in being a pedestrian's town. No one lived more than an hour's brisk walk from anyone else. Except for the few who could afford to keep a country estate or townhouse in addition to a counting house and workshop, people lived where they worked. Thus homes, shops, inns, markets, warehouses, and people tended to bunch around key points of economic activity. A merchant might find a shoemaker living on his right, a lawyer on his left, and a drayman across the street. He may not have liked having these people so close, but not until the advent of the street railway later in the nineteenth century could he escape to his own homogeneous neighborhood. But Baltimoreans still had a choice about where to live and, taken together, their decisions tell us much about the city's social structure. Preindustrial Baltimore had its own patterns of residential segregation, which endured in the face of the massive influx of new people in the late eighteenth and early nineteenth centuries.

There were actually three Baltimores. The oldest, largest, wealthiest, and most populated was the original settlement, sometimes called "Baltimore West" but usually just "Baltimore." It began as a cluster of buildings strung along Baltimore Street, the main commercial axis, running east-west. The eastern border of Baltimore was formed by Jones' Falls, which effectively split the town into two parts. Hills presented an obstacle to northern settlement. According to a 1792 city map, the population spread no further than four or five blocks north of Baltimore Street. It proved easier for newcomers to push west along Baltimore Street, until by 1792 they had reached Union Street. At the same time they crowded into the waterfront area south of Baltimore Street, which now became the bustling site of counting houses, warehouses, and wharves. Circling the southwest rim of the "basin," the residents found homes on Federal Hill overlooking the entire city and marking its southern limits.[12]

The newcomers gave Baltimore a different physical appearance but they did nothing to alter its occupational make-up. In 1796 and 1814 the area's occupational profile, displayed in Table 7, was about the same. The decline in the percentage of unskilled workers occurred everywhere in the city, adding extra weight to the supposition that the directories neglected a growing portion of the lower classes. Mechanics were the largest single group in

TABLE 7
OCCUPATIONAL STRUCTURE OF BALTIMORE BY
COMMUNITY: 1796, 1814

Occupation	Baltimore		Fell's Point		Old Town	
	1796	1814	1796	1814	1796	1814
Merchant	22%	25%	5%	2%	9%	7%
Mechanic	43	45	45	48	57	59
Service	11	13	15	22	8	14
Trader	8	12	11	10	5	10
Laborer	16	7	24	18	21	10
Total	100%	100%	100%	100%	100%	100%
N	1,607	2,209	532	972	340	819

SOURCES: See Table 1.

Baltimore, as they were everywhere in the city. In particular Baltimore attracted craftsmen who specialized in luxury trades, as Table 8 suggests. The reason is probably that goldsmiths, silversmiths, and watch and clock makers wanted to be near their affluent customers. Baltimore also drew brickmakers and potters because clay deposits were located on the town's western extremities. The next largest group were merchants, whose influence far exceeded their numbers. Merchants were practically synonymous with Baltimore, setting the tone of life as they did nowhere else in the city. In 1796 and 1814 a fourth of Baltimore's residents in the directories called themselves merchants. Stating it another way, in both years eight or nine out of every ten merchants lived west of the Falls. In 1796 four of ten lived on Baltimore Street alone. The biggest townhouses, busiest counting houses, and best coffee houses—the places where merchants made their money and spent it—all were in Baltimore.

On the east side of Jones' Falls was Old Town. Founded as the independent settlement of Jones' Town, it was officially incorporated into Baltimore in 1745. Old Town ran from French Street in the north to the basin in the south, and from the Falls in the west to Harford Street in the east. According to an 1801 city map, most Old Town residents lived within four or five blocks of Bridge Street, which spanned the Falls and supplied the main connect-

TABLE 8
CRAFT STRUCTURE OF BALTIMORE BY COMMUNITY: 1796

Community	Con- struction	Ship- building	Metal	Food
Baltimore	61%	18%	60%	66%
Old Town	22	1	17	18
Fell's Point	14	77	23	12
Federal Hill	3	4	—	4
Total	100%	100%	100%	100%
N	319	110	77	126

SOURCES: *Baltimore Town and Fell's Point Directory.*

ing link with Baltimore. Another map published a few decades later revealed that the population had filled the area south of Great York Street. As Table 7 shows, the occupational structure of Old Town experienced no more change than Baltimore's. Anyone crossing Bridge Street from Baltimore into Old Town would immediately notice counting houses giving way to workshops. Although it could never hope to match Baltimore politically or economically, Old Town maintained its distinctive identity as a community of the "middling classes," "leather aprons," "mechanicks and tradesmen." Mechanics constituted about three-fifths of the residents listed in the directories, a figure higher than for any other part of town. The craft which above all concentrated in Old Town was leather making (see Table 8). Since several country roads entered the city at Old Town, tanners, curriers, and saddlers may have established their businesses there to seize advantage of the ready traffic in hides. Only a handful of merchants made their homes in this predominantly laboring men's community.[13]

The city's third community was in many ways the most distinctive of all. From its beginnings Fell's Point was a product of nature. About a mile and a half's walk from downtown Baltimore, the Point jutted into the Patapsco River to form the southeast corner of the basin. The river ran deep off the Point, giving the area a critical advantage over Baltimore with its mud-congested waters. Ships destined for Baltimore would have to anchor off the Point and unload their holds into smaller craft, which either sailed di-

Stone/ Clay	Leather	Clothing	Wood	Luxury
81%	26%	65%	66%	86%
15	39	15	20	5
2	26	18	13	7
2	9	2	1	2
100%	100%	100%	100%	100%
41	31	301	93	65

rectly to town or transferred the cargos into wagons making the overland run to Baltimore. As early as 1763 William Fell, whose father had purchased land east of Baltimore forty years before, began surveying his holdings and named them "Fell's Prospect," which somehow failed to stick. Within a decade the task of surveying the land had been completed and the area, now called "Fell's Point," was swallowed by Baltimore as Jones' Town had been three decades earlier. The Revolution exposed the strategically vital position that the Point held in the town's commercial life, for soon hundreds of vessels were converging there to gather supplies and provisions for the army. From 1776 to 1783 the Point's population soared from over 800 to about 1,500. By the turn of the century streets had been laid out to Hampstead in the north and Harford in the west, although nearly everyone stayed within eyesight of the docks. As late as 1801 settlement had not pushed far north of Wilks Street.[14]

Yet the Point always remained a world apart. The spatial gap separating the affluent downtown neighborhoods from the Point's busy docks, shipyards, ropewalks, taverns, and shops magnified the social and cultural distance between them. The Point developed into a vibrant waterfront community—the home of shipbuilders, dockworkers, and day laborers; a roisterous and sometimes riotous place where sailors, slaves, and servants jostled in the streets; a reputedly plebeian haunt where the great merchants were ready to make money, not homes. The Point's merchant population was practically nonexistent (see Table 7). On the other hand, unskilled workers made up a greater percentage of this dockside community than they did in either Baltimore or Old Town. Perhaps the most conspicuous element in the Point's population was the shipbuilders. Nearly the entire shipbuilding community found homes at the Point, close to the yards off Philpot, Thames, and Fell's streets (see Table 8).

An early assessment list permits a close look at the Point's social structure. It underscores the two fundamental facts of life along the waterfront. The first was that outsiders held enormous economic power. Of the 435 people who in 1783 owned property at the Point, 212 (49 percent) did not live there. These nonresidents owned about half of everything assessed: £136,312 of the total £279,509 (47 percent). Who were they? Judging from the richest ones, they were who we should expect: big Baltimore merchants. With the exception of Thomas Worthington, who operated a substantial ropewalk at the Point, the top thirteen nonresidents were merchants from across the Falls, including such politically prominent figures as William Patterson, Isaac and Abraham Vanbibber, John Sterett, Samuel and Robert Purviance, and Jesse Hollingsworth. Patterson had accumulated £11,134 in Point property—nobody, resident or nonresident, could come within £4,000 of him.

One man who probably typified the Baltimore merchant speculating at the Point was John Sterett. He had joined the Scotch-Irish migration of merchants from Pennsylvania who arrived in Baltimore in the 1760s. The 1783 tax lists shows Sterett with five unimproved lots worth a total of £3,200, making him the seventh-ranking nonresident property holder. Three years later he composed a will that divided two Point water lots and a few Baltimore town lots between his sons, while providing that additional Point property be offered at public sale.

The outsiders like Sterett, who specialized in unimproved lots, did not go bankrupt developing their land. They owned just 35 percent of the total value of improved lots and 41 percent of the value of improved lots yielding rent. On the other hand, they held 72 percent of the value of unimproved lots and 67 percent of the value of unimproved lots yielding rent. Of the Point's 117 unimproved lots, the outsiders owned 72 (62 percent). Of the 209 improved lots, they had 65 (31 percent). If nonresidents tended to sit on their land while residents built theirs up, poor location was not to blame. On the contrary: the outsiders' unimproved lots probably occupied choice spots on the waterfront or near it. Such is suggested from the mean value of their lots, which at £401 was £156 more than the residents'. To a great extent, then, the fundamental economic decisions affecting the Point were being made downtown. And as many Point residents insisted, these decisions may not have been in the best interests of their community.[15]

The second feature of the Point's social structure that emerges from the tax list is inequality. Of the 283 residents whose names appear in the tax list, 90 either were listed as "paupers" who owned less than £10 in taxable property or were single men assessed at a set rate of 15s. a head. The bottom half of the householders possessed a mere 1 percent of the Point's wealth while the top tenth had 65 percent (see Table 9). Arranged according to the type of property they owned, the householders fell into five groups. The first included 52 people who had at least one improved lot as well as some rental property. They were assessed at £1,979 each, and probably consisted of families who, in addition to owning their own home and land, acquired speculative prop-

TABLE 9
WEALTH DISTRIBUTION OF FELL'S POINT
RESIDENTS: 1783

Decile	Wealth Range	Percentage of Total Wealth
Bottom Tenth	£0	0%
2nd	0	0
3rd	0	0
4th	0–20	0
5th	25–50	1
6th	50–125	2
7th	127–250	4
8th	260–542	8
9th	550–1,795	20
Top Tenth	1,880–6,417	65
Total		100%

SOURCES: *Maryland Tax List 1783: Baltimore County* (Philadelphia, 1970).

erty as well. The next group encompassed 8 householders who owned rental property but no improved lots. Worth £525 each, these persons may have occupied a rented house or built their homes on leased land. Another 63 men and women, assessed at £497 a head, succeeded in obtaining an improved lot and usually some personal property as well, but did not own rental property. Here was the group for whom property signified a home and plot of earth, not speculative income. Substantially below them were individuals who owned nothing but personal property. To these 70 residents, taxed at £68 apiece, land and house must have seemed a dream. And then there were the 90 who did not have anything the assessors deemed worth assessing. In short, 79 percent of the Point's householders did not own rental property; 79 percent did not own a house; 57 percent did not own land; and 32 percent did not own anything at all. Who owned Fell's Point? To those who didn't, the answer must have seemed as inequitable as it was incontestable: a few dozen privileged residents together with a few hundred outsiders.

The seaport of 1812, boasting a population near 40,000, had come a long way from the straggling village of a few hundred souls. But the surface changes, dramatic as they were, masked a deeper stability. First, the conditions fostering Baltimore's explosive growth did not change from 1763 or 1776 to 1812. Not only did wheat continue to hold primacy of place among the city's exports, but it also continued to funnel into the same markets across the Atlantic, along the eastern seaboard, and in the West Indies. Second, the antagonism between Baltimore and Annapolis was burning no less brightly in 1812 as in 1776 or 1763. Although the conservative assembly was fighting a rearguard action that could not defeat Baltimore's demands for independence and autonomy, it continued to resist whenever and wherever possible. Finally, from 1796 to 1815 Baltimore's occupational structure, wealth distribution, and residential patterns underwent no major alterations. The tens of thousands of people inundating Baltimore simply found niches in the old social order rather than creating a new one. Baltimore had changed—but it had remained the same too.

NOTES

1. Col. J. Thomas Scharf, *The Chronicles of Baltimore; Being a Complete History of "Baltimore Town" and Baltimore City from the Earliest Period to the Present Time* (Baltimore, 1874), pp. 43–44, 58; Paul Kent Walker, "The Baltimore Community and the American Revolution: A Study in Urban Development, 1763–1783" (Ph.D. diss., University of North Carolina at Chapel Hill, 1973), pp. 8–11, 13–14.

2. David T. Gilchrist, ed., *The Growth of the Seaport Cities, 1790–1825: Proceedings of a Conference Sponsored by the Eleutherian Mills–Hagley Foundation, March 17–19, 1966* (Charlottesville, Va., 1967), pp. 34–35.

3. *Ibid.*

4. The best discussion of Baltimore's early economic development remains Clarence P. Gould, "The Economic Causes of the Rise of Baltimore," in *Essays in Colonial History Presented to Charles McLean Andrews by His Students* (New Haven, Conn., 1931), pp. 225–51. For ethnic composition, see Howard F. Baker, "National Stocks in the Population of the United States as Indicated by Surnames in the Census of 1790," American Historical Association, *Annual Report*, 1 (Washington, D.C., 1932): 307; Wayland Fuller Dunaway, "Pennsylvania as an Early Distributing Center of Population," *Pennsylvania Magazine of History and Biography*, 55 (Apr., 1931): 135–37. For wheat output, see *A Statement of the Arts and Manufactures of the United States for the Year 1810* (Philadelphia, 1814). The southern counties include Anne Arundel, Charles, Calvert, Montgomery, Prince George, and St. Mary's; the northern counties include Baltimore, Allegany, Harford, Frederick, Washington, and Baltimore City; the Eastern Shore consists of Cecil, Caroline, Kent, Queen Anne, Talbot, Dorchester, Somerset, and Worcester. For transportation, see J. Thomas Scharf, *History of Western Maryland* (Philadelphia, 1882), 2:994–1000; Clarence P. Gould, *Money and Transportation in Maryland, 1720–1765* (Baltimore, 1915), pp. 122–70. The quote is from Gould, *Money and Transportation*, p. 126.

5. Walker, "Baltimore Community," pp. 54–71.

6. Gary Lawson Browne, *Baltimore in the New Nation, 1789–1861* (Chapel Hill, N.C., 1980), pp. 17–68, esp. chap. 1.

7. Edward C. Papenfuse, *In Pursuit of Profit: The Annapolis Merchants in the Era of the American Revolution, 1763–1805* (Baltimore, 1975), pp. 16–34. The rise of the planter gentry is the main theme in Charles Albro Barker, *The Background of the Revolution in Maryland* (New Haven, Conn., 1940). For the efforts of Maryland's ruling class to preserve their hegemony during the Revolution, see Ronald Hoffman, *A Spirit of Dissension: Economics, Politics, and the Revolution in Maryland* (Baltimore, 1973).

8. *First Records of Baltimore Town and Jones' Town, 1729–1797* (Baltimore, 1905), p. xx; Gary B. Nash, *The Urban Crucible: Social Change, Political Consciousness, and the Origins of the American Revolution* (Cambridge, Mass., 1979), pp. 30–32.

9. David Curtis Skaggs, *Roots of Maryland Democracy* (Westport, Conn.,

1973), p. 19; Hoffman, *Spirit of Dissension*, p. 14; Newton D. Mereness, *Maryland as a Proprietary Province* (London, 1901), pp. 418–21.

10. The best analysis of Baltimore politics is Frank A. Cassell, "The Structure of Baltimore's Politics in the Age of Jefferson, 1795–1812," in Aubrey C. Land, Lois Green Carr, and Edward C. Papenfuse, eds., *Law, Society, and Politics in Early Maryland: Proceedings of the First Conference on Maryland History, June 14–15, 1974* (Baltimore, 1977), pp. 277–96.

11. *Baltimore Directory and Register, for 1817* (Baltimore, 1817).

12. Map available at Maryland Historical Society, Baltimore.

13. *Ibid.*

14. Scharf, *Chronicles of Baltimore*, pp. 23, 54; Walker, "Baltimore Community," pp. 92–93; "Census of Deptford Hundred or Fell's Point, 1776," *Maryland Historical Magazine*, 25 (1930): 271–75; *Maryland Tax List 1783: Baltimore County* (Philadelphia, 1970).

15. Walker, "Baltimore Community," pp. 39–40.

2

RECRUITING A MECHANIC
WORK FORCE

In preindustrial Baltimore most white men and many black men
made their livings at a skilled trade. Laboring in small workshops
and construction crews, these mechanics plied their trades with
the same tools that generations of craftsmen had used before
them and repeated many of the same work routines. Where did
the mechanics recruit their work force? From 1790 to 1812 most
masters relied on the traditional apprenticeship system, which
supplied new workmen within a familial setting. Until his twenty-
first birthday the apprentice labored in his master's shop, often
lived in his home, and immersed himself in the "mysteries" of his
trade. Although apprenticeship breathed an almost medieval spirit
with its archaic terminology, in at least one trade it was being de-
graded into a thinly disguised form of child labor. Master shoemakers began to substitute apprentices for their journeymen to
manufacture low-grade boots and shoes, "market work," which
they sold in the backcountry and West Indies. In a city where one
person in ten was not free, slaves provided a second source of laborers. At the shipyards of Fell's Point, master shipwrights relied
increasingly on blacks as caulkers and laborers. This practice
caused little disruption because white craftsmen preserved their
privileged status as carpenters and joiners. Another pool of easily
exploitable workers was poor women. At the same time that shoemakers eroded the economic security of their skilled workingmen,
master tailors were replacing journeymen with indigent seamstresses, who did "slop work" at subsistence-level piece rates.

Thus, while Baltimore's mechanic community continued to
operate within a preindustrial framework in the early national
era, it developed several trouble spots. Shoemakers and tailors
constituted perhaps only 15 to 20 percent of the artisan popula-

27

tion, hardly "typical." But their ordeal had a greater impact than mere numbers would suggest, for it served to forewarn all crafts-men about the specter of "cheap" labor.

The sheer growth of Baltimore must have strained the cus-tomary apprenticeship system. The Maryland assembly appar-ently thought so, for in 1794 it revamped the laws regarding apprenticeship and centralized the new system under the juris-diction of the Baltimore County Orphans Court. In part the new law attempted to address the problem of the swelling number of parentless children wandering the streets. It provided that if a magistrate, constable, or watchman found one of these youths in his regular rounds, he should turn the orphan over to the judges of the court. At each of its quarterly sessions the orphans court bound out the dependent children to families in the community. Furthermore, the court strove to bring coherence to the informal and unsystematic way that apprentice contracts had long been handled. Every master in Baltimore city and county was required by law to record his apprentice indenture at the court on pain of a £3 fine. Some masters may have ducked the law to avoid paying the small fee charged by the court's register, but the thousands of indentures recorded during the next two decades suggest that most people cooperated.[1]

In devising a standard indenture form, the orphans court de-liberately invoked centuries-old wording and style. The appren-tice was enjoined to behave like a faithful son or daughter, to guard the master's "secrets," to obey his lawful commands, and to respect his worldly possessions. The apprentice swore to remain celibate and single. For his part the master pledged to instruct his charge in reading, writing, and arithmetic; to supply him with ad-equate food, shelter, and clothing; to teach him the trade; and to provide the "customary freedom dues" at the end of the contract. Although most of the indentures read the same, a few spelled out special provisions. A number of the girls bound out to learn "housewifry, common needle work, and plain sewing"—in other words, they were maids—entered contracts that required regular attendance at church service. The indenture of Mendes J. Cohen, a Jew, exempted him from work on Saturdays and Hebrew holi-days. Only a handful of indentures specified the apprentice's freedom dues. Apprentice Levi Haggerty, who was bound out to a shoemaker, was to receive "a set of tools suitable for a Journeyman Cordwayner," while John Britton, a blacksmith's apprentice, got "one Bellows one Anvil two pair of tongs two hammers and a set of Shoeing tools."[2]

Apprentices entered the families of men who, theoretically, exercised the same paternalistic authority they would with any son or daughter. Such was the ideal, and it seems to have corresponded closely with the reality. Yet the familial arrangement sometimes broke down, forcing the state to intervene. When either apprentice or master felt aggrieved, he could bring his case before the Baltimore County Court, whose dockets bristle with apprentice "protests." In the great majority of cases the apprentices complained of physical abuse, and the court usually ruled in their favor. The judges then bound out the apprentice to another master of the same trade. Recourse to the courts was not taken lightly, for when an apprentice lost his case, as did Joseph Wilson, he had to pay a fine plus court costs. There was nothing to stop a master from dragging his apprentice before the court. After listening to Thomas Kelly's case the court agreed that his apprentice was "a very incorrigible boy" and released him from the indenture.[3]

After 1794 the orphans court became a central clearinghouse for artisan labor. From 1794 through 1800 it recorded an annual average of 148 indentures. This figure jumped to 353 in 1801–5, 360 in 1806–10, and 419 in 1811–15. During the entire period a total of 6,688 masters came before the court to register their indentures, of whom 6,420 identified the trade of the apprentice: 78 percent went for mechanics, 14 percent for maids, 5 percent for merchants and nonprofessional services, and 3 percent for farmers. From 1794–1800 to 1811–15 the annual average of mechanic indentures rose from 109 to 325. One reason was simply the growth of the mechanic population. In 1796 the city directory listed 1,069 mechanics and, in 1814, 1,931. But it also appears that the number of apprentices per workshop was increasing, for while the directories indicated an 81 percent advance in the mechanic population, the yearly average of mechanic indentures ballooned by 198 percent.[4]

To a greater or lesser extent all trades depended on apprentice labor. Only construction workers and shipbuilders obtained fewer apprentice indentures than their relative numbers in the total mechanic population would lead us to expect (see Table 10). By its nature construction work, whether at the building site or shipyard, did not adapt itself ideally to the apprenticeship system. Construction workers always had an eye out for new jobs, which kept them on the road. Because apprenticeship was designed around the family and workshop, it did not fit easily into their peripatetic lifestyle. Other factors related specifically to these trades may also have come into play. As we shall see, shipbuilders recruited large numbers of free blacks and slave workers, who fell largely outside the apprenticeship system, thus reducing their dependency on it. Construction workers seem to have faced a depressed housing market, especially after 1807, which may have discouraged them from taking on a dependent apprentice. Such is the picture suggested by the decline in construction workers from 25 percent of the mechanic population in 1796 to 21 percent in 1814 (see Table 10). It is also supported by Table 11, which reveals that the percentage of indentures taken by construction workers

TABLE 10
APPRENTICE DISTRIBUTION BY CRAFT: 1794–1815

Craft	1794–1815 Percentage Apprentices	1796 Percentage Craftsmen	1814 Percentage Craftsmen
Shoemaking	20%	9%	14%
Clothing	16	19	14
Construction	16	25	21
Wood	14	9	9
Metal	7	7	8
Food	7	10	8
Leather	6	4	4
Luxury	6	4	6
Shipbuilding	5	11	12
Stone/Clay	3	2	4
Total	100%	100%	100%
N	4,991	1,069	1,931

SOURCES: Vols. 1–10, Indentures, Orphans Court, Baltimore County Register of Wills, MHR; *Baltimore Town and Fell's Point Directory* (Baltimore, n.d. [1796]); *Baltimore Directory and Register, for 1814–15* (Baltimore, 1814).

TABLE 11
CHANGES IN APPRENTICE DISTRIBUTION BY CRAFT:
1794–1815

Craft	1794–1800	1801–5	1806–10	1811–15
Shoemaking	19%	19%	21%	22%
Clothing	13	12	15	19
Construction	22	18	16	11
Wood	13	20	14	12
Metal	6	6	9	7
Food	5	7	7	8
Leather	6	6	7	7
Luxury	5	6	5	6
Shipbuilding	6	4	4	5
Stone/Clay	5	2	2	3
Total	100%	100%	100%	100%
N	754	1,272	1,340	1,625

SOURCES: See Table 10.

fell steadily from 22 percent in 1794–1800, a figure roughly
equivalent to their share in the total mechanic population, to
11 percent during the War of 1812. The steepest drop came after
1806, when building activity in Baltimore felt the damaging re-
percussions of the Embargo Act and subsequent measures of
commercial retaliation against France and Great Britain.[5]

Two trades accounted for a disproportionate number of apprentice indentures, wood and clothing. Cabinet makers and
coopers, the big two among the wood-working trades, were as
sedentary as the construction workers were mobile. They faced
none of the obstacles that hindered house carpenters and ship
joiners from assuming responsibility over an apprentice. Organized in relatively large-scale manufactories, the coopers could
pool their resources to supervise and train sizable crews of apprentices that might have proved unwieldy and ungovernable in
the workshops.

The clothing trades also drew heavily on apprentice labor.
They not only acquired a larger percentage of mechanic indentures than their percentage in the mechanic population but also
increased their share of the indentures in the early national era.
In the decade after 1794 the clothing trades accounted for 31 or

32 percent of all mechanic indentures, which jumped to 36 percent in 1806–10 and 41 percent in 1811–15. The main impetus behind this surge was the establishment of a half-dozen textile factories outside of Baltimore after 1807. The new mill owners sought a readily available, cheap work force and they found it at the orphans court. By the end of 1815 the Union Manufacturing Company had taken fifty-seven apprentices as carders, spinners, and weavers; the Baltimore Manufacturing Company forty-nine; Edward Gray and Company nineteen; the Baltimore County Cotton Manufacturers thirteen; and the Washington Cotton Manufacturing Company seven. No other trade increased its share of the total indentures from 1794 to 1815. Thus the single noteworthy alteration reflected in Table 11 stemmed not from the traditional handicraft system but, rather, from a radically different mode of production.[6]

Shoemaking merits special attention because it developed a unique relationship with the apprenticeship system. According to the city directories, shoemakers constituted 9 percent of the mechanic population in 1796 and 14 percent two decades later. Yet they obtained 20 percent of all mechanic indentures during roughly the same period. From 1794 through 1815, 385 master shoemakers registered 909 apprentice indentures at the orphans court. Nearly two-fifths of these youths worked in large-scale shops that employed five or more apprentices (see Table 12). Master William Duncan, whose shop stood at the patriotic sign of the "Boot and Eagle," was the top employer with a maximum of fifteen apprentices under his supervision at one time. Then came John Vernon with twelve; Henry Peck, James Ives, and Alexander Briscoe with eleven each; and William McCleary, Rezin Pool, and Benjamin Waters with ten each. The mean age of the shoemakers' apprentices was 14.7 years, which meant that each youth could count on six or seven years of service. Almost half of them were orphans, presumably with little choice about their trade or master. Only nineteen were identified as black or mulatto, three of whom worked for Henry Folkes, a free black shoemaker.[7]

The big shoemakers like William Duncan were cutting the heart out of the apprenticeship system while preserving its familiar form. Can we imagine this man teaching his fifteen apprentices the three R's, ensuring their proper Christian upbringing,

TABLE 12
APPRENTICE HOLDINGS OF
SHOEMAKERS: 1794–1815

N of Apprentices	Percentage Masters	Percentage Apprentices
1	49%	21%
2	22	19
3	9	12
4	9	15
5	3	6
6	2	5
7	3	8
8	1	4
10+	2	10
Total	100%	100%
N	385	909

SOURCES: See Table 10.

or fulfilling his other obligations set down in the indentures? Can we imagine a dozen teenagers living with him under the same roof? What led men like William Duncan to transform a fundamentally familial institution into a device for securing cheap labor was the rising demand for low-quality shoes and boots. Shoemakers had traditionally hammered out custom-made footware for individual buyers, people they probably knew. This "bespoke" work was left to the steady hands of a highly skilled mechanic, for a bad stitch or uneven cut could ruin a valuable piece of leather as well as waste several days' work. Only the masters and journeymen handled these orders; an apprentice might make a mess of the job. In the early national era, however, these customary arrangements were growing obsolete as Baltimore's merchants established commercial ties to the West Indies and to the agricultural backcountry. Black slaves and poor farmers needed shoes—and cheap ones. They settled for ready-made boots and shoes, available in several standard sizes and shipped by the barrel. The journeyman shoemaker faced a dilemma, for this "market" work obviated the careful craftsmanship of the bespoke era. An apprentice churned out low-grade shoes just as well—or badly—as he could and at a considerably lower cost to the employer and purchaser.[8]

By the early nineteenth century Baltimore had risen to become the center of "market" shoe production in Maryland and probably the entire Chesapeake. The 1810 federal manufacturing census for Maryland, which admittedly suffers from numerous gaps and inaccuracies, revealed that 331 manufactories were operating across the state, producing a total of 281,688 pairs of "Shoes, boots and slippers," valued at $482,426. Baltimore City accounted for 64 of the manufactories (19 percent), 120,000 of the pairs (43 percent), and $212,000 of the value (43 percent). Baltimore's manufactories carried on production on a much larger scale than the shops elsewhere in the state. An average establishment turned out 1,875 pairs annually, worth $3,313. By contrast, the productive capacity of the average shop elsewhere fell to just 606 pairs, valued at $1,050.[9]

Baltimore's top shoemakers converted to "market" production without hesitation. In 1808 John Vernon, the second largest apprentice holder, who operated a manufactory on South Street, announced in the newspapers: "Orders from any part of the country, or for the West-Indies, to any amount, will be punctually attended to; his frequent dealings to any of the different W. I. Islands, has rendered him perfectly intimate with their prevailing fashions." A kindred spirit was Rezin Pool, who had only two fewer apprentices than Vernon. He boasted that his boots were "of materials and workmanship far superior to those generally made for exportation, but will be sold at the usual prices of exportation work." Pool and Vernon had entered an extremely competitive market, for industrial communities like Lynn, Massachusetts, were already shipping their shoes and boots throughout the nation. Every spring coasting vessels carrying packaged Lynn shoes sailed up the Patapsco River to Baltimore, while from all other directions came country traders with their yearly orders of provisions. To get the attention and business of these merchants, a number of shoe sellers who were probably working on commission for New England firms advertised their wares in the newspapers, like Amos Brown and Alexander Finnister.

Not a few of Baltimore's shoemakers resisted this Yankee interloping. In April, 1807, two "Cheap Shoe Stores" opened their doors on Market Street (later Baltimore Street), proclaiming their merchandise "fresh and good; and chiefly of Baltimore Manufacture." In the same year Robert Sands established a ladies' shoe manufactory under his "immediate direction and notice." Also rising to the challenge was John W. Keirle, who in 1809 opened a shoe manufactory at the Point and announced his determination "to sell ladies' Shoes of his own manufacturing, by retail, lower than they can obtain those imported from the New-England states." Some shoe sellers offered a mixed assortment of home-made and imported goods. In May, 1807, Fuller and Wright notified the public of "A complete assortment of SHOES for retailing of their own manufacturing both in Baltimore and to the northward." Koone and Hughes also combined their own products with the "best of NORTHERN SHOES."[10]

A few examples serve to illustrate how these shoemakers rose to the level where they were marketing their wares at home as well as overseas. Many were self-made men. William Mc-Cleary was one of the city's biggest shoemakers. He began as a journeyman under the employ of James Sloan, another big shoemaker. McCleary apparently ran a tight shop, for Sloan made him foreman. By 1805 McCleary had saved up enough to open his own manufactory on the corner of Water and South streets, just a few blocks down from his old employer. Within a year he had signed three apprentice indentures at the court. From 1805 through 1815 McCleary obtained fourteen apprentices. When he opened his shop, McCleary placed an advertisement in the newspapers offering jobs to five or six journeymen. Thus, while he initially depended on journeymen, McCleary gradually shifted to apprentice labor as the youths gained greater skill at their trade. The career of John Duncan provides a parallel case. He had served as foreman in the shop of William Duncan, the foremost apprentice holder in Baltimore. In the same year that McCleary struck out on his own, John established a workshop and soon gathered a crew of apprentices. Another shop foreman who made good was James Lambie, who in 1808 left James Tannoch's employ to open a boot factory on South Street. Lambie hired Robert Beatty to manage his shop, a thirty-eight-year-old journeyman from England via Bermuda. Before the end of the year Beatty had his own shop.[11]

These were the success stories, of course. Perhaps more typical were the small-scale shoemakers whose workshops included no more than a few apprentices. Of the 385 master shoemakers who obtained indentures, 71 percent took just one or two. Consider the case of Alexander McMechin. Born in 1784, McMechin was apprenticed to Joshua Inloes at the age of fourteen. In 1806, a year after his apprenticeship expired, McMechin joined the newly formed Union Society of Journeymen Cordwainers, one of the most militant trade societies of the early national period. Within a few months McMechin had been elected to the society's standing committee. By 1811 he was twenty-seven years old and ready to open his own workshop, obtaining his first apprentice indenture at the orphans court. During the next five years McMechin accumulated a small estate, which the city assessors estimated at $150, placing him in the bottom quarter of Baltimore's property holders. It is interesting to speculate about why McMechin never returned to the orphans court for another apprentice. Perhaps he could support only one. Perhaps, too, he nursed a lingering loyalty to the cause of the journeymen, whose place on the workbench was jeopardized by the growing number of apprentices.[12]

A second source of mechanic labor was slaves. By the standards of urban America Baltimore was a slave society. After the Revolution New York and Philadelphia steadily phased out the institution while Boston ended it for good. Baltimore, however, went its own way. Not until the decade of 1810–20 did Baltimore's slave population fail to keep pace with its free population. During the first decades of the early national era, slaves ordinarily represented about 10 percent of the city's population, their numbers advancing from 1,255 in 1790, to 2,843 in 1800, to 4,672 in 1810. But even these figures fail to convey how completely slavery permeated Baltimore society. In 1800 a third of the city's households—1,064 of 3,301—included at least one slave. Furthermore, many persons who did not own a slave hired one from somebody who did, and this common practice spread the influence of slavery more widely. Urban slaveholding was less concentrated than the plantation variety. In 1800 Baltimore's mean slaveholding was only 2.7. Just 2 percent of slaveholding households had over ten slaves, 4 percent seven to nine, 9 percent five or six, 24 percent three or four, and 61 percent one or two. The largest single slaveholding was twenty-two.[13]

Slaves did three types of work. House servants cleaned,

washed, cooked, and cared for the children of their masters. The small size of slaveholdings suggests that most households acquired a slave or two for home chores. Another indication of the predominance of domestic servants is the disproportionate number of female slaves, who shouldered the greatest burden of household duties. The 1820 federal census, the first to identify blacks by age and sex, revealed that 55 percent of Baltimore's 4,357 slaves were females, in contrast to just 50 percent of the 48,055 whites. The female slave population bulged in the fourteen to twenty-five age group, the natural recruiting ground for maids, cooks, and nurses. This category included 36 percent of female slaves, compared to approximately 28 percent of white females. An analysis of the slaveholders' occupations also points to the predominance of domestic workers (see Table 13). The two groups most likely to employ slaves outside of household work were mechanics, who might use them around the shop, and nonprofessional service trades, which included ship captains who often owned slave sailors. Together, these groups accounted for only 33 percent of the city's slaves in 1800. More inclined to acquire household servants were the merchants, traders, public officials, and professionals. For these groups, who owned two-thirds of the total, slaves symbolized badges of social status and the amenities of townhouse life.[14]

A second group of slaves scoured the town in search of odd jobs, a small army of black handymen doing all but the most highly skilled tasks. Masters who had fallen on hard times might hire out their slaves by the day, month, or year. Inhabiting a gray area where the boundaries between slavery and freedom interlaced, some masters permitted their slaves to find work wherever they could, to live on their own, and to take a share of their earnings. In such cases masters and bondsmen hammered out their own financial arrangements. A considerable number of slaves must have made enough to buy their way out of bondage. Their efforts undoubtedly contributed to the surge of manumissions in the early national era. Indeed, the free black community multiplied faster than either the slave or white segments of the population did.

Although white and black Baltimoreans left little record of the slaves' struggle for self-liberation, we occasionally catch a

TABLE 13
SLAVE DISTRIBUTION BY OCCUPATION: 1800

Occupation	Percentage Total Slaves	Mean Slaveholding	Percentage Slaveholders
Wholesale merchant	32%	3.3	73%
Mechanic	28	2.5	27
Trader	14	2.6	35
Retail merchant	9	2.5	47
Professional	6	3.5	71
Public official	5	3.0	39
Nonprofessional	5	2.2	39
Laborer	1	4.0	3

SOURCES: Second Census of the United States, 1800, Baltimore City; *New Baltimore Directory and Annual Register, for 1800 and 1801* (Baltimore, n.d. [1800]).

Notes: Of the 3,301 white male household heads in the census, 1,072 were identified in the directory by occupation.

glimpse of it. In 1799 physician Alexander Robinson opened his business ledger and began an account with his slave, Anthony Dowding. Over the next six months he recorded, in a handful of laconic entries, a quest for freedom that must have repeated itself many times in Baltimore. Dowding was earning money, and the reason was clear—to purchase his freedom. He spent a month at a brickyard where he probably joined a crew digging out clay and wheeling it to the kilns for firing. Dowding also took jobs around his master's house. In August he plastered the ceiling of the townhouse. In October he glazed the windows, repaired a ladder, and mended the roof of a back building. In November he fixed the fence gates. From July through December, when Robinson finally closed accounts with his indefatigable slave, Dowding had earned the $122 pegged as his purchase price and became a free man.[15]

Standing at the top of the slave occupational hierarchy was the skilled worker. It seems fair to infer that the city's mechanics, who together owned 28 percent of the slaves in 1800, generated the greatest demand for skilled bondsmen. Of course, not all or even most white mechanics could afford to buy a slave. In 1800 only one of four were slaveholders, compared to three of four wholesale merchants. Not surprisingly, rich mechanics were usually slaveholders. In 1800 two-thirds of the wealthiest fifty-two craftsmen owned at least one slave. Whether a mechanic had a slave depended not only on his wealth but also on his trade. In Table 14 we see that shipbuilders stood well above their fellow mechanics in slaveholding, with a mean average of 5.6. In 1800 they supplied five of the top nineteen slaveholders whose occupations are known; the others included five innkeepers, four rentiers, one nail manufacturer, one boarding house proprietor, one revenue supervisor, one merchant, and one brewer. Shipbuilders outdistanced even this elite group. The foremost slaveholder in Baltimore was shipwright William Price with twenty-two, in second place shipwright David Stodder with seventeen, in third shipwright John Steele with twelve, and in fifth shipwrights David Burke and James Biays with ten each.[16]

Slaveholding was nothing new to shipbuilders at the Point. The 1783 tax list identifies 276 slaves at the Point, but there were really more. For some reason the assessor failed to enumerate male slaves over the age of forty-five and females over thirty-six. Most masters seem to have put their slaves to work around the docks rather than in the homes. Of the 276 slaves, 114 (41 percent) were working-age males between the ages of fourteen and forty-five, while only 68 (25 percent) were females from fourteen to thirty-six. Although the assessors did not specify the sex of slaves below the age of fourteen, it appears that males far outnumbered females, in contrast to the sex composition of the city's slave population seventeen years later. The Point's largest slave-

TABLE 14
SLAVE DISTRIBUTION BY CRAFT: 1800

Craft	Mean Slaveholding	Percentage Slaveholders
Shipbuilding	5.6	48%
Stone/Clay	3.5	20
Metal	3.4	23
Food	2.6	44
Leather	2.1	63
Construction	2.0	23
Clothing	1.8	22
Wood	1.6	21
Luxury	1.4	40

SOURCES: See Table 13.

holders were master craftsmen in the maritime trades whose bondsmen were probably skilled hands. The top one was block-maker William Hays with sixteen slaves, followed by ropemaker Thomas Worthington with fifteen, shipbuilders Stodder and John Chapple with twelve each, and shipwright Steele with nine. These men also owned the most working-age male slaves: Worth-ington had twelve, Stodder ten, Hays and Steele eight each, Chapple five.[17]

While the institution of slavery put deep roots into the ship-building trade, it nonetheless underwent a significant structural alteration in the early national era. At the start of the nineteenth century slaveownership was fairly widespread among shipbuild-ers of all ranks, from the big contractors who operated the yards to the skilled hands who worked there. In 1800 seventeen of the thirty-five (49 percent) shipbuilders identified in the federal cen-sus were slaveholders. Six had five slaves or more. Within two decades, however, the number of slaveholding shipbuilders had plunged to thirty-two of 129 (25 percent). Eight had five or more slaves. Price was still in the lead with twenty-four. Then came William Duke with seventeen, Joseph Despeaux with eight, and John Wilson and John Golden with seven each. The big men in the trade not only carved out a larger share of the total number of slaves but also acquired a greater proportion of males. In 1820, 54 percent of slaves owned by shipbuilders were males, compared to 45 percent for the city as a whole. The top shipwrights had an even higher percentage of male slaves: sixteen of Price's twenty-four, thirteen of Duke's seventeen, six of Despeaux's eight. In part through their access to slave labor, a few men had risen to dominance in the shipbuilding trade.[18]

The big shipwrights walked a fine line with striking success. While cornering the supply of slave labor and consolidating their pre-eminence in the trade, they avoided seriously disrupting working arrangements at the yards. The business records of Joseph Despeaux reveal how they brought it off. Born in France in 1758, Despeaux emigrated to colonial St. Domingue, where by the early 1790s he was operating a thriving shipyard at Cape François. Despeaux did not belong to the planter class but, like them, he was a slaveholder. Thus he and his family narrowly es-caped death by fleeing when in 1793 the island's slaves rose up against the master class. Despeaux first tried settling in Philadelphia, whose prosperous maritime industries offered a strong appeal to a shipwright, but the state laws discouraging the importation of slaves convinced him to seek a new home elsewhere. Baltimore was a good second choice, for it was a center of both shipbuilding and slavery. In 1805 Despeaux took an oath as a U.S. citizen. Until his death fifteen years later Despeaux ran one of the busiest shipyards at the Point, which achieved fame by reportedly constructing an early Baltimore clipper.[19]

Like his fellow shipbuilders, Despeaux recruited slave and free black workers without fomenting unrest among his white mechanics. His strategy has a familiar ring: blacks got the worst jobs, whites the best. The aristocrats of the yards were the carpenters, who consistently earned $2.00 a day in the years around 1812. Not a single black seems to have broken into this privileged elite. Beneath the carpenters were the caulkers, and it was here that blacks gained entry into the trade. The 1822 city directory contains the names of twenty caulkers, nineteen of whom were free blacks. Although none of the early directories listed slaves or their occupations, the bondsmen also found jobs next to their free brethren. From 1810 to 1815 Despeaux probably employed eleven slaves as caulkers. Free caulkers usually made $1.50 a day, though in the four months after October, 1812, when Baltimore's shipyards were gearing up for war, their wages rose to $1.67½. Slave caulkers had to settle for between $1.25 and $1.31¼ a day. The bottom stratum at the yards encompassed a wide range of unskilled workers, blacks and whites: poor women spinning oakum, poor men boiling pitch, young boys helping the carpenters. They made bottom wages, 75¢ to $1.00 a day. The differential in wages represented one device for pacifying white mechanics who might otherwise resent the intrusion of black laborers, but perhaps equally important was the expectation of steady work. In 1812 Despeaux recorded wage disbursements for 1,629¾ man-days for carpenters but only 576½ for caulkers.[20]

Slavery was flexible at the yards. Sometimes Despeaux landed a big contract and needed extra hands. He could draw from a ready pool of slave caulkers, hiring them from his fellow shipbuilders at the Point. Usually Despeaux needed only one slave for a day or two, but he might hire as many as five. Slaves were available for both short and long terms. In February, 1811, Despeaux paid shipwright Isaac Sutton $3.00 for the labor of his "black boy Clem" at 75¢ a day. Later in the year he credited $96 to the account of William James for the hire of his "Black boy Daniel," which at prevailing rates would cover four or five months of work. Although Despeaux might seek out workers, he was usually sought out by others. Indeed, his slave caulkers seem to have been in great demand at the Point. In 1813 five shipbuilders hired them: William Parsons, George Gardner, William Flannigan, Steven Benillant, and James Cordery. Despeaux was far wealthier than any of these men. In 1815 he was assessed at $3,030, which placed him in the top 6 percent of Baltimore's property holders. By contrast, Flannigan was worth only $1,756, Gardner $270, and Parsons $80. Benillant and Cordery did not appear on the tax list, either because they did not have enough property to assess or because they had left town. Here we see the subtle forms of dependency that slavery created in the trade, for where else could a small-time ship carpenter go for a relatively cheap slave caulker than to a big contractor like Despeaux?[21]

Brickmakers also relied heavily on slave labor. With a mean average of 3.5 slaves, they were second only to the shipbuilders. Slavery at the yards, whether brick or ship, conformed to a common pattern. Like the slave caulkers, slave brickmakers could not climb to the top rungs of the occupational ladder. Most of them seem to have been diggers and wheelers, shoveling raw clay into barrows and hauling it to the kilns for tempering. The temperers mixed the clay with water, sand, and other ingredients until they judged it the proper consistency. Then the clay went to the molders, the brickyard elite who most closely resembled the ship carpenters. After "cutting down" the clay and filling the molds, they handed the malleable bricks to an "off bearer" who took them to the sheds for drying. A boy was assigned this task, since his small and nimble fingers could handle the bricks without leaving damaging impressions on them. After a day of drying the bricks headed to the kilns for firing. In a petition delivered to the Baltimore city council in 1798, the town's leading brickmakers testified to the prevalence of black workers at their yards:

> If any of you gentlemen have been at our brickyard, you have no doubt observed four black Men for one white man, this is not

owing to wages, no labour in this City affords better wages than brickmakers give to their labourers, but merely because of the ex- tream hard labour, if this could be lessened, it would incourage poor white men and boys to come to the brickyard for imployment. Bricks would then be made better and give more satisfaction to the buyer and Seller.

The master brickmakers were protesting a proposed city ordinance that would increase the standard size of bricks and, they claimed, heap another burden on their already overtaxed workmen.[22]

Among the signers was John Allbright. In 1801 the printing partnership of Warner and Hanna published a map of Baltimore and its environs that identified a number of prominent residences within a mile or two of the city. The map showed a small three- story structure just outside of town, in a clay-rich area of the west- ern precincts called "Ridgely's Delight." This was the home of "J. Allbright." Many of Baltimore's brickmakers lived in the vicin- ity; right down the road from Allbright was a larger house occu- pied by George Warner, whose name also appears on the 1798 petition. Allbright left an account book that reveals the operations of a typical Baltimore brickyard and exposes the trade's strong links to slavery. Like shipwright Despeaux, Allbright hired slaves from fellow mechanics. In 1796 he paid brickmaker John Berry £37 10s. for the hire of each of his slaves, William and Sam. Wages varied from $15 to $20 a month, about what an unskilled laborer could expect at Despeaux's yard but considerably below a caulker's earnings. Brickmaking was dangerous work, especially around the scorching heat of the kilns. In the early 1790s the hired slave Harry suffered what must have been a common type of injury—a "scalded foot." Harry was laid up for nearly two weeks. Allbright's behavior in this case reminds us more of a modern-day employer than a paternalistic slaveholder. He not only deducted the lost time from Harry's earnings but also charged the slave's master 13s. 9d. a week for board until he was back on his feet.[23]

The master brickmakers strove earnestly to discipline their work force, but they were hampered by the primitive technology of the industry as well as erratic shifts in production. The weather and seasons dictated the pace of work, shutting down the yards almost entirely during winter and on overcast and rainy days. In 1791–92 Allbright's yard manufactured 52 percent of its annual output of bricks between April and July, 43 percent between August and November, and 5 percent between December and March. With such unpredictable employment the brickyards were beset with labor absenteeism. The problem reached such proportions that in the early nineteenth century the master brickmakers leagued together to issue a common list of regulations for their workingmen, which prohibited any laborer from leaving the yard without his foreman's permission. Yet, as the case of Joe Hinton suggests, black brickmakers continued to enjoy a substantial degree of *de facto* freedom. In February, 1798, Hinton ran away from his owner, Christopher Hughes, who placed a reward notice in the newspapers. Hughes painted a colorful portrait of his "daring and resolute" slave. Hinton was described as a thirty-eight-year-old fancy dresser and smooth talker. He lived alone in a brick house that Hughes complained cost him $60 a year. An avid gaming man, Hinton was said to have lost $16 at the card table in a single night—close to a full month's wages. Hughes suspected that his slave would be found "lurking about some of the Negro houses card-playing and cock-fighting, for which amusements he has a great passion, and keeps a number of game cocks at different walks." Hinton had a long record of running away, and usually wound up with his father in Baltimore or kinsfolk in Harford County.[24]

Women formed a third source of mechanic labor. We cannot analyze female labor with the precision that has been possible for apprentice and slave labor, for there is no set of documentation corresponding to the apprentice indentures or the federal censuses. Yet from indirect and admittedly impressionistic sources it seems that at least one group of mechanics, the master tailors, was growing increasingly dependent on female workers. In the late eighteenth and early nineteenth centuries the same economic forces that reshaped the shoemaking trade were wreaking havoc among the tailors. At home and overseas the demand for cheap ready-made clothing was on the rise. One indication of this growing market was the sudden emergence of "slop shops" throughout the city, which manufactured a few standard types of cheap clothing and provided precarious employment for seamstresses. The slop-sellers distributed the coarse cloth to women, who brought the material to their cramped rooms and stitched it into duck trousers and shirts. A small piece-rate payment waited for them when they returned the finished product to the slop seller.

Tailors traditionally viewed themselves above "slop" work, which fast became a term of opprobrium in the trade, but several masters could not resist the tempting profits to be made in the market for cheap clothes. Thomas Sheppard and Nathaniel Childs were only two big master tailors who began calling themselves "tailor and slop seller." Seamstresses found work not only at the slop shops but also in the tailors' workshops. To their chagrin journeymen tailors discovered that jobs they had always done were going to poor seamstresses in the community, who were willing to work at desperate wages. Thus the masters could slash their costs while foisting a shoddy product on their customers at the same price. Journeymen tailors sounded such protests again and again in the early national era, bewailing the corruption of their skills just as journeymen shoemakers lashed out at apprentice labor.[25]

Long-term demographic changes in Baltimore may have facilitated the tailors' movement toward female labor. From 1790 to 1820 females increased from 46 percent of the city's white population to 50 percent. A substantial number of these women were household heads, whose husbands may have died or disappeared, leaving them to eke out a living in whatever way possible. In 1800 women headed 8 percent of Baltimore's over 3,000 white households. While the relative and absolute number of potential seamstresses was growing, the number of master tailors remained the same and may have actually dropped. According to the city directories, tailors numbered 138 in 1804 and 129 in 1814. From the perspective of master tailors seeking cheap female labor, Baltimore seems to have been an employer's market.[26]

Another indirect indication that female poverty was becoming a greater problem, compelling women to seek needlework, was the explosion of private charity organizations after 1800. Although few of these associations left any permanent mark on Baltimore's institutional history, they testified to the plight of indigent women. As "The Widow's Friend" observed in 1805, the same conditions that led women to the dole also drove them to the tailors:

Dependent females are almost limited to one branch of business—indeed, they may literally be said to be bound for life to the needle and thread. In this city, however, the remark applies with peculiar force; for here, this numerous class of women derive their daily support almost entirely from such small pieces of work as can be had occasionally from the tailors, or on the very precarious employment to be procured from the shelves of the slophouse.

Such sentiments lay behind the establishment of charitable agencies designed to assist poor women and their children. The pioneer was the Female Humane Association, set up in 1800 to educate the children of destitute women. Two years later the Impartial Society for the Relief of Widows also offered schooling to needy orphans. Within a short time these agencies stopped distributing alms and started demanding work from their recipients. Eight years after its founding the Impartial Society proposed to buy a warehouse for the storage of sewing materials that could be distributed to idle seamstresses. Another group of prominent citizens pled for the creation of a Benevolent Society for the Benefit of Females. Once they had rented a storehouse, the society planned to provide cloth to unemployed seamstresses along with a quarterly dividend on any profits arising from the sale of the finished products. To foster the correct working habits, the organizers planned to offer "premiums to the most industrious and deserving." They also proposed to appoint thirty overseers whose duty was to "advise any female, whom they may visit, against the dangers and folly of idleness and dissipation and to encourage them steadily to pursue the path of virtue and honest industry as the only means by which they can maintain an unspotted character or acquire with any credit to themselves, the common necessaries and comforts of life." By May, 1805, the society's capital stock was nearly complete.[27]

The most ambitious charity scheme was the School of Industry. Like other agencies, it was fashioned primarily to help poor women. In August, 1804, Mayor Thorowgood Smith chaired a meeting of interested citizens who desired a comprehensive charity program. According to the plan as it finally emerged, the School of Industry would be an omnibus institution. It included a soup house, which opened its doors during the particularly harsh winter of 1805. The soup house was supplied with pork, lard, and bacon that had been donated by the subscribers. To get a free meal, a poor person had to obtain a meal ticket from one of these subscribers. The organizers also hoped to purchase a storehouse where seamstresses could find enough work to tide them over the slack winter months. If the storehouse proved successful, the subscribers planned to add a workhouse to gather all the recipients under the same roof. Not only would this device permit closer supervision of the seamstresses, but it would also save them the expense of heating their small homes during the day. Since the School of Industry aimed at the moral regeneration of the women, the founders envisioned purchasing books on both religious instruction and the mechanical arts. If all went well, this small library might one day become the nucleus of an orphans' school. The subscribers proposed to contribute any excess profit to the support of the incapacitated poor who failed to qualify for the Baltimore County almshouse.[28]

How can we assess the economic impact of the recruitment of apprentices, slaves, and women upon the trades it touched most directly? One way is to examine the patterns of property holding in the shoemaking, shipbuilding, and tailoring trades. As Table 15 reveals, the relative number of mechanics in these branches who did not acquire taxable property grew. The shipbuilding trade experienced the least change, probably because slaves did not compete directly with white carpenters and joiners. Slavery may have contributed to the increase in poverty, but the relationship was indirect: master shipwrights cornered the supply of slave caulkers, depriving small ship carpenters of taxable property and a source of income. Shoemakers and tailors, as we might expect, felt the intrusion of cheap labor most painfully. If the shoemakers are representative, the vast majority of those mechanics who fell into the propertyless category were journeymen. At least nine members of the Union Society of Journeymen Cordwainers, which disbanded in 1809, were still living in Baltimore during the 1815 assessment. None of them had taxable property.[29]

By the early national era Baltimore's mechanic population had come of age. It now numbered in the thousands; one would have to visit New York, Philadelphia, or Boston to find a comparable concentration of craftsmen. Even the state legislature could

TABLE 15

ESTIMATES OF PROPERTYLESS MECHANICS: 1804, 1815

	Tailors		Shoemakers		Shipbuilders	
	1804	1815	1804	1815	1804	1815
Propertyless	54%	73%	43%	65%	44%	52%
N in Sample	83	90	96	145	98	155
Unidentified	55	38	76	108	87	73

SOURCES: Alphabetical Lists of Assessed Persons, 1804, Baltimore County Commissioners, MHR; Baltimore Assessment Record Book, MS. 55, MHS; *Baltimore Directory, for 1803* (Baltimore, n.d. [1803]); *Baltimore Directory, for 1804* (Baltimore, n.d. [1804]); *Baltimore Directory and Register, for 1814–15*; *Baltimore Directory and Register, for 1816* (Baltimore, 1816).

Notes: If a mechanic was listed in the city directories of 1803 and 1804, it was assumed he lived in Baltimore at the time of the 1804 assessment. He was placed in the sample category. If he was listed in one directory but not the other, it could not be assumed he was living in Baltimore in 1804. He was placed in the unidentified category. The same procedure was used in estimating the propertyless mechanics in 1815.

not ignore them. Perhaps under pressure from the workmen themselves, the assembly in 1794 shored up what most mechanics must have considered the institutional foundation of their community—the apprenticeship system. For the next generation apprentices poured into the workshops to imbibe the skills and values there, in time to strike out as independent journeymen, and ultimately to establish shops of their own, where a new generation of apprentices would renew the cycle. Over 6,000 mechanic indentures gave ample testimony to the vigor of the traditional handicraft system. Even where the mechanics drew on nonapprentice slave labor, as did the shipbuilding and brickmaking trades, they did not threaten the customary status of skilled working men. In two trades, however, the old ways were not working. Master shoemakers and tailors resorted to "cheap" labor—children and women respectively—to produce a low-grade product for a new mass market. In each of these trades the growing polarization of wealth bore witness to the ordeal of journeymen who found their skills becoming obsolete. By the early national period the human material for a politically conscious mechanic community was in place, but so too was the potential for conflict.

NOTES

1. Chap. XLV, "An Act for the better regulation of apprentices," Nov., 1793, Session, William Kilty, ed., *Laws of Maryland* (Annapolis, 1800).

2. Vol. 8, fo. 33, vol. 3, fos. 192–93, 20, Indentures, Orphans Court, Baltimore County Register of Wills, Maryland Hall of Records (hereafter cited as MHR).

3. Petition Docket, July, 1809, Session, pp. 13, 27, Criminal Dockets of the Court of Oyer and Terminer, Baltimore City Criminal Court, MHR.

4. *Baltimore Town and Fell's Point Directory* (Baltimore, n.d. [1796]); *Baltimore Directory and Register, for 1814–15* (Baltimore, 1814).

5. *Ibid.*

6. Indentures; Richard W. Griffin, "An Origin of the Industrial Revolution in Maryland: I, The Textile Industry," *Maryland Historical Magazine*, 61 (Mar. 1966): 24–36.

7. *American* (Baltimore), Apr. 4, 1805; vol. 8, fos. 475–76, vol. 9, fos. 198, 347–48, 371, Indentures.

8. John R. Commons, "American Shoemakers, 1648–1895: A Sketch of Industrial Evolution," *Quarterly Journal of Economics*, 24 (Nov., 1909): 39–84.

9. Calculated from *A Statement of the Arts and Manufactures of the United States for the Year 1810* (Philadelphia, 1814).

10. *American*, Nov. 20, 1805, Apr. 9, 1806, Apr. 16, May 6, 29, 1807, May 7, 1808, Jan. 5, 1809; *Whig* (Baltimore), Nov. 10, 1808.

11. *American*, Apr. 6, Aug. 16, 1805, Sept. 8, 1808, Dec. 18, 1810; *Federal Gazette* (Baltimore), Oct. 28, 1808.

12. July 20, 1807, Apr. 18, 1808, Constitution and Bye Laws of the Union Society of Journeymen Cordwainers of the City and Precincts of Baltimore, Baltimore County Commissioners, Private Commissioners, MHR; vol. 7, fo. 132, vol. 8, fos. 238–39, Indentures.

13. Data on slaveholding compiled from Second Census of the United States, 1800, Baltimore City.

14. David Gilchrist, ed., *The Growth of the Seaport Cities, 1790–1825: Proceedings of a Conference Sponsored by the Eleutherian Mills–Hagley Foundation, March 17–19, 1966* (Charlottesville, Va., 1967), pp. 34–35.

15. Alexander Robinson Ledger, MS. 699, p. 45, Maryland Historical Society (hereafter cited as MHS).

16. The estimate on the slaveholdings of wealthy mechanics was calculated by cross-referencing the 1804 city tax list, which contains the names of 2,988 property holders, with the 1803 city directory. This procedure identified the occupations of 1,237 property holders, of whom 476 were craftsmen. Of the 118 craftsmen who ranked in the top 30 percent of the city's property holders, 52 appear in the 1800 census and 28 of them owned slaves. See 1800 Census; Alphabetical Lists of Assessed Persons, 1804, Baltimore County Commissioners, MHR; *Baltimore Directory, for 1803* (Baltimore, n.d. [1803]).

17. *Maryland Tax List 1783: Baltimore County* (Philadelphia, 1970).

18. 1800 Census; Fourth Census of the United States, 1820, Baltimore City; *New Baltimore Directory and Annual Register; for 1800 and 1801* (Baltimore, n.d. [1800]); *Baltimore Directory, for 1822 & '23* (Baltimore, 1822).

19. For biographical information, see Despeaux Papers, MS. 260, MHS.

20. Despeaux Account Book, Oct. 26, 1812, Feb. 16, Sept. 1, 1813.

21. *Ibid.*, Feb. 25, Aug. 19, 1811; Baltimore Assessment Record Book, MS. 55, MHS

22. Petition is reprinted in Lee H. Nelson, "Brickmaking in Baltimore, 1798," *Journal of the Society of Architectural Historians*, 18 (Mar., 1959): 34.

23. Allbright Account Book, Dec. 30, 1795, June 22, Nov. 29, 1798, MS. 12, MHS; vol. 5, fo. 393, Indentures.

24. Allbright Account Book; *Rules To be Observed by the Hands Employed in the Brick-Making Business* (Baltimore, 1812), MHS; *Federal Gazette*, Feb. 2, 1798.

25. *American*, June 4, 1810; John R. Commons et al., *The History of Labour in the United States* (New York, 1918), 1: 104–6.

26. 1800 Census; *Baltimore Directory, for 1804* (Baltimore, n.d. [1804]); *Baltimore Directory and Register, for 1814–15.*

27. *American*, Feb. 3, Mar. 15, 1805, May 5, 1806, Nov. 30, 1804, June 4, 1810; *A Plan of the Female Humane Association Charity School* (Baltimore, 1800).

28. *American*, Aug. 22, 1804, Apr. 2, Dec. 16, 1805.

29. By combining the membership of the Union Society with the journeymen indicted in the 1809 strike, it is possible to identify the names of sixty-two journeymen shoemakers. Of these sixty-two, nine appear in both the 1814 and 1816 city directories. Therefore it is assumed that they were residing in Baltimore at the time of the 1815 assessment. See Baltimore Assessment Record Book; Constitution and Bye Laws of the Union Society; July, 1809, Session, Criminal Dockets, Baltimore City Criminal Court; *Baltimore Directory and Register, for 1814–15; Baltimore Directory and Register, for 1816* (Baltimore, 1816).

PART TWO

THE MAKING OF
THE MECHANIC COMMUNITY,
1763–1800

3

THE LEGACY OF THE REVOLUTION

From 1763 to 1800 Baltimore's mechanics transformed themselves into a politically conscious community. It was not a sudden awakening. Nor did it happen automatically once Baltimore had reached some predetermined level of material development. Political maturity came slowly and often painfully, as workingmen struggled to win recognition in the new republic. Before the independence movement Baltimore's mechanics lacked the numbers, experience, and elan of their brethren in the older cities. Not until 1763 did they ally with merchants in the Baltimore Mechanical Company, an early experiment in self-government that challenged the assembly's efforts to throttle local autonomy. Merchants had the upper hand in this popular coalition. Furthermore, after 1767 they continued to dominate the local leadership of the independence struggle.

Yet the mechanics were mobilizing on their own. By 1773 the first mechanic had been elected president of the Mechanical Company, and two years later workingmen formed the Baltimore Mechanical Volunteers. This was more than a militia unit; it was a "school of democracy" where mechanics gained confidence in themselves, their abilities to command, and their right to be heard. Irresistibly, the Volunteers were drawn into politics. Having concluded that Maryland's leadership was hopelessly compromised by its ties to tories, mechanic militia officers joined radical merchants in founding the Baltimore Whig Club. For several tense months the club set out to purge toryism from the Baltimore area. By 1777 the new state and town authorities had combined to destroy the radical organization, which seemed to embody the social upheaval spreading across Maryland. Yet they could not destroy the legacy of the Mechanical Company, Mechanical Volunteers, and Whig Club: the mechanics had emerged from the Revolution as a political force.

By 1763 nearly everyone could see that Baltimore was a town with a future, not a glorified village whose internal affairs could be handled informally. Certainly Baltimoreans saw things this way. Their streets needed policing, the harbor needed maintenance, the markets needed regulation—and all of this required a municipal authority invested with the power to raise revenue through taxation. Thus it became all the more nettling that the Maryland assembly refused to grant Baltimore the right of self-governance, while favoring Annapolis with the privileged status of incorporation. The town commission which handled land and street disputes may have been a gesture toward local autonomy, but few Baltimoreans could have been satisfied with commissioners appointed by the assembly. Luckily, the townspeople were not completely powerless, for they did have the right to organize on a voluntary basis to provide services over which the commission had no power. In 1763 they formed the Baltimore Mechanical Company. While none of its founders openly challenged the assembly, the challenge was there nonetheless. Baltimoreans had made a statement: they would have self-government, even if it lacked formal legal standing.

The chief function of the company seems to have been training the militia, which implied more than military preparation against foreign foes because the militia was the only effective policing agency overseeing the town's internal affairs. On regular occasions the membership mustered for drills, and fines were meted out to those who failed to attend. The company envisioned its duties as going beyond strictly military matters; sometimes it acted as judge, jury, and executioner when townspeople violated the accepted norms of the community. For example, John Brown received a ducking at a "horse-pond" for abusing his "good wife and industrious woman." He had to endure this watery justice despite the fact that he had never enrolled in the organization, suggesting that the company regarded any errant townsman as fair game.

In the period 1763–76, when the townspeople were organizing frantically against imperial policy, the Mechanical Company's

membership multiplied three-fold, from 49 to 155. Six years after
the founding of the parent organization, the townspeople organized the Baltimore Mechanical Fire Company. Drawing on the
same membership as the Mechanical Company, the new fire brigade was also designed to supplement the powers of the town
commissioners. It held frequent meetings and imposed regular
fines to maintain discipline. In addition to keeping the engine in
smooth running order, each member was obliged to have two
good leather buckets on hand.[1]

Perhaps the most striking feature of the Mechanical Company is its name. In the eighteenth century the word "mechanic"
possessed several connotations, the most uncharitable of which
conjured up an image of crudity, coarseness, and vulgarity. This
was not the way mechanics liked to think of themselves. They
preferred to associate the term "mechanic" with skill, industry,
and ingenuity. That they succeeded in bestowing their name on
Baltimore's foremost voluntary society suggests that the mechanics' self-perception was prevailing. The Mechanical Company
benefited craftsmen in ways more tangible than semantics. It
served as a training ground for master mechanics, providing their
first opportunity to polish their verbal and organizational skills
within an institutional setting. Of the original forty-nine members,
fourteen can be identified as craftsmen, although there were undoubtedly more: five shoemakers, two saddlers, a breeches maker,
peruke maker, cooper, tailor, hatter, cabinet and chair maker, and
one mechanic whose trade is unknown. These men seem to have
represented the cream of their trades. Consider the five shoemakers. In 1773 all of them published a piece in the town newspapers, offering employment to journeymen who would accept
the wages that their own workmen apparently refused. These
Mechanical Company shoemakers were masters of their craft,
employers of apprentices and journeymen, owners of workshops,
and heads of households. Among the masters who got their start
in the Mechanical Company and later enjoyed prominent political
careers were tailor James Cox, hatter David Shields, spinning
wheel maker David Poe, blacksmith John McClellan, saddler
Erasmus Uhler, tailor Cornelius Garritson, and watch and clock
makers Thomas Morgan and John McCabe.[2]

Yet the Mechanical Company was rather a misnomer, for its

appeal reached beyond workingmen to some of Baltimore's leading merchants. Although it has not been possible to identify the
occupations of most members, it appears that merchants constituted a large part, perhaps the largest, of the company. Of the
company members who in 1766 joined the Baltimore Sons of Liberty, the great majority were merchants. It was a merchant, Mark
Alexander, who originally suggested the organization's name to
honor the mechanics who had enlisted. Another merchant, Melchior Keener, called the company's first meeting in 1763 at his
store. Most important, merchant Keener was elected the first
president. Having migrated to Baltimore from Germany via Pennsylvania in 1761, Keener had succeeded in constructing a wharf
and warehouse as well as a dry goods store downtown. He retained his office for a decade until his loyalist sentiments finally
drove him out of the company. Thus while mechanics constituted
a large share of the membership and while they derived invalu-
able experience in its activities, merchants were in command. For
many of these merchants affiliation with the Mechanical Company became a steppingstone to higher political office. All of the
city's early mayors elected after 1797 were merchants; all of them
belonged to the Mechanical Company. James Calhoun, William
Lux, Samuel Hollingsworth, Daniel Bowly, and William Spear
are some of the merchant names that appear on the company's
membership lists.[3]

These were also the men who led Baltimore during the imperial crisis of 1765–66. When news reached Maryland that Par-
liament had enacted a new stamp tax, the merchant community of
Baltimore allied with anti-proprietary elements in Annapolis
against the measure. For several months this coalition orches-
trated the provincial opposition to the Stamp Act. It was a political marriage of convenience. The anti-proprietary group, led by
lawyer Samuel Chase, intended to ride the crisis to political office. Solidifying his popular support in the provincial capital,
Chase directed the anger of mechanics and tradesmen not only
against imperial policy but also against the proprietary favorites
who monopolized municipal government.

Baltimore's merchants also expected concrete gains from
their opposition to the Stamp Act. After 1763 they faced a severe
economic contraction, as European and English creditors began

demanding remittances from overextended colonial merchants. The merchants of Baltimore simply couldn't pay. Trade plummeted, exchange rates soared, currency disappeared, inventories mounted. In the midst of this commercial crunch came reports of new taxes, which only promised to exacerbate the situation. Yet the Stamp Act also provided a way out of the credit squeeze. For Baltimore's merchants who were watching stock gather on their shelves, a nonimportation measure against the new taxes offered hope of relief. It would enable them to reduce inventories while discouraging competition among themselves. "Thus," writes the ablest historian of the Revolutionary era in Maryland, "the merchant protest against the new taxes conveniently justified the implementation of policies necessitated by economic troubles." By November, 1765, Baltimore's merchants had joined their colleagues in Philadelphia and New York in agreeing not to import a specified list of goods until repeal of the taxes.[4]

Since the Mechanical Company was the closest thing Baltimore had to representative town government, it could not avoid entanglement in the Stamp Act controversy. After some prodding from New York, Baltimoreans in February, 1766, formed their own chapter of the Sons of Liberty. Merchant William Lux was the main man behind the move; his own business had been buffeted badly in the commercial crisis, which disposed him to favor forceful measures against the Stamp Act. The Sons of Liberty was really a rechristened Mechanical Company. Thirty-six company members are known to have joined the Sons. Of the thirty-three whose occupations can be identified, twenty-four were merchants and two were innkeepers. The remaining seven were mechanics: two tailors, a hatter, tanner, cooper, watch and clock maker, and an artisan whose craft is uncertain. Thus, while mechanics were visible in the new organization, they hardly stood out. Merchants were still in control, having exploited the momentary derangement in imperial relations to set their business affairs in order and to assert their leadership in the community. With Chase and Lux cooperating to forge a provincial-wide protest, the enemies of the new taxes forced proprietary officials to open their offices and transact business without stamps, in violation of the act. It did not matter, for a few days later, on April 3, 1766, news reached Maryland that the Stamp Act had been rescinded.[5]

The Stamp Act was just the opening salvo. For the next decade the mother country continued to fashion a more rigid imperial system than the colonies had ever seen, while Baltimore continued to resist. The Sons of Liberty disbanded after the repeal of the Stamp Act, but new bodies arose to take its place as imperial relations lurched from one crisis to another. In 1769, despite lukewarm support from the town's merchants who were enjoying commercial prosperity, Baltimoreans appointed a committee of inspection to enforce a provincial-wide boycott against Great Britain in retaliation against the Townshend Duties Act. In November, 1774, when the Coercive Acts became public knowledge, they formed a committee of correspondence to keep abreast of happenings through the colonies. In the same year the Continental Congress declared a new boycott against the mother country and urged all localities to execute it, prompting the townspeople to choose two committees of observation in May, 1774, and September, 1775. The composition of the committees accurately indicates who was in control over the independence struggle. A total of ninety-two positions were available on the committees. They went to fifty-four men, thirty of whom served on only one committee, fifteen on two, four on three, and five on four. Not a single mechanic received a seat on any of the committees. The merchants had clearly lost none of the initiative they exhibited in the Sons of Liberty.[6]

The top five committeemen were John Smith, William Smith, William Buchanan, Samuel Purviance, Jr., and William Lux. To a man they were merchants. They also formed a closely knit elite. In 1759 John Smith migrated to Baltimore from Carlisle County, Pennsylvania. He did not rise from rags to riches. On the contrary: John Smith had prospered in Pennsylvania and served in the provincial assembly. What brought him to Baltimore was the lure of the wheat trade and the hope of making a big fortune even bigger. John Smith came with his friend and partner, William Buchanan. Their families had been linked for years. Both of their fathers had served as Lancaster County sheriffs before packing west to Carlisle. Armed with $40,000 to invest, John Smith and Buchanan built several houses and the two longest wharves in Baltimore. By the Revolution John Smith was called "the richest Merchant in Baltimore." William Smith, another committeeman, was John's brother. He followed the same path from Pennsylvania to Baltimore, arriving in 1761 and investing heavily in shipping. Samuel Purviance left Philadelphia for Baltimore a few years later. With his brother, Robert, he constructed a wharf and a rum distillery that was touted as one of the finest in the colonies. Of the top five committeemen, only William Lux was Baltimore-born and -bred. His father, Darby, had early recognized the potential growth of Baltimore and settled there. When Darby died in 1750, William took over the family business and diversified it into manufacturing by acquiring a ropewalk.

Most of these families were interconnected through marriage. John Smith was married to William Buchanan's daughter, giving them a triple bond as friends, partners, and in-laws. One of the sons of John Smith married a daughter of William Smith, his first cousin. With the exception of the Anglo-Anglican Lux, the leading committeemen were Scotch-Irish and Presbyterian. In 1763 they founded the first Presbyterian church in Baltimore. John Smith, William Buchanan, and William Smith received appointments to the six-man committee delegated to oversee the congregation's finances.[7]

Yet as merchants consolidated and formalized their authority through the committee structure, new conditions were arising that would eventually call their leadership into question. First, the Baltimore-Annapolis coalition came under increasing strain. During the Stamp Act imbroglio the town's merchants had entered into a successful political alliance with anti-proprietary elements in Annapolis. For all the surface harmony, though, the coalition masked a fatal flaw. All of the political factions jockeying for position at the provincial capital were committed to preserving the hegemony of southern Maryland. From their perspective the rapid rise of Baltimore threatened to upset the traditional balance of power in the province in favor of the booming northern and western areas. While the deep-rooted antagonism between Baltimore and Annapolis went into eclipse in 1765 and 1766, it burst into the open a few years later. In 1770 Baltimore's merchants, thankfully following the lead of their northern colleagues, abandoned the provincial nonimportation agreement that had been adopted against the Townshend duties. The assembly and a few Eastern Shore representatives met at Annapolis and condemned the merchants' withdrawal as cynical and selfish, producing a rupture in Baltimore-Annapolis relations that never entirely healed.

By 1773 a new "popular party" had seized the initiative at Annapolis, centering around Charles Carroll of Carrollton, a wealthy Catholic planter who gained instant recognition by assailing in the leading newspaper the decision of Governor Robert Eden to set the fees of proprietary officials without the assembly's consent. Soon Carroll had gathered around him a knot of ambitious politicians that included the rising lawyer triumvirate, Samuel Chase, Thomas Johnson, and William Paca. To these men the fee controversy appeared as a weapon to demolish the proprietary system of privilege that had denied them political patronage. Fundamentally conservative in outlook, the popular party consisted of political "outs" who wanted in.[8]

With the popular party congealing at the provincial level after 1773, a second political realignment emerged in Baltimore. For the past decade mechanics had failed to strike an independent stance on the major questions rocking imperial relations. While they had participated in the Mechanical Company and Sons of Liberty, they never rose into the leadership ranks. They could not get even a toehold in the committees. Although documentation is spotty before 1773 when the first newspaper was established in Baltimore, it does not appear that mechanics attacked merchants in 1770 for abandoning nonimportation, as they did in New York and Philadelphia. Nor could Baltimore offer an equivalent of the mechanics' committees that appeared in Philadelphia in 1770 and New York four years later. But in 1773 the mechanics took a crucial step in declaring their own political independence by electing a brother craftsman as president of the Mechanical Company. In finding a replacement for the loyalist merchant Melchior Keener, the company turned to Gerard Hopkins, one of Baltimore's premier cabinet makers and an original member of the organization. Hopkins served less than a year when for unknown reasons new elections were held. This event was critical, for the mechanics were obliged to defend the position they had so recently won. They rose to the challenge, electing the wool card manufacturer Adam Fonerden. When Fonerden stepped down in 1775, the mechanics did not let the presidency slip from their hands. Hatter David Shields took over, the first treasurer of the Mechanical Fire Company.

What caused this shift in the leadership of the Mechanical Company is unknown. Perhaps the mechanics inherited the presidency by default, as merchants were preoccupied with their committee assignments. Perhaps the merchants bowed out in a mood of apprehension and anxiety over the mounting independence movement. Perhaps the mechanics, emboldened by the liberating atmosphere of the opposition struggle against Great Britain, rejected the merchants' claims to leadership while asserting their own.[9]

By late 1775 Baltimoreans were stirring to arms. They had discovered from the engagements at Lexington and Concord the previous spring how easily confrontation might explode into bloodshed. Perhaps Baltimore was intended for the next showdown. The town buzzed with rumors about a planned British invasion of the Chesapeake, where Lord Dunmore, the royal governor of Virginia, was inflaming the minds of disaffected slaves and servants with promises of liberation. Who could ignore the possibility of attack? The townspeople responded to the threat by mobilizing the militia, their traditional bulwark of self-defense. In retrospect, the mechanics had been preparing for this moment for over a decade. In December they organized a unit and proudly named it the Baltimore Mechanical Volunteer Company. This action put the mechanics at the forefront of mobilization, for six months later Baltimore had only five other units. The Volunteers' enrollment stood at 64; the total for the other companies was 284.

Who were the Volunteers? It has not been possible to determine the occupations of all but a handful of troops, but they appear to have been mechanic in fact as well as name. Perhaps the man in the best position to know was General William Smallwood, commander of the Maryland line. In 1777 he wrote to the state governor on behalf of the Volunteers, requesting that they be relieved. "They are entitled to this indulgence," the general said, "from their station (being mostly tradesmen), having served their time out faithfully."[10]

The Revolutionary militia was the single most important institution politicizing the mechanics. At a time when Baltimore had no local elective offices, privates were suddenly choosing their own officers. As late as the Seven Years' War the assembly had monopolized the power of appointing militia officers. But as the independence movement reached its culmination, the new provincial authorities could no longer hope to generate sufficient enthusiasm among the troops without making concessions. In 1775 the provincial convention permitted companies to elect officers below the battalion level. Across Maryland the new militia law sparked a revolution within the units, as soldiers debated openly the merits of their prospective commanders. In the words of one historian, "the Convention unwittingly opened a Pandora's box leading eventually to democratization of the militia." Of the twelve officers elected by the Volunteers, the occupations of five are known: Captain James Cox was a tailor, Lieutenant John Mc-Clellan a blacksmith, Sergeant David Evans a watch and clock maker, Corporal Aaron Mattison a saddler, and Corporal John Shrim a cooper. The Volunteers had entrusted leadership to fellow mechanics, not to merchants, lawyers, or physicians; only a decade of experience in the Mechanical Company, Sons of Liberty, and Mechanical Fire Company could have prompted such independent action.[11]

While Baltimore and its mechanics were ready for the coming struggle, Annapolis continued to hedge. By late 1775 the "popular party," which had coalesced during the fee controversy, had secured the top positions in the new provincial convention and council of safety, the supreme executive authority. But they were not sanguine about the future. They had grown alarmed over the social upheaval that the opposition movement seemed to be fomenting. On the Eastern Shore slaves, servants, and tenants were becoming openly rebellious. Throughout the province the militia's mobilization was producing social discord. To the convention and council, it seemed that the movement they had helped to create would overwhelm them. As late as spring 1776 many of them opposed independence. To Baltimoreans the provincial leadership was swaying between excessive caution and plain cowardice. Some townspeople could discern even more sinister forces at work. Many of the new provincial leaders had formerly belonged to the proprietary interest and presumably maintained close ties to suspected loyalists. Had toryism infected the province's highest governing body?[12]

Baltimoreans seemed pinned between a tyrannical government abroad and a submissive one at home. Their frustrations surfaced in April. Military authorities in Virginia had seized a packet of correspondence which suggested that Governor Robert Eden of Maryland was supplying information to the British government on the feasibility of landing troops in the Chesapeake. The incriminating material was sent not to the Maryland council of safety but rather to the Baltimore committee of observation. The committee chairman, Samuel Purviance, dispatched the material to the Continental Congress at Philadelphia, enclosing a letter that accused the council of lukewarm patriotism. Without obtaining the committee's official consent Purviance ordered a ship and armed guard to Annapolis to apprehend the governor if he should attempt an escape. The chairman doubted that "the Council would take so spirited a step as to seize the Governor." Captain Samuel Smith and his men shipped out for Annapolis, only to find the governor at home and unpacked.

When they discovered everything that had occurred behind their back, the council of safety burst into anger. Their indignation did not subside upon receiving a letter from John Hancock of the Congress ordering them to arrest Eden. The council felt dishonored and refused to seize the governor. More important, the affair had exposed how tenuous were the council's claims on the loyalties of the province. "We are to be plunged into all the Horrors of Anarchy," they exclaimed. While the council reprimanded all of the principal characters involved in the abortive abduction, the Baltimore committee applauded Purviance's "warm and zealous Attachment to our distressed and perhaps betrayed Country." The Eden incident left animosity and mistrust on all sides. To Baltimore's most rabid patriots the provincial authorities had shown their true colors.[13]

If a timid council of safety balked at the extraordinary measures the occasion demanded, some Baltimoreans were ready to take matters into their own hands. Within a few months of the Eden affair disgruntled patriot elements in the Baltimore area were mobilizing to weed out the traitors they saw in their midst.

In February, 1777, they proclaimed the formation of the Baltimore Whig Club and, in an effort to rally popular support and allay popular suspicion, printed their constitution in the town newspapers. The new republic, said the Whigs, teemed with "secret and disguised enemies, whom we have fostered in our bosoms," "artful villains," and "dignified Tories, under the cloak of moderation." With such insidious forces gnawing at America's patriotic fiber, it was imperative that "the true friends to the ountry, who have stood, and are still determined to stand, forth, at the risk of their lives and fortunes, should take every step in their power to strengthen the hands and encourage the spirit of their friends at this critical period." Wasn't this simple vigilanteeism? Wasn't the club abrogating powers that rightfully belonged to the council of safety and committee of observation? To these questions the Whigs answered no; it was not their intention "to reflect on the present governing powers, or rob them of any of the prerogatives." But such disclaimers rang hollow. They could not hide the challenge that the Whigs posed, for the club had insinuated that the "present governing powers" lacked the backbone to enforce anti-tory legislation.[14]

The Whigs voiced their commitment to republicanism as loudly as their detestation of toryism. They designed their club as a model of republican governance. The constitution provided for frequent elections of officers; a new president, vice-president, and secretary were chosen four times a year. In theory the meetings were orderly, sober, and characterized by republican decorum. Before addressing the club, each member was obliged to rise to his feet and receive the recognition of the president, who might fine any troublemakers for "indecent behavior and personal altercation." To safeguard unanimity of sentiment, two-thirds of the club had to vote their approval of prospective members before they could become full-fledged Whigs. The constitution also outlined the procedure to be followed in executing the club's chief objective, the elimination of tories. Any member who wished could demand a general meeting and condemn "an enemy to America." If the membership agreed that the evidence warranted further investigation, the president was empowered to set a date for a trial. Here, before the assembled Whigs, the accused tory could present his defense. After hearing testimony from both sides, the club adjourned to deliberate and issued a guilty verdict if two-thirds of the membership concurred. Although the constitution did not specify the punishment in store for the guilty party, the Whigs always sentenced their victims to banishment.[15]

The Whig Club revived the popular coalition between mechanics and merchants that had operated intermittently since 1763, flowing naturally out of the Mechanical Company and Sons of Liberty. Yet the mechanics had a much greater voice in the Whig Club than in the earlier organizations. We have a membership list of the club, complete with occupations, compiled by one of its most vocal enemies, newspaper editor William Goddard. He identified thirty-one Whigs, the largest number of which were mechanics: tailors James Cox and Cornelius Garritson, watch and clock makers John McCabe and Thomas Morgan, spinning wheel maker David Poe, saddler John Gordon, and shipwright Daniel Lawrence. Although his occupation made shallopman John Slaymaker a small-time entrepreneur and petty proprietor, he probably fell within the mechanic fold for having served an apprenticeship. Goddard listed Benjamin Griffith as a stone mason and Mark Alexander as a cooper, even though both men invariably called themselves merchants in the 1770s. It is probable that Goddard was dragging out their plebeian origins to discredit them. Griffith practiced the stone mason's trade upon arriving in Baltimore in the 1760s, contracting to rebuild a stone bridge spanning the Falls. While there is no evidence that Alexander was a practicing cooper or owned a cooperage, he may have been apprenticed to the trade before settling in town. Goddard did not specify the occupation of James French, other than saying he was a former servant of watch and clock maker Morgan. It was a common practice for master mechanics to acquire indentured servants trained in their own trades who could provide cheap labor at the workshops; Garritson, for example, had several servant tailors. Thus French may have been a watch and clock maker like his master. In addition to these mechanics and near-mechanics, two manufacturers joined the club, distillers Robert Purviance and Nathaniel Smith, who had not undergone the formal apprenticeships of the mechanics but who nonetheless shared many of their interests and concerns. At the other end of the occupational spectrum the club drew from unskilled workers, who seem to have been ostracized from the Mechanical Company and Sons of Liberty, including a pair of common sailors from the Point.[16]

The Whig Club was missing the big merchant names that had commanded attention in the earlier organizations. Goddard identified only five men as merchants, deriding them as "haberdashers." Most of them were newcomers to politics: only Daniel Bowly and David Stewart had joined the Mechanical Company and Sons of Liberty. The Whigs also encompassed five ship captains from the Point, who were probably small-time traders on their own accounts. At least two of them permanently left the quarter deck for the counting house: James Nicholson, a native of the Eastern Shore who earned a reputation in the navy during the War for Independence, and George Woolsey, referred to as a "merchant" in his obituary in 1781. Another five Whigs were lawyers, "pettifoggers," Goddard quipped. The last Whig was George Welch, a schoolteacher, who probably felt more at home in the company of mechanics than merchants. He belonged to the Mechanical Company, rose to become a lieutenant in the Mechanical Volunteers, and was an intimate companion of James Cox, the company's commander and a fellow Whig. Thus the Whig Club brought together mechanics whose political experience and outlook had been maturing for over a decade and a group of relatively unknown merchants, ship captains, and lawyers, few of whom had stood out in the independence movement before 1777.[17]

The Revolutionary militia welded these disparate elements into a single-minded organization. It is here that the politicizing role of the militia, especially for mechanics, comes into view. In addition to supplying more Whigs than any other militia unit, the Mechanical Volunteer Company provided more of its officers. Of the five Whigs belonging to the Volunteers, three were officers between 1776 and 1789: Captain Cox, Lieutenant Welch, and Corporal Poe. At least one other officer, John McClellan, participated in Whig-inspired actions without formally joining the club. Elected as the Volunteers' first lieutenant, he advanced to captain at Cox's death in 1777. The Mechanical Volunteers were the most conspicuous unit in the club but not the sole one. John McCabe served in the Ninth Company of Light Infantry, and other mechanics undoubtedly enlisted in units whose muster rolls have not survived. The Whig Club also attracted seamen from the company of the provincial warship *Defence*, which mobilized the Point's maritime population. From September, 1776, to January, 1778, the ship's pay accounts record the names of 194 seamen receiving wages, while at least 125 more passed through the company's ranks before then. Five members of the club served aboard the *Defence*, three of whom were officers: Captain Nicholson, Captain C. George Turnbull, and Lieutenant Slaymaker. No fewer than three other Whigs attained officer rank in the militia: Captain Nathaniel Smith in the First Company of Matrosses and Captain Nathaniel Ramsey and Lieutenant David Plunket in the Fifth Company.[18]

Initially the Whig Club may have enjoyed the silent support of the committee of observation, which continued to burn over the Eden affair and the censure of the council of safety. One of the committeemen, lawyer Benjamin Nicholson, actually joined the club. Having received a reprimand from the council for his actions in the Eden incident, Nicholson may have seen the club as a way of evening the score. Two other Whigs had indirect ties to the committee: Robert Purviance was the brother of chairman Samuel Purviance, while Daniel Bowly was the uncle and partner of deputy chairman William Lux. Although they did not belong to the committee, James Nicholson and David Plunket had also participated in the attempted seizure of the governor and felt the sting of the council's censure. As commander of the *Defence*, Nicholson had ordered the ship's tender to Annapolis under the command of his younger brother. For his part Plunket, on orders from the committee, delivered the incriminating material to the Continental Congress at Philadelphia. To the committee the Whig Club may have appeared as a means of combatting toryism without openly challenging the provincial authorities and as a device for placating the most militantly patriotic townsmen without openly backing them.[19]

From December, 1776, through April, 1777, the Whig Club attacked a number of tories in the Baltimore area—not just any tories, but rich and powerful ones. Its first victim was merchant Robert Christie, Jr., the sheriff of Baltimore County. Together with his brother James, Robert led all the town's merchants in the number of ships trading to Great Britain. Both men were loyalists. As early as 1775 the Baltimore committee had banished

James from the province for writing a letter that contained treasonable sentiments. Robert succeeded in eluding his brother's fate until the summer of 1776, when he refused to read the newly adopted Declaration of Independence at the county courthouse. He was soon receiving threats. Whether the Whig Club was responsible for the anonymous letters is uncertain; not until December do we have unequivocal evidence of the club's existence. Christie appealed for protection to the Baltimore committee, which issued a declaration in the newspapers urging all citizens "to assist them in their Endeavours to preserve the Peace and good Order of Society, and to prevent all Riots and Tumults, and personal Abuse and Violence to individuals." The committee's decree may have calmed tempers temporarily, but on the night of December 4 Robert Christie and Hugh Scott, another suspected tory, received the following note: "Your conduct has been such in this State during our struggle for Liberty, that we are at this present moment determined that unless you leave Town instantly & the State within six days your life shall be sacrificed by an injured people." The note was signed "Legion," the code word for the Whig Club.[20]

"Legion" sounded ominous, invoking images of a monolithic army of patriots. It expressed an ideal, not a reality. The first action of the Whig Club exposed underlying tensions and potential conflicts between merchants and mechanics. When Christie and Scott received their sentence of exile, they rode into town to present their cases before the club. Meeting at Grant's tavern, they pleaded for a day's reprieve to put their affairs in order. Not only did the Whigs refuse leniency, but many of them felt Christie and Scott deserved sterner punishment than what they had received. Seeing that further talk was pointless, the two men walked out of Grant's tavern and prepared to mount their horses. The club followed them into the street. Tempers were hot. At this volatile point the president of the club, merchant and ship captain James Nicholson, intervened. "In justice to Commodore Nicholson," Christie later testified, "I must observe that he declared in my presence, his sole reason for coming there was to prevent injury to our persons, & he actually forbid the people from insulting us when we went to mount our horses." Nicholson had gone to

Grant's that night to help Christie, not hurt him; to restrain the club, not rouse them.

Who was causing the trouble? Christie blamed David Poe, who "seemed at the head of the lower class." A recent immigrant from northern Ireland, Poe was then just twenty years old. Already he was a corporal in the Mechanical Volunteers and would later rise through the ranks of the Continental Army. Such was Poe's martial temperament that after the war he was nicknamed the "General." From Christie's account it seems that "General" Poe and his "lower class" followers advocated stiffer measures than the club's merchant president could tolerate.[21]

A second target on the Whigs' list was merchant Melchior Keener. No other figure illustrates more clearly the transformation in the mechanics' attitude toward the preindependence elite leadership. Garritson, Cox, Poe, and Morgan had belonged to the Mechanical Company when Keener was president. Now they repudiated him. In early December Keener, like Christie and Scott, received an anonymous ultimatum from "Legion" promising dire consequences if he should refuse to leave town. Rather than appealing to the Baltimore committee, which Keener may have suspected of masterminding the Whigs' actions, he sought protection from the council of safety. On December 13 the council issued the first of several attacks on the club, which seemed "to assume to themselves not only Legislative but even Executive powers." Picturing the club as a harbinger of "anarchy and a total end of all regular Government," the council prodded the Baltimore committee to crush the menace before it was too late. By withholding its reply for a month, the committee may have fueled suspicions that it was using the club as a stalking horse.[22]

In the meantime Henry Stevenson and William Smith were battling the forces of "Legion." A resident of Baltimore County since 1752, Stevenson was probably the best-known physician in the area. He also invested in commerce along with his brother John, a physician turned merchant. Stevenson was an unrepentant loyalist, describing himself after the war as "the Principal person of Character Interest and Influence on the western Shore in the said province of Maryland that openly opposed & resisted the Ringleaders of the Insurgents." William Smith (not the committeeman) settled in Baltimore in 1769 and within a few years had constructed a house, three warehouses, and a ropewalk. By late 1776 Stevenson and Smith were facing harassment. A few months later Stevenson and nine of his friends barricaded themselves inside his Baltimore County mansion to repulse an attack by patriots, perhaps fomented by the Whigs. By August the skirmishes had escalated into full-scale military operations, with a hundred men massing outside his estate, prepared to lay siege with a pair of cannons. Both Stevenson and Smith fled Baltimore and ultimately escaped to the British army. By the end of the war they were petitioning the British government to compensate them for their confiscated property.[23]

In January, 1777, the council heard further complaints about the Whigs. It shot a second letter to the Baltimore committee detailing the latest reports of Whig harassment. Several privates in the militia unit of Captain William Galbraith had been driven from town, while Keener's home had been broken into and ransacked. The Whigs did not claim credit for the Keener incident, but the two men implicated by the council—David Welsh and "Harry the Drummer"—belonged to the company of a Whig, Captain Nathaniel Smith. Harry may have been black, which would elicit disquiet among the council of slaveholders. On January 18 the council ordered three of Baltimore's militia companies to assist the committee in "putting a speedy End to all Riots and Tumults within the said County, or Baltimore Town." On the same day the council finally received a reply from the committee, who explained they were doing the best they could under difficult circumstances. This was hardly reassuring. As if to defy both the state and local authorities, the Whig Club on February 11 printed its constitution in the town newspapers.[24]

William Goddard was next in line. In 1773 he had moved to Baltimore from Philadelphia to establish the town's first newspaper, the *Maryland Journal*. Although Goddard turned over management of the paper to his sister a few years later, he continued to submit pieces for publication and shape editorial policy. In February, 1777, Goddard received an essay from Samuel Chase, which tongue-in-cheek praised the latest peace offerings of the British. The piece appeared in the newspaper anonymously. Fearing that unperceptive readers might fail to see the

satire, the Whig Club on March 3 demanded that Goddard tell
them the identity of the author. He refused. The Whigs then ordered him to appear before the assembled club the next evening.
When the designated hour arrived and Goddard did not, a Whig
delegation forced its way into his home and dragged the editor
back to Rusk's tavern to stand trial. With president Nicholson in
the chair and David Stewart taking minutes, the club again attempted to uncover the author's identity. Goddard continued to
hold his tongue. When the confrontation reached an impasse,
Nicholson sent Goddard and a few guards to the bar room while
the club deliberated in the hall. It took little time to reach a verdict. Later that night Goddard received the official sentence at his
home: "*Resolved*, That Mr. William Goddard, do leave this Town
by twelve o'clock to-morrow morning, and the County in three
days. Should he refuse due obedience to this notice, he will be
subject to the resentment of a LEGION."[25]

Goddard saw himself as a beleaguered defender of freedom
of the press. Perhaps he was, but he was also a defender of an
elitist politics that Baltimore's mechanics were struggling to overturn. At his trial at Rusk's Goddard suggested in a typical supercilious remark that the Whigs "resume their awls and needles."
He dismissed them as "*deluded artists*." A few months later Goddard published a pamphlet in which he acknowledged that his
remarks had enraged the mechanics. But his defense only made
matters worse. "I have been blamed by some," Goddard wrote,

> for throwing out a sarcasm on the *Mechanics* in *Whig Club*, by ad-
> vising them to resume their "awls and needles!" To this I answer,
> that I respect that class of men as much as any other, whose situa-
> tion in life is considered, abstractedly of their moral characters,
> and view them as brethren; but, when a man who is only fit to
> "patch a shoe," attempts "to patch the State," fancies himself a
> *Solon*, or *Lycurgus*, and usurps the executive power, he cannot fail
> to meet with contempt.

We can only imagine what the Whig mechanics thought as they
read Goddard's pamphlet.[26]

Goddard ignored the Whigs' ultimatum. Three weeks passed
before president Nicholson appeared at Goddard's printing office,
together with a group of fellow Whigs. The editor and his work-

men barricaded the door; Nicholson and his men broke it down; the two groups scuffled inside the office. Overcome by the Whigs, Goddard relented and accompanied them back to Rusk's tavern. In the meantime the editor's sister had been appealing to the militia, the only force that could resist the Whigs. Captain William Galbraith, who a month earlier had received orders from the council to suppress the club, told her he could do nothing without directions from the Baltimore committee. After repeated pleas from Goddard's sister, he finally consented to mobilize his troops on the condition that Captain Nathaniel Smith do the same. The response of Whig Smith was predictable: "D—— my blood! if my commission was worth ten thousand a year I would throw it up before I would fire upon any of those gentlemen." Some talked about tarring and feathering Goddard; in fact, Whigs David Mc-Mechen and Daniel Bowly had already secured a cart to haul Goddard through town.

With the Whigs considering such measures and the local militia refusing to oppose them, Goddard agreed to leave town and set out for Annapolis to put his case before the council. After hearing his account, the council referred the matter to a committee of the assembly, which condemned the Whig Club and urged the governor to abolish it. On April 17 the governor declared "all bodies of men associating together, or meeting for the purpose of usurping any of the powers of government, and presuming to exercise any powers over the persons or property of any subject of this State, or to carry into execution any of the laws thereof on their own authorities, unlawful assemblies." This meant the Whig Club. After April the Whigs dropped from the Baltimore scene. The governor's decree may have been the killing blow. More likely, the club would have disbanded anyway as its militia members were called to the battlelines.[27]

While the War for Independence distracted Baltimoreans from internal issues and riveted their attention on the British enemy, the popular coalition that underlay the Whig Club could be called into action when the necessity arose. On June 6, 1779, the irascible William Goddard was at the center of controversy again, publishing another anonymous article that criticized Washington, the Pennsylvania assembly, and the French nation. Two days later a number of people, enraged by the disloyalty Goddard seemed to be inciting, burst into the editor's home. Although Goddard was sick and in bed, he nevertheless brandished a sword at his attackers. He finally surrendered and consented to appear before another extralegal trial at one of the town's coffee houses the next morning. His elitism as biting as ever, Goddard described the plebeian composition of the several dozen men who assailed him: "a Band of Ruffians, composed of Continental Recruits, Mulattoes, or Negroes, Fifers and Drummers." To Goddard the Whig Club was stirring to life again: "*Vermin* who have crept out of the *putrid* Carcass of that many-headed Monster LEGION."

The next morning, instead of going to the coffee house where his accusers were waiting, Goddard sought out the local magistrates to plead for protection. When the assembly at the coffee house got word of Goddard's flight, they poured into the streets determined to hold their ad hoc proceedings wherever they happened to find him. Meanwhile Goddard was standing on the doorstep of William Spear, a justice of the peace and prominent merchant, recounting his predicament and begging for help. When Spear caught sight of the crowd pushing up toward his house, he closed the door in Goddard's face. The crowd wrung from the editor a repudiation of the article he had printed and forced him to beg the forgiveness of General Washington. Another group riffled through his personal papers at his home in search of treasonable correspondence. According to Goddard, several of his neighbors who were foolhardy enough to defend him were "dragged, (amidst the din of insulting music) in carts thro' the streets, with halters about their necks, and occasionally cudgelled for the diversion of the inhuman part of the spectators." Goddard later protested his treatment to the state assembly while disowning the statements he had made under threat of violence.[28]

Two men had stood out in the crowd, John McClellan and Samuel Smith, and they personified the popular coalition that had shaped the protest movement in Baltimore since 1763. Goddard singled out three militia captains among the eight men who engineered the disturbance, including blacksmith McClellan. Exhibiting his characteristic elitism, Goddard called him a "Horse Shoe-Maker." McClellan could make as strong a claim as anyone to being the mechanics' foremost spokesman. Two years earlier he had been awarded the highest position the mechanic community had to offer, the command of the Mechanical Volunteers. Like his predecessor, James Cox, McClellan had joined the Mechanical Company in the 1760s and supported the Whig Club a decade later. Among the eighteen men Robert Christie identified as his assailants in December, 1776, one was John McClellan. The similarities between Cox and McClellan went deeper, for both men had helped to found Baltimore's first Baptist church, where they undoubtedly acquired organizational experience. During the 1770s McClellan frequently received room and board at the Coxes' home, and the ties of affection continued after the war. As late as the 1790s one of Cox's sons was writing his mother in Baltimore inquiring about the health of the McClellan family.[29]

The merchant equivalent to McClellan was Samuel Smith. A new generation of merchants had come of age during the Revolutionary war, bringing a new style of popular politics and a new recognition of the power of the mechanic community. Smith was their spokesman. Born in 1752, Samuel was the eldest son of merchant John Smith. He early resolved to make himself a name in politics and the military, which actually amounted to the same thing, and earned a reputation for bravery in the Continental Army. In 1776 Smith won a promotion from captain to lieutenant-colonel of the Fourth Maryland Regiment, but had to resign it three years later to salvage his faltering business affairs in Baltimore. Upon returning to town, Smith launched a meteoric career in the state militia. He immediately received an appointment as commander of the Baltimore Town Battalion and eventually rose to colonel and brigadier general.

The careers of McClellan and Smith intersected in the militia, where both mechanics and merchants were creating a popular politics that would flower fully after the war. The scene before the house of William Spear dramatically revealed the changing political tactics of the merchant leadership. As Goddard beseeched Spear for help, Smith and his followers gathered around the house demanding justice. What would Spear do? He belonged to the first generation of Baltimore merchants, a Scotch-Irish Presbyterian who had played a prominent role in the town's committees of observation but who avoided the street politics he now saw before him. It is difficult to suppose Spear liked what he saw. Yet he abandoned Goddard to the crowd. Samuel Smith and John

McClellan may have been violating the law, but other considerations were paramount: Smith was Spear's son-in-law.[30]

Few documents have survived to illuminate the personal impact of the independence struggle on Baltimore's mechanics. We can trace the broad outlines of their public activities, but the inner revolution that reshaped their private lives is largely lost to us. One exception is James Cox, probably the most popular mechanic in Revolutionary Baltimore. Born in 1737, Cox married Mary Purviance and by the age of forty had five children from two to ten years old. He was a successful master craftsman, described by one nineteenth-century historian as "the most fashionable tailor in Baltimore town." Cox diversified his investments as much as he could, purchasing forty-six acres of land north of town, turning his home into a boarding house where rooms rented from 12s. to 15s. a week, and loaning money at interest. He had at least one Irish indentured servant and perhaps a slave or two.

Judging from his account book for the years 1768 to 1771, Cox must have been one of Baltimore's most sought after tradesmen. In 1770 alone he received 915 orders for making and mending breeches, waistcoats, suits, vests, and greatcoats. The orders were not large, less than a pound each, but accounted for annual receipts of over £890. Like most master craftsmen in the clothing trades, Cox catered to wealthy customers. Of his 319 patrons in 1770, 54 percent placed one order, 20 percent two or three, 20 percent four to nine, and 6 percent ten to twenty-two. The top tenth of his customers accounted for 40 percent of his total receipts. They consisted of twenty-one merchants, three ship captains, two lawyers, two ministers, two physicians, a planter, and a planter's wife. Cox's largest customer was merchant Mark Alexander, who was also his landlord and creditor. However this economic dependency may have affected their relationship, one thing is clear: it did not foster antagonism or resentment. Indeed, James and Mary named their second son Mark Alexander.[31]

The career of James Cox encapsulates the institutional development of the mechanic community. In addition to serving in the Mechanical Company, Mechanical Fire Company, Sons of Liberty, and Whig Club, Cox was a leading figure in the Baptist church. His penchant for preaching has led one Maryland genealogist to describe him as "a tailor by vocation and a minister by avocation." In 1775 Cox was the logical choice for captain of the newly formed Mechanical Volunteers. By itself his election to this office might justify us in calling Cox the most popular mechanic in Baltimore, but we have other evidence as well. In September, 1775, when the townspeople elected a committee of observation, Cox received more votes than any other mechanic. He was an uncompromising patriot, as is evidenced in a poem he wrote a month after the battle of Lexington and Concord:

> Cursed be the wretch that's bought and sold,
> And barters liberty for gold;
> For when elections are not free,
> In vain we boast for Liberty.
> And he who sells his single right,
> Would sell his Country, if he might;
> When liberty is put to sale
> For wine, for money or for ale,
> The sellers must be abject slaves—
> The buyers, vile designing knaves.

In this piece Captain Cox admonishes freeborn men to form their political loyalties without regard to the rich and powerful. He tells his readers to resist the blandishments of those who can buy popularity. Perhaps Cox read his poem before his troops, for it seems to contain a special meaning for them. Deliberately or not, the captain was justifying the independent behavior of mechanics in the Volunteers, whose ideological zeal and patriotic commitment won the praise of no less a person than General Smallwood. "These men," he told the governor, "have behaved better than any corps of militia from Maryland, and have had far less desertions among them."[32]

On October 4, 1777, at the battle of Germantown, James Cox fell while leading his men in an assault on a British breastworks. For nearly an hour he lay dying. At his side were his old friends Benjamin Griffith and George Welch, fellow members of the Mechanical Company and Whig Club. Only two weeks before, Cox had received a promotion to major, making him the highest-ranking mechanic officer in Baltimore. He did not live to hear the news. Pressed by British troops who had wheeled on the Americans, Griffith and Welch retreated after leaving the body with a sympathetic family who promised to provide a Christian burial. Four days later Mary was informed of her husband's death by breeches maker Richard Lemmon, one of Cox's fellow Baptists in the Volunteers.

Even the successful master mechanic could not protect his family against the economic disaster that now befell Mary and the children. James left only £50, about a half-month's receipts, at the shop. Having "lived Comfortably" before his death, Mary now had to sell the family furniture and take up shopkeeping. The business never prospered. For over a decade Mary petitioned the Baltimore County Orphans Court for the financial assistance she believed the government owed her. Not until 1788 did the state assembly grant her wish. Meanwhile Mary strove to guide her sons into what she described as "Genteel" livelihoods; none of them chose the mechanic life of his father. During these difficult years Alexander, Welch, and Griffith stood behind Mary and the children, sponsoring her petitions and co-signing her loans. In 1787 Mary asked Griffith to pay one last respect. He journeyed back to the site of James's death to retrieve the body for reburial in Baltimore. Mary had a new tombstone inscribed with the epitaph:

> Why all this Toil for Triumphs of an hour?
> What tho' we wade in wealth, or soar in Fame?
> Earth's highest Station ends in, "Here he lies"
> And "Dust to Dust" concludes her noblest Song.[33]

In a political sense the mechanic community was born of the independence movement. Although Baltimore did not experience the intense social conflict of the larger northern towns, it nonetheless conformed to the pattern Carl Becker noted long ago. Its Revolution was a struggle over both "home rule" and "who should rule at home." Having followed the leadership of merchants in the Mechanical Company and the Sons of Liberty, mechanics organized on their own in the Mechanical Volunteers. For the first time workingmen elected their own officers, met regularly for drills, and paraded with merchant-led companies on a basis of equality. Undoubtedly they debated the political issues of the day. From the militia it was a short step to the radical patriot Whig Club, where mechanics and merchants formed a popular coalition that continued beyond the war itself. That coalition would be tested in the years to come.

NOTES

1. Mechanical Fire Company Day Book, Mechanical Fire Company Record Books, MS. 584, MHS; George W. McCreary, *The Ancient and Honorable Mechanical Company, of Baltimore* (Baltimore, 1901), pp. 15, 26–28.

2. Mechanical Fire Company Day Book, Dec. 4, 1769; McCreary, *Mechanical Company*, pp. 13, 15; Thomas W. Griffith, *Annals of Baltimore* (Baltimore, 1829), p. 38. For occupations of original mechanic members, see *Maryland Journal* (Baltimore), Aug. 20, 21, 1773, Jan. 17, 1776, June 23, 1778, Dec. 7, 1784; Ronald Hoffman, *A Spirit of Dissension: Economics, Politics, and the Revolution in Maryland* (Baltimore, 1973), p. 40; William Goddard, *The Prowess of the Whig Club, and the Manoeuvres of Legion* (Baltimore, 1777), appendix; Paul Kent Walker, "The Baltimore Community and the American Revolution: A Study in Urban Development, 1763–1783" (Ph.D. diss., University of North Carolina at Chapel Hill, 1973), pp. 46, 71.

3. McCreary, *Mechanical Company*, pp. 13, 15.

4. Here and throughout this chapter I have relied heavily on Hoffman's excellent *Spirit of Dissension*, chaps. 2 and 3. Quote from p. 38.

5. *Ibid.*, p. 40. I have altered a few of the occupations listed by Hoffman.

6. *Maryland Gazette* (Baltimore), Nov. 1, 1770; Resolves of Baltimore County, May 31, 1774, Purviance Papers, MS. 1394, MHS, *Maryland Journal*, Nov. 30, 1774, Sept. 27, 1775.

7. A Sketch of the Life of General Samuel Smith during the war of the Revolution, Box 6, p. 1, Samuel Smith Letter Books, Library of Congress; Col. J. Thomas Scharf, *The Chronicles of Baltimore; Being a Complete History of "Baltimore Town" and Baltimore City from the Earliest Period to the Present Time* (Baltimore, 1874), pp. 52, 53, 56; Griffith, *Annals of Baltimore*, pp. 27, 37, 38, 42–44; Robert Purviance, *A Narrative of Events Which Occurred in Baltimore Town during the Revolutionary War* (Baltimore, 1849), pp. 30–33, 38–39; William Reynolds, *A Brief History of the First Presbyterian Church of Baltimore* (Baltimore, 1913), pp. 9, 122; *Maryland Journal*, Oct. 21, 1785, Jan. 6, 1786.

8. Hoffman, *Spirit of Dissension*, chaps. 4 and 5.

9. McCreary, *Mechanical Company*, p. vii.

10. General Smallwood to Gov. Johnson, Oct. 14, 1777, in *ibid.*, pp. 20–21.

11. David Curtis Skaggs, *Roots of Maryland Democracy, 1753–1776* (Westport, Conn., 1973), p. 157.

12. Hoffman, *Spirit of Dissension*, chap. 6.

13. William Hand Browne, ed., *Archives of Maryland*, 11 (Baltimore, 1892): 365, 369. For documents relative to the Eden incident, see *ibid.*, pp. 354–92.

14. *Maryland Journal*, Feb. 11, 1777.

15. *Ibid.*

16. Goddard, *Prowess of the Whig Club*, appendix; Geo. Welsh to [Mary Cox], Oct. 7, 1777, in Scharf, *Chronicles of Baltimore*, pp. 165–66; George Welch and David Rusk Certificate in Support of Mary Cox, Apr. 11, 1786, Cox Papers, MS. 1909, MHS.

17. Scharf, *Chronicles of Baltimore*, pp. 39, 141; *Maryland Journal*, Nov. 6, 1781.

18. Goddard, *Prowess of the Whig Club*, appendix; McCreary, *Mechanical Company*, pp. 21–22, 23–25; *Archives of Maryland*, 18 (Baltimore, 1900): 19, 23, 655, 639, 659, 660.

19. *Archives of Maryland*, 11: 354–93; Walker, "Baltimore Community," p. 30.

20. *Maryland Journal*, July 31, 1776; Walker, "Baltimore Community," p. 55.

21. William Hand Browne, ed., *Archives of Maryland*, 12 (Baltimore, 1893): 517–18; *Federal Gazette* (Baltimore), Oct. 18, 1816.

22. *Archives of Maryland*, 12: 526–27.

23. Memorial of Henry Stevenson, Memorial of William Smith, pp. 341–43, 423–27, Transcript of Manuscript Books and Papers of the Commission of Enquiry into the Losses of Services of the American Loyalists, MHS (on microfilm); Scharf, *Chronicles of Baltimore*, p. 50.

24. William Hand Browne, ed., *Archives of Maryland*, 16 (Baltimore, 1897): 31, 58–60.

25. Goddard, *Prowess of the Whig Club*, pp. 4–11, quote from p. 11; George Welch and David Rusk Certificate in Support of Mary Cox.

26. Goddard, *Prowess of the Whig Club*, p. 7.

27. Scharf, *Chronicles of Baltimore*, pp. 160, 161, 162.

28. *Maryland Journal*, July 20, Aug. 3, 1779.

29. *Archives of Maryland*, 12: 518; McCreary, *Mechanical Company*, pp. 21, 23; Cox Account Book, MS. 262, MHS; William Cox to his brother, James Cox, Jr., Dec. 27, 1790, Cox Papers.

30. Frank A. Cassell, *Merchant Congressman in the Young Republic: Samuel Smith of Maryland, 1752–1839* (Madison, Wis., 1971), p. 36 and passim.

31. Scharf, *Chronicles of Baltimore*, p. 187; George Welch and David Rusk Certificate in Support of Mary Cox, James Cox Agreement with Dennis Malone, Nov. 27, 1776, Cox Papers. For references to boarders, see last leaf of Cox Account Book, and July 14, Sept. 16, 1769, Nov. 20, Dec. 6, 1770. William B. Bayre, "Some Baltimore City Place Names: Huntington or Huntingdon, the Two Liliendales and Sumwalt Run," *Maryland Historical Magazine*, 54 (Dec., 1959): 354; Walker, "Baltimore Community," p. 46.

32. McCreary, *Mechanical Company*, pp. 19, 21, 27; George F. Adams et al., *History of Baptist Churches in Maryland Connected with the Maryland Baptist Union Association* (Baltimore, 1885), p. 31; Reiman Steuart, *A History of the Maryland Line in the Revolutionary War* (Towson, Md., 1969), p. 69; Bal-

timore Town and Baltimore County, Committee of Observation Proceedings, 1774–76, Sept. 12, 1775, MHS.

33. Mary Cox to Darby Lux, Apr. 5, 1779; Petition of Mary Cox, Dec. 12, 1779; Act for the benefit of Mary Cox, Dec. 22, 1788; Petition of Mary Cox to the General Assembly of Maryland (1779?); Darby Lux to Mary Cox, June 8, 1779; Mary Cox and Carey and Tilghman, Agreement of Apprenticeship of James Cox, Jr., Aug. 9, 1786; William Cox to his brother, James Cox, Jr., Dec. 27, 1790; Mary Cox to Mark Alexander, July 29, 1784; Inscription on Tombstone of James Cox—all in Cox Papers.

4

THE MECHANIC INTEREST EMERGES:
THE CONSTITUTION

The formation of the Mechanical Company, Mechanical Volunteers, and Whig Club represented the first stage in the development of a self-conscious community of skilled workingmen. In the 1780s mechanics continued to build on the Revolutionary legacy, stepping up their organizational activities in pursuit of a protective tariff. The protectionist movement plunged craftsmen into election politics for the first time and eventually turned them into unwavering supporters of the new federal Constitution.

In 1785 workingmen launched an unprecedented effort at mobilization, calling meetings of the individual trades and appointing delegates to a general assembly that founded the Association of Tradesmen and Manufacturers. The association immediately set out to petition the state legislature for a tariff. Not surprisingly, the petition drive foundered in the rural-oriented and planter-dominated assembly. The association responded by taking the novel step of urging its members to vote only for candidates who had declared their support of a tariff. In the annual assembly elections the association was forced to broaden its political outlook beyond the issue of protectionism to include other matters concerning mechanics. By late 1787 the association had despaired of securing a state tariff and aligned itself with the movement for a new federal government empowered to implement a national tariff. The overwhelmingly federalist sympathies of Baltimore's mechanics became clear in April, 1788, when, in celebration of the ratification of the Constitution, they staged a general parade, marching by craft behind the chosen leaders of the trades and displaying flags that reflected a strong craft and patriotic consciousness. Six months later the mechanics reaffirmed their federalism by helping to defeat an assembly candidate who, despite his reputation as a champion of the "laboring and middling classes," had committed the unpardonable political sin of opposing the Constitution. In its final action the Baltimore association led a nationwide drive for a federal tariff, which was enacted in 1789. It is difficult to exaggerate the importance of the years 1785 to 1789, for they witnessed the emergence of a "mechanic interest" that no politician could afford to ignore.

The movement for a protective tariff began in Boston. In April, 1785, a committee appointed by Boston's tradesmen and manufacturers notified the merchant community of their intention to petition the assembly for higher tariff duties. They asked for the merchants' support. Speaking for his colleagues, John Hancock assured the committee that merchants would stand behind all efforts to ameliorate the depressed state of manufacturing. In May Baltimore's newspapers printed an account of the proceedings, at whose direction is unknown, but it must have spurred the town's mechanics to consider a tariff as an answer to their troubles. Three months later came more news from Boston. In a circular letter the newly formed Association of Tradesmen and Manufactures of Boston decried the massive importation of British manufacturers since the end of the war, which "unless speedily checked by the prudent Exertions of those who are more particularly interested, must eventually prove ruinous to every Mechanical Branch in America." Boston's mechanics explained how since April they had organized, circulated petitions favoring manufacturing, and convinced the assembly to lift tariff rates on certain articles produced at home. The strategy had worked for them; they now recommended it to the mechanics of Baltimore and elsewhere. "We therefore apply to you, Gentlemen," the association wrote, "to send us your Assistance, and like a Band of Brothers, whose Interests are connected, we beg you to join in such Measures to advance the general Good, as your Prudence shall suggest and your Wisdom dictate."[1]

The circular stands as a landmark in American labor history. It was the call precipitating the creation of a network of organizations dedicated to the promotion of domestic manufacturing in the major urban centers. Each association chose a corresponding committee to keep abreast of activities in other states. Loosely coordinated and often short-lived, these organizations nonetheless contributed to a broader identity among mechanics throughout the republic. According to the Boston association, organization would overcome two obstacles that had dogged the mechanics in their efforts to secure protective legislation. It would end interstate rivalry. "An Association, established in your State," the Boston mechanics wrote, "we shall ever be happy to correspond with, and we flatter ourselves from this social Intercourse, a general Harmony will prevail throughout the whole Manufacturing Interest of this Country." Organization would also allay jealousies within the mechanic community arising from the diverging interests of different trades. In associations patterned on the Boston model, the circular said, shipbuilders and shoemakers, coopers and carpenters, would cooperate as "each Man becomes interested not only in his own Branch but in those of his Brethren." The Boston association was trying to do nothing less than convey "the United Voice of the Tradesmen and Manufacturers of America."[2]

Baltimore's mechanics had not been idle before receiving the call from Boston. That summer they had held two general meetings, but nothing definite had been decided. The circular stirred them to sustained action. On September 19 a number of mechanics gathered at the "Lodge-Room" at Fell's Point and resolved that during the coming week each trade should hold a meeting and appoint two delegates to a general assembly. When the mechanic representatives convened on September 26 at the market house, they founded the Association of Tradesmen and Manufacturers of Baltimore. The association appointed a corresponding committee which on October 4 sent a message to Boston thanking its mechanics for their encouragement and informing them that they had associated along the lines suggested in the circular. The Baltimore committee expressed its hope to establish a regular correspondence with Boston that would help "to counteract the insidious schemes which have been formed against our country, and to promote by encouraging our own manufactures, its real prosperity, and true political and commercial independence." The committee passed along the circular to other Maryland towns, enclosing a covering letter that outlined a plan of action to petition the legislature for protective duties. From the mechanics of Frederick Town came a prompt reply. They had already appointed their own corresponding committee and were distributing a petition favoring American manufacturing to be presented to the Maryland assembly.[3]

Baltimore's mechanics were making a revolution in their own self-perception and potential for collective political action. The two general meetings held between May and August were the first such in Baltimore's history, and by October there were two more. With the membership of the Mechanical Company dwindling to a few dozen by 1783 and the Mechanical Volunteers disbanding, the Association of Tradesmen and Manufacturers inherited the task of bringing workingmen within an institutional framework that crossed craft boundaries. The meetings of the individual trades in September were also unprecedented. Indeed, Baltimore's mechanics had yet to form a craft association like those in New York, Philadelphia, and Boston. For leadership the Baltimore association turned to prominent mechanics and manufacturers. The chairman at the September 26 meeting was shipwright David Stodder, one of the kingpins of his trade. He also served on the corresponding committee along with card maker Adam Fonerden and hatter John Gray. No newcomer to politics, Fonerden had joined the Mechanical Company in the 1760s and rose to become its president a decade later. Another veteran mechanic was coppersmith William Clemm, the secretary of the Baltimore association, who had been one of the original members of the Mechanical Company and Sons of Liberty.[4]

The Baltimore association set out its arguments for protective tariffs in a series of articles published in the newspapers by "A PLAIN, AND REAL, FRIEND TO AMERICA." By his own admission the author was speaking for the association; in October, 1785, he claimed to be "authorized from the associated Body of Mechanics, in this Town." "A Friend" catalogued a half-dozen reasons why the assembly should boost tariffs: it would prevent rural destitution, employ the urban poor, forestall an overabundance of merchants, reduce America's dependence on Great Britain, lessen the flow of cash out of the republic, and strengthen the nation's military. Through all these arguments ran two consistent themes. One was the notion of "decency." At the very least, according to "A Friend," decency implied the right of all mechanics "to produce bread and support for their families." A mechanic who enjoyed a decent living was an independent household head, a father and husband, a man who could maintain his wife and children in comfort if not luxury. A decent living carried the expectation that diligent work would advance the mechanic through the ranks from apprentice, to journeyman, and finally to master status. A decent workshop was one where the master could "get more hands to work, and take more apprentices."

To "A Friend" decency also imposed restrictions and obligations on the mechanic. If the tradesman had the right to a decent price for his labor, the community could demand that he not exceed it. "A Friend" assured the public that the mechanics had already agreed not "to act like extortioners, or to ask what they please for such articles as they make." Taking advantage of a protective tariff by driving up the price of labor was "extortion," even if the market permitted it. Here we see a key assumption underlying "A Friend"'s concept of decency. The impersonal forces of the marketplace must not become the arbiter of wages and prices, but rather producers and consumers should conduct themselves according to ethical precepts that have been called the "moral economy."[5]

A second theme in the essays was "idleness." "A Friend" attributed to the mechanic community a moral resilience that he could not find in other classes; he saw the mechanics as a bulwark against idleness and "luxury." The decline of manufacturing, he argued, would drive men into rural poverty or, even worse, lead them into the merchant profession. The towns would swarm with would-be entrepreneurs, young men clamoring for a place in the counting houses. The result? "He gets a clerk's place; he dresses, powders, and waits upon the ladies!" Contrast this image of the merchant as frivolous, idle, and effeminate with the diligent mechanic, the father at the dinner table surrounded by his family, the master at his workshop overseeing his apprentices and journeymen. Left to themselves, "A Friend" insinuated, the merchants would destroy the very values embodied in the mechanic community. "What can we promise ourselves if we still puruse the same extensive trade? What, but total destruction of our manners, and the entire loss of our virtue?" Unless checked by a protective tariff, merchants would continue to inundate America with foreign manufactures, throw mechanics out of work, and create the idleness antithetical to the mechanics' self-perception. From the writings of "A Friend" emerges more than a special-interest plea for higher duties. They present a picture of the mechanic as he saw himself—diligent, disciplined, industrious, the republic's best hope against "luxury, effeminancy and extravagance."[6]

The prospects seemed favorable that the assembly would enact legislation in response to the petition drive at its November, 1785, session. By October the legislatures of Massachusetts, Pennsylvania, Rhode Island, and New Hampshire had adopted measures to encourage manufacturing. Five years earlier the Maryland assembly had imposed a 1 percent ad valorem tax on most imports and higher duties on a few enumerated goods, while in 1784 it raised the duty to 2 percent. But the assembly would go no further. Despite the nearly one thousand signatures attached to the association's petition, the assembly made only a nominal bow toward higher tariffs. It raised the duties on coaches, carriages, and mahogany furniture but cut the ad valorem rate to .5 percent. As the assembly session closed, few could doubt that the legislature still reflected the interests of southern planters who feared protective tariffs would spur a commercial war with Great Britain and jeopardize their own tobacco trade.[7]

The setback forced the association to devise a new strategy by taking their cause directly into the political arena. Before 1785 local politics in Baltimore was relatively tranquil, almost pro forma. But the emergence of the mechanics as an organized political bloc turned the once peaceful assembly elections into tense, sometimes riotous, confrontations. In 1784 merchant John Sterett and lawyer David McMechen had been elected to the assembly from Baltimore; no one even opposed them. A year later the town's voters "*unanimously*" returned them to their seats. Although both representatives agreed informally to press the petition before the assembly, the session ended without a tariff bill coming up for consideration. For a year the association harbored the suspicion that their delegates had not given the measure the commitment it deserved. By 1786 the mechanics were ready to name their own candidates for office.

In August, with elections scheduled two months away, "*A real Friend to Maryland*" addressed the association in the town newspapers. He could not understand why an assembly willing to enact laws benefiting farmers and merchants should spurn the mechanics, especially in view of the consequences. "Look around," he told the mechanics, "behold the injustice, extravagance, luxury, dissipation, loose morals, idleness, extortion, corruption, &c. are stalking through the land." Sterett and McMechen, the author implied, had forgotten their promise to the mechanics; now it was time to ask "whether a change of men is not at present really necessary." "A real Friend" urged the association to choose delegates, *"tell them the business you want done, and order them to do it—* thus be free and happy."[8]

The association's candidate was physician James McHenry, whose mechanic support seems to have sprung from three sources. McHenry was a military man, having earned a reputation during the war, which gave him credibility among the militia-minded mechanics. He lived at Fell's Point, which many believed made him sympathetic with the needs of the heavily laboring-class population. He was a physician rather than a lawyer or merchant. "A real Friend" had expressed the popular contempt for lawyers, condemning them as "voluptous, or refined and modish gentlemen." In September the townspeople were called upon to elect an elector for the state senate, and the association proposed McHenry as its candidate, recommending him "to the different branches of TRADESMEN in particular, and to the INHABITANTS of the Town in general."

For several reasons the association opposed Richard Ridgely, who was also running for the office. It feared that his election would strengthen the "Ridgely connection," which dominated Baltimore County politics. More controversial was Ridgely's behavior while serving on the board of trustees of the Baltimore College, a public institution established in 1784. Although the supporters of the Episcopal institution argued that it would stop students from leaving Maryland and thus benefit the entire state, its enemies saw the college as a first step toward "establishing Deans, Prebends, Canons, and Archdeacons in this State, and maintaining them at the public expence." The Baltimore association, whose leadership included Presbyterian Stodder and Methodist minister Fonerden, was alarmed at this movement toward an established church. In a letter printed in the newspapers before the election, one anonymous individual wrote about "the Mechanics, who swear-off against all Church-men, and hate *Ridgely* ever since, he was a Trustee for the College." A year before "A Mechanic" feared that the college portended "more Burdens preparing for the Back of the poorer Part of the Community."[9]

The September election revealed that the association was more than a single-issue forum. It was a vehicle expressing a broad range of mechanic interests—protective tariffs, religious freedom, government without "connections." McHenry lost the election, though, which is not surprising. The association had endorsed him on the issue of religious liberty and thereby diverted attention from the protectionism question, the logical point around which to organize the mechanics. A month later McMechen was re-elected to the assembly along with merchant Jesse Hollingsworth. On November 13 the association met and drew up a new petition, instructing the two delegates to fight for legislation "in favour of American Manufactures." Nonetheless, the assembly could not be moved and another session passed without a tariff law.[10]

Their petition rejected again, the mechanics prepared for the October, 1787, assembly elections. The campaign set it apart from all previous elections. Never before had all candidates felt obliged to campaign openly for the mechanics' support or to justify their political views as those best serving the mechanics' interests. One correspondent in the newspapers, "A Mechanic," resented the "impertinent scribblers" who were suddenly presuming to tell mechanics what was best for them. The workingmen blamed their delegates for the petition's defeat, especially Hollingsworth, who belonged to a prominent merchant family specializing in the grain trade. According to one of several authors assuming the pen name "A Mechanic," Hollingsworth had trampled the mechanics' interests to further his own by sacrificing the country's "*best security*, viz. her manufactures, for the sake of the paltry commissions of a wagon load of wheat, flour, &c." Nor was this the sole example of Hollingsworth's misconduct. He had also supported a bill that would have imposed a period of servitude on indigent debtors, shackling many workingmen to what "A Mechanic" called "temporary slavery."[11]

It was easier to reject McMechen and Hollingsworth than to

agree on alternatives to them. Complicating matters was the fact
that two men had announced their candidacies, both of whom enjoyed popularity among skilled workingmen. One was Samuel
Chase, a lawyer who had recently moved from Annapolis to Baltimore. Declaring his candidacy on September 14, Chase had ample reason to expect the mechanics' support. He ranked among
Maryland's best-known political figures. In the 1760s and 1770s
he had been a leader against proprietary and imperial policies,
developing a close relationship with the workingmen of Annapolis. More recently, Chase had opposed the same insolvency bill
that had gotten Hollingsworth into trouble among the mechanics.
There was reason to expect that Chase would be more amenable
to a tariff than Hollingsworth had been. "The man," "A Mechanic" said in reference to Chase, "is not employed in the purchasing of produce as remittances to pay for foreign gewgaws and
triffles, therefore, more protection and encouragement to American manufactures may be expected."

On the other hand, Chase had occupied the center of political controversy too long not to make enemies. During the War for
Independence Alexander Hamilton and others had accused him
of exploiting his confidential political position to corner the Baltimore wheat market and drive up the price of grain. Chase's views
on religion were also suspect. He had once supported a bill in
the assembly that placed a head tax on Maryland inhabitants for
the support of the church. Those congregations with fewer than
thirty male members were prohibited from drawing on the fund,
which lent credence to the charge that the bill was designed to
weaken the smaller non-Episcopal churches. Chase's own father
had been an Anglican minister.[12]

James McHenry was also campaigning for mechanic votes.
Selecting Philip Rogers as his running mate, the McHenry ticket
touted itself as "well known Friends to the Federal Constitution"
that had been recently drawn up at Philadelphia. On this issue
they clashed with Chase, who had opposed the Philadelphia convention, arguing that the states individually could best deal with
the faltering finances of the republic. When the Constitution was
submitted to the states for ratification, Chase called for substantial amendments. He and his running mate, David McMechen,
hedged on the constitution question before the assembly elec-

tion. In a speech delivered at the Baltimore County court house Chase declared: "I have not formed my Opinion, whether the Plan proposed ought to be accepted as it stands, without any Amendment or Alteration." Chase was a tried politician. To have frankly professed his antifederalism in federalist Baltimore would have damaged his hopes for election.[13]

The mechanic vote seems to have been divided. When the polls closed on October 3, Chase and McMechen were declared the winners. The margin of victory was impressive: they had received 612 and 593 votes respectively, to McHenry's 206 and Rogers's 168. Although the Baltimore association had not endorsed candidates in the newspapers, it had apparently supported the McHenry-Rogers ticket. William Goddard, a vocal Chase man, congratulated the mechanics on their defiance of certain "Gentlemen" who had been "extremely mistaken in their supposed Weight and Consequence with the People." These were the same words used to describe the association a year before. We can only speculate about the dilemma facing the association in the 1787 assembly election. As its petitions continued to meet defeat in the assembly, the association pinned its hopes on the newly proposed national government to enact a federal tariff. Thus the McHenry-Rogers ticket, outspoken federalists, seemed more attractive than Chase and McMechen, whose position on ratification was dubious. Yet Chase had sidestepped the ratification issue and diverted attention to his past record as a popular spokesman. It would seem, then, that while the leadership of the association supported the federalist candidates on the matter of ratification, they could not persuade the mechanics generally to renounce a proven Revolutionary hero. Perhaps it was this very dilemma that convinced the association to avoid an open endorsement.[14]

In the months following the assembly elections, as each state debated the proposed Constitution, federalism gained ground in Baltimore. By the spring of 1788 the townspeople's attention was fastened on the state ratifying convention that was scheduled to meet in Annapolis on April 21. Special elections were held for the convention, with each county, Baltimore, and Annapolis choosing two delegates. In most cases the assemblymen returned to their home districts and stood for election to the convention. The notable exception was Samuel Chase, Baltimore's representative, who preferred to run as a convention representative in his old political bailiwick of Anne Arundel County. Baltimoreans protested Chase's action. Why should he snub the voters who had just honored him with an assembly seat? Many accused Chase of violating the residency requirement of the state constitution. Chase's enemies maintained that he was betraying himself as the political cynic he had always been. During the 1787 assembly campaign Chase had been hard pressed defending his opposition to the constitution. He finally explained that he had no choice, for as an assemblyman from Anne Arundel and Annapolis he was duty-bound to follow the antifederalist sentiments of his old constituents. The implication was clear: as a delegate from Baltimore, Chase could in good conscience switch to the federalist side. By the spring of 1788 Chase's political maneuverings had placed him in a difficult situation. He could not serve as a convention representative from Baltimore, fight ratification of the Constitution, and remain true to his earlier pledges. On the other hand, he could return to Anne Arundel, where antifederalism ran high, and oppose the Constitution in the convention.[15]

In Chase's absence two tickets declared their candidacies for the convention. Assemblyman McMechen joined Samuel Sterett on a platform that demanded amendments as a precondition to ratifying the Constitution, which was widely perceived as a delaying strategy for subverting ratification altogether. On the other side, James McHenry and fellow physician John Coulter rallied their supporters around the position "that the ratification of the Constitution ought to precede any Amendments or Alteration; and that it must be injurious to our common Interests to *delay* its Ratification, in the Hope of obtaining them *in any other Manner* than prescribed by the Constitution." The federalist ticket won; McHenry's persistence finally paid off. He received 962 votes, Coulter 958, Sterett 385, and McMechen 380. The announcement of the election results found the town's mechanics in high spirits. Together with other federalists they staged a parade where, apparently for the first time, they marched separately from the other townspeople: "the Shipbuilders, the Tradesmen concerned in Navigation, the Merchants, the Manufacturers, and several

Thousand Inhabitants, walked in Procession through the different Streets of the Town, preceded with the Flag of the United States, and a small decorated Ship, supported by Sailors."[16]

The election had been wide open. Although the state assembly stipulated that persons eligible to vote for legislators—adult white males who had established a one-year residence and an estate assessed at £30—could vote for the convention delegates, Baltimore's election judges dispensed with the property qualifications. Thus the number of voters, according to one observer who published a close analysis of the voting returns, rose 62 percent from the assembly elections seven months before, from 830 to 1,347. The author's figures demonstrated that the federalist ticket drew its support disproportionately from those who could not meet the property qualification—in other words, poor mechanics and laborers. Of the ballots cast for McHenry and Coulter, 82 percent came from the "ineligible" voters, compared to 69 percent for McMechen and Sterett. The difference was actually greater, though, because 671 persons who were eligible to vote had been prevented from casting their ballots, intimidated by federalist toughs. According to the analyst, these men would have voted overwhelmingly antifederalist. The convention election was unprecedented not only for abandoning the property qualification for voting but also for rioting. On Wednesday, the final day for polling, it was reported that "a very large number of men, among them a great number of *foreign* sailors, and servants, many of them with *bludgeons*, took possession of the polls, and terrified and prevented many peaceable and respectable citizens, chiefly Germans, from coming to the polls, and they did not vote at the election."[17]

On April 26 the state convention voted sixty-three to eleven to ratify the Constitution. Maryland thereby became the seventh state to ratify, giving the Constitution a majority of the states' votes. As in other towns, Baltimore held a huge parade in celebration. On the morning of May 1, 3,000 townspeople gathered at Philpot's Hill at Fell's Point and wound their way across town to Federal Hill, which overlooked Baltimore from the west side of the harbor. The mechanic community was out in full force. "The Mechanics," according to one observer, "anticipating, under the new Government, an Increase of their different Manufactures, from the Operation of uniform Duties, on similar Articles imported into the United States, vied with each other in their Preparations." They arranged themselves into forty trades. In the days leading to the procession each craft met and chose representatives to lead their brethren. Sixty craftsmen received the honor, including many men who for a generation had supplied the mechanics' leadership. David Shields, the former president of the Mechanical Company, led the hatters. John McClellan, the captain of the Mechanical Volunteers, was at the head of the blacksmiths. John Gordon, a one-time member of the Whig Club, was first among the saddlers. William Duncan, an old Son of Liberty, headed up the coopers. Especially visible were the leaders of the Baltimore Association of Tradesmen and Manufacturers, whose demands for protectionism put them at the forefront of the movement for the constitution: David Stodder led the ship joiners, John Gray the hatters, and William Clemm the coppersmiths.[18]

The mechanics carried banners and displays that symbolized their trades, weaving their craft identity with their strong nationalism. The number thirteen for the states appeared consistently. The bakers bore a flag "displaying Two Men Hand-in-Hand;—Thirteen Loaves;—Thirteen Stars and Thirteen Stripes;—the rising Sun;—Sheaf of Wheat.—Motto, 'May our Country never want Bread.'" The ropemakers lined up behind a wagon pulled by thirteen laborers and holding a spinning wheel with thirteen whirls operated by thirteen workmen. The house carpenters probably constructed the most elaborate display, a "grand Tower" of thirteen stories, pillars, arches, pediments, spires, and flutes. The mechanics' banners also demonstrated the importance attached to protective tariffs. The silversmiths and watch makers had a flag that stated bluntly: "No Importation and we shall live." The blacksmiths and nailors drove home the same point:

> May ev'ry Federal Heart,
> Encourage Vulcan's Art.
> And
> While Industry prevails,
> We need no foreign Nails.

No less important was the craft identity that the banners reflected. Despite the absence of craft associations in Baltimore, the mechanics invoked long-standing trade traditions in their flags by exhibiting the patron saints and founding fathers of the trades. The house carpenters carried a banner showing the classical Italian architect Palladio; the shoemakers displayed their third-century patron saint, King Crispin; the printers' flag contained a portrait of Gutenberg, the fifteenth-century pioneer of movable type; on the ropemaker's banner was Queen Catherine, probably the eighth-century Alexandrian martyr who became the patron saint of many trades. One of the clearest indications of the mechanics' unity was the decision of masters, journeymen, and apprentices to march together rather than by status. When the parade reached Federal Hill, the marchers sat down to feast at an enormous circular table. The festivities cost £600, disregarding what individual organizations spent.[19]

The debate over the Constitution had crystalized the differences between "federalists," as they continued to call themselves, and "antifederalists," a term of opprobrium they saddled on their opponents. This political polarization provided the backdrop for the October, 1788, assembly elections. Samuel Chase was up for re-election along with David McMechen, and they now faced the consequences of Chase's political machinations. In April Chase had seemed to desert his Baltimore constituents. What was worse, as a convention delegate from Anne Arundel he had been one of the eleven who had voted against ratification. Try as he might, Chase could no longer hedge on the constitution question. On the opposing side were Baltimore's proven federalists, McHenry and Coulter, members of the "virtuous sixty-three" who had voted in favor of the constitution. Although they had lost to the Chase-McMechen ticket a year before, running as "friends to the constitution," the political scenario had changed radically since then. Their earlier attacks on Chase's questionable politics now seemed vindicated.[20]

In the assembly campaigning, Chase resorted to the same strategy that had worked so well during his years at Annapolis. He appealed to the "poor." Some of the boldest calls for plebeian support came from the pen of "An old German." On September 16 he declared that the "aristocratic party, the great and the rich men" had leagued together against Chase. The aristocrats must be resisted, for Chase "had always been the friend of the poor man."

By early October the warnings of "An Irishman" had grown more ominous: "Ye poor men! Stand by Mr. Chase, against whom the rage of malice, the fury of persecution and unjust resentment boil over." Underlying these appeals was a strategy to undermine the two political alliances behind Baltimore's federalist bloc: the first between rich and poor mechanics, the second between mechanics and merchants. By convincing poor mechanics and laborers that their successful fellow tradesmen were their enemies and by persuading the mechanics generally that merchants were behind their woes, Chase could draw attention away from his own antifederalism, where he was most vulnerable.[21]

In August "A Citizen" published the antifederalists' clearest attempt to rally poor mechanics against rich ones. He said that the federalist leadership consisted of "wealthy Mechanics" and "Merchants," who had joined forces for their own selfish ends. "Some *few* Mechanics," he explained,

> who have acquired wealth, and who are able to carry on business extensively, wish the Government to take place; they sound aloud its praise wherever they go; cry out that manufactories must be encouraged—home manufactories will be the salvation of our country—the importation of foreign luxuries must be restrained—duties—heavy duties must be imposed—and this cannot be done without a general Government; all forsooth that they may get it in their power to make fortunes themselves, at the expence of their fellow-citizens, by charging exorbitant prices for their flimsy work.

"A Citizen" claimed that the patrician mechanics and merchants were attempting to cajole and coerce the lower classes into supporting them, and "generally the poor and the ignorant have fallen prey to their designs." He warned the "labouring People" about their self-styled friends: protective tariffs might prove a boon to wealthy mechanics but they would harm everyone else by raising the prices of all "necessaries."[22]

The Chase faction also attempted to inflame animosities between mechanics and merchants. A series of articles written by Chase men protested that federalist merchants were threatening mechanics with economic retaliation should they fail to vote the McHenry-Coulter ticket. Addressing himself to "the TRADESMEN, MECHANICKS, and MANUFACTURERS of BALTIMORE-TOWN,"

"Adze" described several instances of intimidation. "Now I do not like the threatening of some *great folks* not to employ any of us *Mechanicks*," he wrote, "or to take away work from us, unless we vote as the great men please." His own employer, a master carpenter, threatened to lay off any of his workmen who voted for Chase. "Adze" also claimed to know a sailmaker who lost his job by expressing his preference for Chase; the employer had been a hatter, personifying the collusion between merchant and "wealthy Mechanic." "One of my neighbours, a carpenter," "Adze" continued, "is as silent as a mouse from threats of one of his employers." Another correspondent calling himself "A Mechanic" wrote that his federalist landlord had not too subtly dropped by to remind him that rent was due soon. "By this it seems to me," "A Mechanic" concluded, "that after all our talk and fighting about LIBERTY, the poor must submit to be directed by the rich, or he will have a poor time of it!"[23]

The McHenry men responded in kind. On September 9 "A federal Mechanic" blasted the attempts of the Chase faction to split the federalists: "I am told that I ought to hate all merchants and rich mechanics, despise my landlord, and listen only to a few men who make a trade of electioneering." Merchants and mechanics, employers and employed, shared the same basic interests. "I have always thought," "A federal Mechanic" wrote,

> that whatever did an injury to those who employed me, must sooner or later do me an injury; and I have always found that when trade flourished most, I had most to do; could pay my rent without feeling it, and get my money without dunning for it; and this proved to me clearer than anything in print, that *trade* was the best friend to the mechanic and poor man; so that, if I vote as my brother mechanics and merchants vote, I shall do nothing but what is very natural and very much to my interest.

Another writer, "Vice," took up the accusations of "Adze" and showed them to be empty. He spoke to the workingmen allegedly threatened, who denied the fact. McHenry himself strove to discredit Chase in the eyes of the poorer classes. After meeting with him in early September, McHenry accused his rival of endorsing a bill in the assembly "to assess and tax the tools of the mechanics and tradesmen, and also to tax poor mechanics and labourers."

The charge hit the mark, for one correspondent warned Chase that unless he cleared himself, "it will go hard with him."[24]

The debates moved into the streets. In the week before the election a rumor circulated at the Point that "those merchants, *particularly interested in vessels and shipping*" supported Chase and McMechen. In response forty-six prominent merchants published an open statement denying the charge, including John and Samuel Smith, David Stewart, and David Plunket—veterans of the independence movement. In addition, the merchants paraded through the Point to proclaim their federalism to the community. The Chase faction was enraged; the federalists had concocted the rumors themselves, they claimed, which then served as a pretext to further intimidate the Point's laboring classes. "What does such a parade mean," asked "An Irishman": "The language is so plain that a child may understand it. Coopers! we buy your cases; tradesmen! we are your employers; retailers! we give you credit; draymen! we give you bread; you *must* have no voice of your own; our representatives have incurred our displeasure; you *must* be on our side." "An Irishman" asked the mechanics what would have happened if they had similarly approached the merchants—"what treatment would you have received?"[25]

The election reached new levels not only in the bitterness of the campaign rhetoric but also in violence in the streets and hustings. Two days before the polls were scheduled to open, McMechen reportedly visited each of the taverns at the Point, dressed "in the shabby tarred dress of a sailor." He treated the seamen to grog and urged them "to parade on Monday morning, in his and Mr. *Chase*'s favour." At the designated hour Chase and McMechen gathered their supporters at the Point and "marched from the Point to the place of election, with a flag, a liberty cap, and a representation of a pilot-boat." Upon arriving at the hustings, they found a group of hostile McHenry sailors already in possession of the polls. The Chase faction stationed itself at the entrance to the building and patroled until the polls had closed for the evening. Before sunrise the next morning a group of Chase supporters assembled at the entrance and built a new scaffolding with "a flag with a inscription, implying censure upon their opponents." When the election judges arrived and the voting commenced, the Chase party allegedly blocked the McHenry men from the polls. After an unsuccessful protest to the judges the McHenry faction fought their way to possession of the polls. A few "gentlemen" stepped in quickly and stopped the brawl.

By Wednesday, the third and final day of the election, Chase had apparently realized that the contest was going against him. According to the McHenry party, he planned to provoke a confrontation with his opponents, which he could later cite as evidence in challenging the election results. Between ten and eleven o'clock he led 500 supporters to the polling place and demanded free access. Although the federalists later claimed that only a quarter of these men were eligible voters, they nonetheless allowed them to cast their ballots and thereby eluded Chase's ploy. By seven o'clock that evening the Baltimore County sheriff obtained the permission of both sets of candidates to close the polls. The votes were tallied and the sheriff announced a federalist victory: McHenry 635 votes, Coulter 622, Chase 502, and McMechen 494. As everyone expected, Chase petitioned the assembly to disallow the election. He lost his case.[26]

The 1788 assembly election symbolized a great step in the political maturation of the mechanic community. For the master craftsmen striving to make the mechanics a politically conscious entity, Chase's campaign had posed a formidable threat. The old hero of the Revolution had attempted to undermine mechanic unity by rallying the "labouring poor," who included skilled and unskilled workingmen, against the successful masters. Chase was pitting the struggling apprentice, destitute journeyman, and disappointed master against their wealthy brethren. His campaign became an assault on the mechanic leadership that had risen since the independence movement, for who were the "wealthy Mechanics" the Chase faction assailed if not the former spokesmen of the Mechanical Company and Mechanical Volunteers and the present officers of the Association of Tradesmen and Manufacturers? Weren't the antifederalists blackening the reputations of such men as hatter David Shields, shipwright David Stodder, blacksmith John McClellan, hatter John Gray, coppersmith William Clemm, and card maker Adam Fonerden?

That Baltimore's poorer mechanics failed to respond to Chase's call—at least in sufficient numbers to elect him and McMechen to office—testified to the strides the mechanic leadership had made in inculcating an awareness of the collective interests of all skilled workingmen. Samuel Chase had served his political apprenticeship in an earlier era when appeals to the "labouring poor" produced better results. In the new postindependence era such appeals became less compelling. In a sense Chase was lost in this world. His defeat in 1788 marked the end of one phase of his career; afterward he would rise in appointive rather than elective office, the judiciary rather than the legislature. He would metamorphose into one of the republic's most outspoken conservatives, an almost hysterical enemy of what he perceived as the "rabble" who had rejected him.[27]

After the assembly election the Associaton of Tradesmen and Manufacturers resumed its petition drive, now five years old. By February 17, 1789, a committee appointed by the association to draft a petition to Congress presented the measure before a "GENERAL MEETING of the TRADESMEN and MANUFACTURERS." It met approval and circulated through the state. Each of the trades appointed representatives who met on February 24 to identify those manufactured goods that stood in greatest need of protective duties. Two days later a newly appointed corresponding committee of the association—which included the veterans Fonerden, Stodder, and Gray—sent a copy of the petition to the Society of Mechanics and Manufacturers of New York. In a separate letter the committee explained how Baltimore's workingmen had waited for another organization to take the initiative in petitioning the Congress, but as none had stepped forward it now offered its own petition as a model. On April 21 the association laid its petition before the House of Representatives.[28]

The document described how tradesmen across the country had turned to their state legislatures for assistance after the war. It recounted their growing disillusionment as the realization dawned that "no effectual provision could reasonably be expected, until one uniform, efficient government should pervade this wide-extended country." Now that the citizens had created this government, the association rejoiced "at the prospect this affords them, that America, freed from the commercial shackles which have so long bound her, will see and pursue her true interest, becoming independent in fact as well as in name." Appended to the petition was a list of articles crying out for protection. Under the category of metal goods fell everything from bar and cast iron to copper, tin and brass ware, silver and gold work. Also suffering under foreign competition were leather goods, including curried leather, sheepskin breeches and gloves, boots and shoes, hats, and saddle ware. Craftsmen in the wood trades hoped to see duties placed on cabinets and household furniture, coaches and carriages, carpenters' planes. The entire line of products in the shipbuilding industries also needed protection: ship blocks, cordage, rope, and twine. Import duties were vital to the watch and clock makers and mathematical instrument makers. Finally the list included a miscellaneous collection of products from wool and cotton cards to stays, brushes, paper, and candles. Signed by over 700 persons, the petition stands as testimony to the efforts of the association to secure economic protectionism.[29]

The years 1785 to 1789 were a watershed. For the first time Baltimore's mechanics held general meetings, assembled in their individual crafts, and elected representatives from the trades to confer on matters affecting all of them. This outburst of organizational activity culminated in the formation of the Association of Tradesmen and Manufacturers of Baltimore, which for the first time brought mechanics into regular contact with their brethren in Boston, New York, and elsewhere. The association initiated the first petition drive to secure a state tariff and, when it failed, it organized the first campaign to elect an assemblyman devoted to the mechanics' interests. When Maryland ratified the federal Constitution upon which protectionist forces had pinned their hopes, the mechanics organized their first parades—huge displays of their commitment to the new national government. Despite the association's failure to elect James McHenry to office in 1786 and 1787, the mechanics helped put him in the assembly in 1788. In rejecting McHenry's opponent, Samuel Chase, the mechanics had proved that the issues outweighed the man. For all his popularity Chase had opposed the Constitution, which damaged his credibility among the federalist mechanics. Finally, in 1789 the Baltimore association drew up the first petition to Congress for a national tariff, which served as a model in New York and elsewhere. From 1785 to 1789 protectionism had provided the issue unifying nearly all skilled workingmen; it had been the rallying point of the "mechanic interest."

NOTES

1. *Maryland Gazette* (Baltimore), May 24, 1785; *Maryland Journal* (Baltimore), Sept. 20, 1785.

2. *Maryland Journal*, Sept. 20, 1785.

3. *Ibid.*, Sept. 20, 30, Oct. 11, 28, 1785; *Maryland Gazette*, Nov. 18, 1785.

4. *Maryland Journal*, Sept. 20, Aug. 4, 1785; *Maryland Gazette*, Nov. 18, 1785.

5. *Maryland Journal*, Aug. 16, Oct. 11, 21, 1785.

6. *Ibid.*

7. Mary Jane Dowd, "The State in the Maryland Economy, 1776–1807," *Maryland Historical Magazine*, 57 (June, 1962): 100–101.

8. *Maryland Journal*, Oct. 8, 1784, Oct. 7, 1785, Aug. 22, 1786.

9. *Ibid.*, Jan. 28, 1785, Sept. 1, 5, 1786; *Maryland Gazette*, Aug. 29, 1786.

10. *Maryland Journal*, Nov. 21, 1786.

11. *Maryland Gazette*, Sept. 18, 1787.

12. *Ibid.*; *Maryland Journal*, Sept. 14, 21, 25, 1787.

13. *Maryland Journal*, Sept. 28, 1787.

14. *Ibid.*, Oct. 5, 1787.

15. *Ibid.*, Apr. 11, 1788; *Maryland Gazette*, Apr. 18, 1788.

16. *Maryland Journal*, Apr. 11, 1788.

17. *Maryland Gazette*, Apr. 15, 22, 1788.

18. *Maryland Journal*, May 2, 6, 1788.

19. *Ibid.*, May 6, 1788.

20. *Maryland Journal*, Sept. 5, 1788.

21. *Maryland Gazette*, July 29, Sept. 17, 1788; *Maryland Journal*, Oct. 4, 1788.

22. *Maryland Gazette*, Aug. 22, 1788.

23. *Ibid.*, Sept. 5, 1788; *Maryland Journal*, Sept. 5, 1788.

24. *Maryland Journal*, Sept. 5, 9, 1788.

25. *Ibid.*, Oct. 4, 1788; *Maryland Gazette*, Sept. 30, Oct. 3, 1788.

26. *Maryland Gazette*, Oct. 10, 24, Nov. 11, 28, 1788; *Maryland Journal*, Nov. 11, 1788.

27. *Dictionary of American Biography*, s.v. "Chase, Samuel."

28. *Maryland Journal*, Feb. 13, 20, 27, Mar. 27, 1789.

29. American State Papers, Finance, Class III, 1:5–8.

5

ORGANIZING THE TRADES

For Baltimore's mechanics the 1780s had been a decade of mobilization. In forming the Association of Tradesmen and Manufacturers, participating in the assembly and convention elections, and staging the federalist parades, the mechanics acquired the experience and confidence that enabled them to launch the first tradesmen's associations. In 1791 the Carpenters' Society of Baltimore appeared. Within five years it was joined by the Association of Master Hatters, United Journeymen Cordwainers, Journeymen Tailors' Society, and United Master Tailors. Although these associations differed in composition and function, most of them established benefit funds for their members. The idea proved so popular that in 1793 skilled workingmen organized the Baltimore Mechanical Society, the central institution reflecting the development of a mechanic community in the 1790s. The society provided benefit payments for all mechanics who joined, irrespective of trade or their status as journeymen and masters.

But the Mechanical Society could hardly control the forces shaping several trades and impoverishing large numbers of journeymen. In 1794 the town witnessed an unprecedented wave of labor strife as journeymen hatters, shoemakers, and tailors demanded better pay and called the first clearly documented strikes in Baltimore's history. Though confined to only a few trades, journeymen militancy nonetheless endangered the unity workingmen had so recently achieved in the Mechanical Society.

The earliest known association of tradesmen in Baltimore was the Carpenters' Society. It was founded no later than 1791, the year a pamphlet came off the local press containing the society's constitution and membership list. With over 200 members the society was probably larger than the tradesmen's organizations that followed. By the end of the decade the journeymen shoemakers and tailors had no more than a hundred members each, and the master hatters considerably fewer. The carpenters were the pioneers of Baltimore's labor movement, building into their society elements that would reappear in subsequent tradesmen's associations. Their society became the model upon which later ones were patterned.[1]

The Carpenters' Society had four functions. The first was to establish and enforce a "price list" for carpentry work that all members pledged to uphold. From its own ranks the society selected several experienced and trusted men as "measurers," whose duty was to assess a job according to the set prices. Theoretically, the procedure benefited all parties. It safeguarded the members against the unscrupulous contractor who undercut what the society deemed fair prices and against the "scab" workingmen willing to accept substandard payment. It also offered the public protection against the master builder who charged extortionate prices. The price list embodied a preindustrial social ideal, maintaining a framework within which both workingmen and customers could expect fair treatment. The prices themselves may have been set in accordance with standards that now seem hopelessly subjective—"justice," "fairness," "decency"—but no one appeared to protest on this count. Although in concrete instances what constituted a just, fair, and decent price could touch off an argument, few voices questioned the concepts as such. The efficacy and legitimacy of a "moral economy" were widely accepted, despite the free market principles of a later era, which remained half-formulated and vaguely disreputable.[2]

The Carpenters' Society also created a formal mechanism for mediating clashes among its own members. It provided that an acting committee of twelve "hearken to the Complaints, redress the Grievances, and decide as equitably and speedily as possible, upon all Matters in dispute between Members of this Society, consistently with the Tenor of this Constitution." The committeemen exercised their authority and made their judgments within guidelines set down in the constitution. No master could employ a slave as either apprentice or journeyman, a measure designed to insulate the free skilled employee—both black and white—from

competition with bonded labor. Nor could a master hire a journeyman who did not belong to the society (unless the job lasted
less than two weeks) without obtaining the permission of the officers. Finally, a master could not fire an employee without "a satisfactory Settlement" and six days' notice. In turn, the journeymen agreed to the following: not to leave the worksite without
their employers' permission, not to work for a master who had refused to join the society, and not to quit their jobs without giving
the customary six days' notice or "adducing to the Committee
such Reasons as they may deem sufficient."[3]

The third of the society's functions was as a mutual benefit
association. Its insurance fund, which could not have exceeded a
few thousand dollars, came from two sources: an initiation fee of
three guineas per master carpenter and $3 per journeyman, and
quarterly dues of 50¢ for each member. If a member lost his job
through "Accident, Misfortune, or Sickness," the officers could
draw upon the fund to tide him over the slack times. How much
an individual received, whether payments were adjusted to family needs, how long they continued—these matters were not addressed in the constitution. Undoubtedly, the society wished to
preserve discretion in individual cases. The widows and orphans
of deceased members could also apply for help, which must have
allayed a fear of all mechanics—dying without providing an adequate estate for their families. The third category of recipients
were "those who cannot procure Employment among the Members of the Society, and wish to seek Employment elsewhere." In
such cases the society offered to pay travel expenses. It would be
difficult to overstate the significance of what the Carpenters' Society was attempting to achieve through its benefit fund. Every
mechanic, master and journeyman, faced economic disaster as a
daily reality. But where could they turn for financial assistance?
The churches each maintained charitable endeavors but mainly
for widows and orphans, the aged and infirm, not healthy men
thrown out of work through no fault of their own. What could
a mechanic, imbued with the value of "independence," have
thought about the church dole or the final alternative of the
almshouse?[4]

The society moved to assume one last function, education. In
March, 1796, a brief notice appeared in the newspapers express-

ing the carpenters' desire "to erect a Hall and Library." Whether the building was started or completed is unknown. The carpenters were not only skilled workingmen. They were building contractors, employers, and incipient architects. Training in accounting, mathematics, geometry, as well as the humanistic sciences became a vital concern of the society. One of its professed goals in the constitution was to keep abreast of the latest building techniques in America and Europe and to disseminate this information to the membership. We can only speculate about the carpenters' hall and library, what sorts of books it would contain, whether apprentices would take their study seats alongside journeymen and masters. But the workingmen's willingness to dip into the dollar or two they earned each day to build a library reflected the Carpenters' Society's broad outlook, the importance it attached to self-improvement, its ability to look beyond the bread and butter issues.[5]

Ideally, the carpenters belonged to a brotherhood. Any grievance, misunderstanding, or controversy that arose within their society was settled there. No one took his troubles outside, appealing to an authority above his fellow workingmen. In practice, too, this seems to have been pretty much the case. In only one recorded instance did a carpenter commit the unpardonable breach of solidarity by airing his complaints before the public in the newspapers. The case reveals the weapons that the Carpenters' Society could level against an errant member.

In March, 1795, Frederick Haifligh, master carpenter, publicly accused the society's measurers of violating the price list by overcharging. At the invitation of someone who had contracted with the society for the construction of a building, Haifligh inspected the assessments given by the measurers and found them to be excessively high. One of the measurers was the society's president, who, when confronted with the charge, called Haifligh a "sneaking fellow." Haifligh responded that by overcharging, the measurers had gouged the public and dealt an injustice to carpenters who, like himself, adhered to the rules instituted by the society.

A few days later Henry F. Hagaman, the society's secretary, issued a rebuttal on behalf of the measurers. His argument was illuminating, for he seemed less worried about salvaging the society's reputation in the eyes of the public than with defending its officers before the rank and file. Ignoring the substance of Haifligh's allegations, the secretary depicted the accuser as an oppressive employer who had a long history of cheating his employees. He cited an episode four years earlier in which Haifligh had contracted to construct a gallery in a public tavern, hiring a number of journeymen at 7s. 6d. a day each. Hagaman charged that when the job was completed and Haifligh had collected his payment, the journeymen were informed that their pay would be only 6s. 3d. The secretary asked the public and, more pointedly, the society's members if such a man could be trusted. Haifligh retorted that he had, admittedly, fallen short of cash on pay day but only because his customers insisted on deducting a sum for wood planks that had not been used. By the next day, he explained, he had sold the planks and settled accounts with each of his workers.[6]

Haifligh had challenged the society's officers for the loyalties of the membership. The contest now shifted to the quarterly meeting scheduled for April. Haifligh said he was anxious to put his case before his brother carpenters, for he felt confident that his true motives would become evident. "As a member of the Carpenters' Society," he wrote, "I look upon myself not only bound to support the constitution which we have adopted, but to oppose every deviation from the regulations we have mutually agreed to: It is therefore with extreme regret I have of late observed so little regard paid to the prices we have established." The meeting apparently saw things differently; it refused to condone Haifligh's disloyalty. Perhaps he had had a legitimate grievance. But by airing it before the public Haifligh had threatened the unity without which the constitution was meaningless. By May Haifligh was back in the newspapers, adding evidence to substantiate his charges, escalating the battle to new levels of bitterness. Once, he claimed, the measurers had overcharged for a building by some £200 or £300; he had the documents to prove it and offered them for the public's inspection. Frequently, Haifligh maintained, the measurers demanded 20 to 25 percent above what the price list warranted.[7]

Having failed to rally support among the members while maligning the integrity of the officers, Haifligh read himself out of the society. In his last public statement he announced he was quitting the society. The leadership, he explained, had whipped up resentment and hostility toward him that raised the prospect of violence. "But these goaded brethren," Haifligh said, "have threatened that on the 4th of July, they will tar and feather me; and I am told that one of the offended junto has offered 50 dollars, to have carried into effect their manly and decent design." Independence Day would have been an appropriate occasion; since 1793 the Carpenters' Society had held its annual meeting on the Saturday following it. In disrepute among the Carpenters' Society, Haifligh joined several other carpenters who had apparently been won to his side and in October, 1795, organized the "Carpenters' Association." Haifligh was named as a manager and, a few months later, as a measurer. With a "book of prices, as a standard of Carpenters' work," he was now in a position to implement what the association claimed to be its objective—"a reformation in their business." How long the Carpenters' Association survived is unknown; there is no trace of it in the newspapers after January, 1796.[8]

A year after the Carpenters' Society published its constitution, a second tradesmen's society appeared. On September 22, 1792, thirteen masters organized the Association of Master Hatters to guarantee a steady supply of properly trained workmen. Because hat making was traditionally among the poorest paid crafts requiring the least skill, it inevitably attracted young workers who had picked up the trade on their own without undergoing a formal apprenticeship. The association proposed to eliminate them. It announced that the masters would require proof that their journeymen had served regular apprenticeships and advised youths entering the trade to register their indentures at the Baltimore County Orphans Court. The association refused to hire any journeyman or apprentice whose training had been under a master who himself had failed to serve a proper apprenticeship. Finally, it demanded that each worker present proof of his having complied with the terms of his previous contract, which was tantamount to a letter of recommendation from his former employer. "The substance of the Resolves," the hatters proclaimed, was to encourage "the regularly qualified Tradesmen, whether Master or Journeymen" and "contribute to the interest of the employer and employed." The hatters hoped their "brother artists, elsewhere" would follow their example and adopt similar measures.[9]

The Association of Master Hatters was a truncated version of the Carpenters' Society. It was explicitly an employers' organization, excluding journeymen and apprentices. It did not profess an interest in education beyond maintaining a strong apprenticeship system; it did not provide benefit payments for either members or their employees; nor did it establish a procedure for resolving disputes that might arise in the workshops. There are grounds, indeed, for questioning the association's true motives. What can be made of its professed commitment to a highly skilled work force when two years later the journeymen hatters accused the masters of degrading their craft by substituting green apprentices for trained workingmen? The association's resolutions, especially the last, could be read as a step against uncooperative workingmen: a blacklist. It is probable, then, that the master hatters were more interested in securing a tractable work force than a skilled one.[10]

Around 1792 a third trade society appeared, the journeymen's counterpart to the Association of Master Hatters. Our knowledge of the United Journeymen Cordwainers is based on a series of newspaper articles printed in the spring and summer of 1794, when one observer remarked that the society "appeared two years ago." The United Journeymen Cordwainers occupies a place beside the earliest journeymen societies in American history. Indeed, it antedates by several years the Federal Society of Journeymen Cordwainers of Philadelphia, which is customarily cited as the first journeymen association. As early as 1773 the shoemakers appear to have clashed with their employers over wages, the first recorded instance of journeymen strife in Baltimore. Behind the singular volatility of the trade stood two related facts: shoemakers were poorer than nearly all other skilled workingmen, and they faced intense competition from apprentice labor.[11]

Although the United Journeymen Cordwainers have left no records before 1794, they must have adopted a constitution, agreed to bylaws, and elected officers. The society resembled the Carpenters' Society in its determination to spread useful information pertaining to the trade and its establishment of a benefit fund. Of course, the shoemakers could never aspire to a library of their own as the carpenters could, for their benefit fund was only a few hundred dollars at most. In 1794 only forty or fifty journeymen were reportedly attending the society's meetings, though the full membership was undoubtedly larger. Quarterly dues must have been small, smaller even than the 25¢ collected by another shoemakers' association founded fourteen years later. Nevertheless, the benefit fund seems to have been the society's main concern. In 1794 the United Journeymen Cordwainers declared that its original goal had been to raise "a fund for the relief of those of our business who are deemed good members of society (for none else were admitted to our body), and who, by some inadvertency, might be disabled from reaping the benefits of their labour."[12]

This flurry of activity—three tradesmen's societies in two years where none had existed before—culminated in 1793 with the formation of the Baltimore Mechanical Society. On December 14, 1792, the newspapers printed a call for a meeting of "MECHANICS and MANUFACTURERS" issued by *their Committee* that had been formed at an earlier date. The gathering took place at Nathan Griffith's tavern, easily recognizable at the sign of "The Rights of Man." On January 8, 1793, the mechanics again assembled at Griffith's "for the Purpose of RATIFYING their CONSTITUTION, and ELECTING MANAGERS." Agreeing on a constitution apparently took more time than expected; in late January and early February the mechanics were still trying to hammer one out. But on Monday morning, February 4, the debate had finished and the association was ready to elect officers. The polls opened at the Lovely Lane Methodist meeting house and the voting continued for four days until Thursday evening. With the election of a president, vice-president, treasurer, secretary, and twelve-man board of managers, the Baltimore Mechanical Society was complete.[13]

The Mechanical Society was a synthesis of the trade associations preceding it, blending their political and economic functions in a new and exciting way. It was the logical successor to the Association of Tradesmen and Manufacturers because both served as vehicles expressing the political sentiments of the entire mechanic community. But the Mechanical Society did not merely take up and carry forward the association's work; it aspired to something greater than its predecessor had. The association had confined its interest largely to securing a protective tariff and disappeared once that objective had been achieved. The Mechanical Society viewed its political role more broadly. While continuing the fight for economic protectionism—which in the 1790s meant tough measures defending America's neutral trade—the society saw this as part of a larger struggle to define republican government and protect it from foreign and domestic enemies.

In addition, the Mechanical Society provided an economic service that the earlier association had never considered, one perhaps suggested by the Carpenters' Society and United Journeymen Cordwainers. The formation of those two tradesmen's societies had reflected a growing concern about the poverty into which mechanics, journeymen above all, seemed to be falling. But their benefit funds addressed the problem in only two trades. The Mechanical Society proposed to establish an insurance system for all skilled workingmen, regardless of their trades, be they masters or journeymen. Like the associations of carpenters and shoemakers, it collected quarterly dues that went to the support of needy members, their widows and orphans. As late as November, 1795, the society's secretary reported that only one member had been expelled for failing to pay his dues and none for "misdemeanors." Nonetheless, the secretary urged all those who had fallen into arrears to settle their debts so that "the benevolent spirit of the society, and their funds, will be adequate to the exigencies of the approaching winter." As a reminder, the society appointed a collector to visit each member whose dues were delinquent. The winters seem to have posed the greatest challenge to the Mechanical Society, for then survival might hinge on financial assistance. In January of 1797 and 1798 the society's board of managers appointed three officers, "to give temporary relief, during the recess of the board, to members, or to widows or orphans of deceased members, whose pressing circumstances may require it." The board urged any member who knew of destitute individuals to inform the special appointees, suggesting the reluctance with which many members accepted what they considered charity.[14]

The Mechanical Society avoided one area at the heart of the concerns of the Carpenters' Society, Association of Master Hatters, and United Journeymen Cordwainers—the internal regulation of the trades. Prices, wages, working conditions, apprenticeship, the relationship between masters and journeymen—these were matters the Mechanical Society did not confront, at least not openly in its public pronouncements. The one exception came in July, 1793, when Baltimore received an influx of "*Aliens*, of the *French Nation*, whose Distresses have compelled them to seek an Asylum and Residence in this Town." The board of managers, unmasking its pro-French sympathies that would remain unshaken until 1797 or 1798, resolved to recommend "to the MECHANICS in general, but *especially* to the MEMBERS of this SOCIETY," not to raise their prices. "They will thereby shew themselves," the managers declared, "to be the Friends of Mankind, and manifest a Disposition to make their Country a desirable Residence to the Virtuous and Industrious, as well as to the Distressed, of every Nation." The circumstances in which the board exhibited such magnanimity were unique, however, because it could ask all mechanics to sacrifice equally without requiring any one segment of them to carry an extra burden. Later, when bitter disputes arose within the mechanic community between masters and journeymen—and, presumably, within the Mechanical Society's membership as well—the board said nothing.[15]

The Mechanical Society differed from the Association of Tradesmen and Manufacturers in composition. Even their titles reflected a shift of emphasis. The term "tradesmen and manufacturers" had been broad and inclusive. It encompassed the ordinary craftsman working in his shop and the substantial manufacturer who owned a slitting mill, textile factory, bleaching operation, flour mill, iron work, comb manufactory—any of the large-scale industrial establishments of the eighteenth century. The term "mechanic" meant something different. A mechanic had undergone an apprenticeship, earned his living at the workbench, and hoped someday to master his trade, buy a shop, and establish an "independency."

In leadership master craftsmen assumed almost exclusive control over the Mechanical Society. This tendency had been in the making for a generation. In the Mechanical Company of the

Revolutionary era merchants had ordinarily held the leading offices until 1773. In the Association of Tradesmen and Manufacturers mechanics obtained most of the top positions but merchants continued to play an important role. In the Mechanical
Society master craftsmen practically monopolized the leadership.
From 1793 until the society's dissolution eight years later forty
men are known to have held office. With the exception of three
merchants, all of the officers were mechanics or manufacturers. It
was probably a matter of prudence to include a merchant on the
governing board, for it parried the allegation that mechanics were
pursuing their own selfish interests at the expense of their fellow
citizens. But the membership never gave a top post to the merchants, who served exclusively as secretaries, treasurers, and
managers. One of the merchant officers was a proven friend of the
mechanics, having served on the committee of the association.
Another was later elected to the board of directors of the Baltimore Mechanics' Bank.[16]

The society's officers represented the elite of the mechanic
community. Thirty-five of the mechanic officers appear on a tax
list of 1804. With a mean assessment of £786, they were three to
four times richer than the ordinary mechanic; many mechanics,
including most journeymen, had no property at all. The mechanic
officers were even a shade wealthier than the average wholesale
merchant, whose assessment was £770. The officers fell into two
groups. One was composed of manufacturers and substantial mechanics who practiced trades requiring heavy investment in tools,
buildings, and labor. This group included four construction workers who were probably building contractors, two metal workers
who owned large-scale manufactories, two shipwrights who operated yards at the Point, and a brickmaker who ran a kiln on the
outskirts of town. These nine men were each assessed at over
£1,000, putting them in the top 5 percent of the city's property
holders. The second group included a larger number of small-
scale craftsmen, like the tailors, shoemakers, and hatters who
formed nearly a quarter of the officers. Of these twenty-six
men, only tailor John McCannon owned property assessed at over
£1,000. Although nothing definite can be said about the social and
cultural background of the society's officers, they seem to have

included a conspicuous number of non-Anglicans. The earliest meetings of the society took place at a Methodist meeting house, while the first president, Adam Fonerden, was a Methodist minister. In addition to Fonerden, the non-Episcopal officers included Baptist John McClellan, Presbyterian David Stodder, and German Reformed Christopher Raborg.[17]

The Mechanical Society was the clearest expression of the collective identity Baltimore's craftsmen had been developing since the Revolution. Many of its officers had been active in mechanic organizations for three decades. For several years hatter David Shields served as president of the Mechanical Society. He had numbered among the founders of the Mechanical Company in 1763 and was the treasurer of the Mechanical Fire Company. Spinning wheel maker David Poe was also a Mechanical Society president in the 1790s. Thirty years earlier he had joined the Mechanical Company, served as an officer in the Revolutionary Mechanical Volunteers, and belonged to the Whig Club. Those mechanics who had led the Association of Tradesmen and Manufacturers stood out in the Mechanical Society: card maker Adam Fonerden and shipbuilder David Stodder, both of whom belonged to the association's standing committee, were elected as society officers. The Mechanical Society was the achievement of master mechanics who had been striving for a generation to make their fellow craftsmen a self-conscious community.[18]

Just a year after the society's formation Baltimore witnessed an outburst of journeymen militancy. Except for a possible strike among the journeymen shoemakers in 1773, Baltimore's history had been free from major labor confrontations, organized protests, and turn-outs. The labor strife of 1794 involving shoemakers, hatters, and tailors was unprecedented. In only one other period before the Jacksonian era, 1805 to 1812, did the workshops become the scene of such angry confrontations.

The problem seems to have started in the hatting trade. Gearing up in March for the busy season that commenced each spring, the journeymen hatters apparently demanded "raising the Wages." There is no evidence that they had organized a society similar to the United Journeymen Cordwainers. According to a letter in the newspapers from "A Friend to the Trade" dated

March 8, the employers resisted the workmen's demands by im-
posing a set of "fixed Prices." "A Friend" assured the masters that
the journeymen would refuse to work under the "fixed Prices."
Nor would they consider "letting any Stranger here Work under
them." The masters, he claimed, had been corrupting the skills
of the trade and foisting shoddy merchandise on their customers
through the practice of replacing journeymen with apprentices.
The largest employers were even scheming to prevent newcomers from acquiring apprentices themselves "so they may engross
the whole Trade in their own Hands." "A Friend" singled out four
employers as leaders, three of whom had belonged to the Association of Master Hatters a few years earlier. How the dispute ended
is unknown, but it does not appear that the journeymen carried
out their implied threat to strike.[19]

The journeymen shoemakers were also at odds with their
employers. Although since its formation the United Journeymen
Cordwainers had averted a confrontation with the masters, by the
spring of 1794 it was considering a strike. The immediate source
of discontent was "the very enhanced prices in every article of
consumption"; their wages could not keep pace with inflation. No
less disturbing was the employers' exploitation of the apprenticeship system. The society claimed that it "is quite customary for
Master Shoemakers to have 8 or 10 apprentices, whom they keep
bungling at, and spoiling so truly valuable a commodity, without
even any person for instructing them; and thus they impose wear-
ables on the public which are not an *tacit*, but a out-crying stigma
on the profession." The society informed the masters that they
would no longer train these unwieldy crews of apprentices; from
now on its members would instruct only two youths per employer. The journeymen raised the possibility that their trade follow the example of certain European associations, where new
workers were apprenticed to journeymen rather than to masters.
Nothing came of this suggestion, as it would have overturned the
apprenticeship system in Baltimore by enabling journeymen to
regulate the recruitment of new workmen into the trade. That the
United Journeymen Cordwainers entertained the idea reflected
the extent to which the apprenticeship system, in its eyes, had
been abused. It also demonstrated the society's knowledge of and

interest in labor trends abroad, not so surprising considering that many of its members must have received their training in England and Europe.[20]

Wages were the key question. In the early 1790s a journeyman shoemaker earned 4s. 2d. per pair of shoes. According to the United Journeymen Cordwainers, each pair involved "a close day's work" and, "in the Winter season, cannot be accomplished by many, until 10 or 11 o'clock." The shoemakers were at the bottom of the mechanics' wage scale. For instance, in 1791 Frederick Haifligh was paying his carpenters 7s. 6d. a day. By April or May there was talk of a turn-out. In the words of one observer speaking for the masters, the employers became "apprehensive of a total suspension of their business, and dreading so formidable a combination, were obliged to indulge their request." The journeymen had won their first battle with the masters. However, they offered a different account of what had happened. The society admitted to the public that it had debated the possibility of a strike, but before a decision could be reached a few masters raised their wages, breaking ranks with their fellow employers who had agreed to maintain the existing prices. The unity of the masters quickly collapsed as each one scrambled for workers; some employers increased wages to 4s. 5d. a pair while one went as high as 5s. Pleased with their own solidarity in contrast to the masters' failure to maintain discipline, the journeymen gloated over the "malicious *jealousy* existing among the Master Shoemakers" that had "saved us the trouble of *turning out.*"[21]

Stung by the journeymen's success, the master shoemakers braced themselves against further demands. In June, only a month or two after the first pay raise, the society threatened another strike for 6s. a pair. The decision prompted a debate among the members, for some journeymen believed it better to wait until the fall season "when the business would be doubly brisk" and their bargaining power twice as great. On June 14 the masters met to discuss the demands of their workers. They rejected them. Thus began the first clearly documented strike in Baltimore's history. Despite its lack of experience, the United Journeymen Cordwainers formulated an effective strike strategy. Those journeymen "whose circumstances did not admit of the suspension of their labour" left Baltimore to find work wherever they could. A second group remained in town and patroled the workshops, guarding against scab shoemakers recruited from outside Baltimore. One critical observer charged the society with terrorizing mechanics who wished to continue working, "threatening them with every kind of persecution." The society also kept an eye on the local shoemakers who had not joined. The number of non-society men was not negligible: forty or fifty shoemakers attended the meeting that declared the strike, but a year later the city directory listed over a hundred shoemakers residing in Baltimore.[22]

A third group of journeymen organized a cooperative undertaking, the first in what would become a long line of such collective enterprises. On June 28 the United Journeymen Cordwainers announced the opening of a "BOOT and SHOE MANUFACTORY" on Market Street, the main commercial artery of town. The manufactory was designed as a model workshop where journeymen could "expect to find speedy employ, and more generous treatment than ever they experienced in their line in Baltimore." The society envisioned its experiment as a large-scale venture and accepted orders from the West Indies as well as locally. It appointed two of its members as "foremen" to oversee the workshop and assured the public that it could expect high-quality shoes, not the "sheepskin boot legs" that "a certain extensive shoemaker" passed onto his unsuspecting customers as deer skin. The workshop also served as a "house of call" where all journeymen seeking employment were told to report. In theory, this establishment gave the United Journeymen Cordwainers control over the work force and allowed it to boycott those shops refusing to meet its demands. Within a few weeks a number of master shoemakers had caved in under the society's pressure. While on June 28 the society had required all journeymen to report to its new manufactory, eight days later it added three more approved shops to the list. Whether the remaining masters ultimately granted the new wage of 6s. a pair is unknown.[23]

In June, 1794, the journeymen tailors also went on strike. Again the issue was wages. Tailors counted their work in "jobs." The masters estimated that a workingman could complete eight to fourteen jobs a week, while the journeyman claimed he could do no more than seven. The journeymen demanded 7s. 6d. a job, which would have placed them two or three shillings ahead of the shoemakers. It is unclear whether the tailors had organized a trade society complete with a constitution, benefit fund, and officers. They did establish a "house of call"; in the midst of the strike when master tailor Jacob Brown advertised for two journeymen, he added that none "need apply that belong to the house of call, in Baltimore."[24]

On June 10 the master tailors assembled to devise a strategy for dealing with the strike. What emerged from this meeting and another six days later was the United Master Tailors, an experiment in benevolent coercion. The employers professed two objectives. The first was to "regulate their business," which presumably meant setting prices and sharing information on tailoring techniques—what the Carpenters' Society and United Journeymen Cordwainers had declared as their aim. In addition, the United Master Tailors proposed "to raise a fund for the benefit of their members," similar to that of the Carpenters' Society. The fund was designed for masters and journeymen, as well as their widows and orphans who otherwise might "become sufferers without a hand to give help to them in their necessitous situation." The coercive element was implied in the organization itself. The master tailors refused to hire any journeyman not belonging to their society. In other words, to qualify for benefits a journeyman had to accept the prices and wages instituted by the society. It was improbable that journeymen would exert much influence in determining wages; they weren't even invited to the June 16 meeting where the masters wrote a constitution and presumably elected officers. The United Master Tailors disappeared after the strike. It could not prevent the journeymen from winning their raise.[25]

The journeyman activity subsided after 1794 but many of the underlying tensions continued to simmer. In January, 1796, the journeymen tailors reiterated their determination to establish a "house of call." The eighteen months that had elapsed since the strike had not softened the masters' opposition to an enterprise depriving them of control over the recruitment of new workers. Nor had it lessened the journeymen's resolve. The tailors declared that starting in March all journeymen should report to their house of call at the tavern of J. B. Mercer in Light Lane. The announcement came over the signature of the journeymen's secretary, Nesbit Slack, indicating that a society of some type was in operation.[26]

In June, 1799, the tailors struck for a second time. The Journeymen Tailors' Society, which led the turn-out, had probably been active since 1796 and perhaps earlier. In its statement to the public the society attacked the "mean spirited wretches who have never joined our associations, commonly the worst workmen." That the society referred to associations in the plural indicates that the tailors had organized several times over the past five years. The journeymen demanded a wage increase from the 7s. 6d. a job they had been earning since 1794. Based on the enthusiastic response to their strike call, they had good reason to hope for success. Over a hundred journeymen walked out of the shops, leaving only twenty on the job. The Journeymen Tailors' Society opened a cooperative workshop on South Street where it proposed selling a suit of clothes for £2, which amounted to 5s. beneath the prevailing price at the masters' shops. Despite the display of unity, the journeymen lost. The strike ended with wages at the old level. Judging from the society's protests, the masters broke the strike by resorting to female labor:

> every Woman whom they are informed can make her own children's clothes, they sedulously hunt up; ney the very slop makers are put in a state of requisition, and they who heretofore, could hardly put together check'd shirts, and duck trowsers are now employed in making vests, breeches, pantaloons, coatees, and summer coats. These are truths which, the work done while we are idle will evidently establish.

The journeymen complained that while women got the easy jobs of sewing vests, pantaloons, and breeches, they received the most onerous and time-consuming task of making suit coats.[27]

The journeymen's militancy from 1794 to 1798 threatened master craftsmen who had been instrumental in founding the Mechanical Society. Of the thirteen employers who founded the Association of Master Hatters, three served as Mechanical Society officers: David Shields, Thomas Bodley, and William Branson. Shields and Bodley were identified as the leaders of the attempt to roll back the journeymen's wages in 1794. Prominent master shoemakers like William Farris and James Osburn and master tailors like John McCannon and James Martin, who were likewise involved in the 1794 strikes, became society officers.

In the first decades of the new republic Baltimore's mechanics mobilized to defend what they perceived as their "interests." From 1785 to 1789 the issue upon which nearly all mechanics could agree was protectionism, the *raison d'être* of the Association of Tradesmen and Manufacturers. After the establishment of a new federal government and the implementation of a national tariff, the mechanics organized in pursuit of a second interest: benefits. Between 1791 and 1794 the Carpenters' Society, United Journeymen Cordwainers, United Master Tailors, and probably Journeymen Tailors' Society all attempted to establish benefit funds for their unemployed or disabled members, their wives and families. In addition, these tradesmen's associations together with the Association of Master Hatters regulated the internal workings of their crafts, setting prices and keeping their members abreast of technological advances in America and abroad. The culmination of this benefit movement came in 1793 with the establishment of the Baltimore Mechanical Society, which provided insurance for all dues-paying members, whatever their trades. The last interest around which mechanics organized also proved to be the most disruptive. In demanding higher wages, the hatters, shoemakers, and tailors raised an issue that threatened the foundations of mechanic unity by pitting journeymen against masters. The 1794 and 1799 strikes were probably the first in Baltimore's history. They were not the last.

NOTES

1. *Constitution of the Carpenters' Society of Baltimore* (Baltimore, 1791).
2. *Ibid.*
3. *Ibid.*, pp. 5, 9.
4. *Ibid.*, pp. 6, 7, 9.
5. *Maryland Journal* (Baltimore), Mar. 22, 1796.
6. *Federal Intelligencer* (Baltimore), Mar. 18, 20, Apr. 1, 1795.

7. *Ibid.*, Apr. 4, May 19, June 1, 1795.

8. *Ibid.*, June 1, Oct. 28, 1795; *Federal Gazette* (Baltimore), Jan. 14, 1796; *Baltimore Daily Repository*, July 1, 1793.

9. *Maryland Journal*, Oct. 2, 1792.

10. *Ibid.*, Mar. 10, 1794.

11. *Edward's Baltimore Daily Advertiser*, July 3, 1794; *Maryland Journal*, July 9, 1794; Selig Perlman, *A History of Trade Unionism in the United States* (New York, 1921), p.4.

12. *Edward's Baltimore Daily Advertiser*, July 3, 1794.

13. *Maryland Journal*, Dec. 14, 1792, Jan. 8, Feb. 1, 12, 1793.

14. *Federal Intelligencer*, Nov. 26, 1795; *Federal Gazette*, Jan. 14, 1797, Jan. 19, 1798.

15. *Maryland Journal*, July 26, 1793.

16. For officers, see *Maryland Journal*, Feb. 12, Dec. 13, 1793; *Federal Intelligencer*, Dec. 3, 1795; *Federal Gazette*, Dec. 9, 1796, Dec. 6, 1797, Dec. 5, 1798; *Baltimore Telgraphe*, Dec. 4, 1799; *American* (Baltimore), Dec. 5, 1800. For merchants, see *Maryland Journal*, Mar. 27, 1789; *American*, June 9, 1809.

17. Alphabetical Lists of Assessed Persons, 1804, Baltimore County Commissioners, MHR

18. George W. McCreary, *The Ancient and Honorable Mechanical Company, of Baltimore* (Baltimore, 1901), pp. 13–19, 26–28; *Maryland Gazette* (Baltimore), Nov. 18, 1785.

19. *Maryland Journal*, Mar. 10, 1794.

20. *Edward's Baltimore Daily Advertiser*, July 3, 1794.

21. *Ibid.*; *Maryland Journal*, July 9, 1794.

22. *Ibid.*; *Baltimore Daily Intelligencer*, June 14, 1794; *Baltimore Town and Fell's Point Directory* (Baltimore, n.d. [1796]).

23. *Baltimore Daily Intelligencer*, June 29, 1794; *Maryland Journal*, July 9, 1794.

24. *Baltimore Daily Intelligencer*, June 10, 20, 1794.

25. *Ibid.*, June 10, 14, 16, 1794.

26. *Federal Gazette*, Jan. 31, 1796.

27. *American*, June 5, 8, 1799, Nov. 16, 1808.

6

MECHANIC REPUBLICANISM AND
THE CITY CHARTER

From 1776 to 1790 Baltimore's population doubled to 13,500, making it the largest town in Maryland. Yet it still lacked a charter of incorporation. By the early 1780s the townspeople were demanding a city charter establishing a regular municipal government that could police and tax the citizenry. For more than a decade the question of incorporation agitated local politics and fueled a debate over the nature of republican government. By the time the issue reached a climax in the mid-1790s Baltimore's mechanics had fashioned the institutional framework within which to articulate their own radical vision of republicanism, a distinctly mechanic republicanism.

Since 1782, proposals had been made to adopt a conservative frame of government with a strong executive branch, bicameral city council, electoral system for the upper chamber, high property qualifications for office holding, and long terms in office. When the conservative measures were aired again in 1793 and 1794, the Baltimore Mechanical Society organized against them and offered its own charter proposal. Heading a coalition that included the Carpenters' Society, Republican Society, and committees of the precincts and Fell's Point, the Mechanical Society offered a plan that would provide for a weak executive, unicameral council, direct elections, low property qualifications or none at all, and rotation in office. Despite the success of the Mechanical Society and its allies in rallying the townspeople to its charter proposal, the state assembly saddled the citizens with the conservative government they had so vehemently opposed. The Mechanical Society had been defeated, but not before demonstrating the vitality of a mechanic republicanism.

The movement for a city charter grew out of the Revolution. Since the struggle for independence Baltimoreans had been steadily weakening the political constraints imposed on them by the planter gentry of Annapolis. By the 1780s they had succeeded in pushing the frontiers of political autonomy further than anyone a generation earlier could have foreseen. Perhaps the quest for home rule stirred first in the Revolutionary committees of inspection and observation in which Baltimore asserted its claim to equality with Annapolis. Facing the specters of a British invasion and servile insurrection among disaffected blacks and whites, Maryland's gentry had no choice but to accommodate the political newcomer. In 1776, over considerable objections and misgivings, the state constitutional convention awarded Baltimore two seats in the House of Delegates, the same number as Annapolis. Four years later the legislators made Baltimore an official port of entry. With a pair of representatives in the assembly and its own customs house, Baltimore could look ahead to growth and development unfettered by the old antagonists in Annapolis.[1]

Notable as these advances were, Baltimore continued to labor under the same make-shift government that the assembly had established in 1729. This was a government designed with a backwater settlement in mind, not the thriving seaport Baltimore had become. The assembly retained the power to appoint the town commissioners in charge of day-to-day administration while they, in turn, continued to handpick their successors. The assembly called upon special commissioners to undertake the extraordinary tasks that fell outside the competence of the regular town commissioners. Thus, despite the political gains of two generations, Baltimore remained in a sense stymied—it still had no elective local office. Earlier this informal arrangement may have sufficed; but now, with Baltimore emerging as one of America's boom towns, it broke down. The streets needed more effective policing. Pigs and dogs rooted and roamed their way through town. Trash piled up in the main streets and backways and congested the basin. Fires posed an ever-present nightmare with ramshackle construction going up unsupervised. Epidemics loomed because nobody had responsibility over public health. The public markets wanted better regulation to generate a revenue and protect the public against extortionate sellers. The shallow basin required dredging as well as measures to prevent silting. These were the problems plaguing any rapidly growing seaport of the period. Baltimoreans struggled with them all but lacked, as many believed, the means of success.[2]

If Baltimore had a regular government, representative officials, adequate income—if it had a city charter providing these things—perhaps orderly growth could be achieved. In 1782 enough people had reached this conclusion that on April 2 a meeting was held that agreed to present an incorporation petition to the next session of the Maryland assembly. There was no disputing the desirability of a charter. The meeting "unanimously" chose a committee to draw up a draft proposal. But before going to the assembly, the petition had to be circulated among the townspeople for their scrutiny and approval. When the document reached the hands of the citizens, it raised such an outcry that all hopes for petitioning the assembly collapsed. Without a surviving copy of the draft, it is impossible to uncover the roots of the protest. Two years later a newspaper correspondent recalling the incident said only that "the town some how or other were never favoured with the draught." One piece of illuminating testimony survives: John Thomas Scharf, the nineteenth-century historian of Baltimore who could peruse documents no longer available, stated that the "laboring classes" killed the charter proposal. By itself the statement could be interpreted in various ways. But when placed within the context of the incorporation movement's subsequent evolution, it conformed to a pattern. At its inception the incorporation drive precipitated a battle along two fronts, neither of which shifted markedly during the next decade—one over political principles, the other between social classes.[3]

The outlines of the conflict surfaced a year and a half later when Baltimore revived the matter of incorporation. In October, 1784, to widespread consternation, a group of citizens took it upon themselves to petition the assembly for a charter. There had been no general meeting, only a blurb in the newspapers that customarily preceded any petition. Disappointed by the earlier setback, these pro-charter men had lost faith with the cumbersome meetings and resolved to circumvent the popular forums.

Indignation mounted. Addressing the townspeople in the news-papers, "Civis" asked why the petition had been concealed; he had been searching for a copy of the document for days without finding one. For the assembly to dictate a charter to the towns-people that they had not read, much less endorsed, "would be a violent infringement of the principles of our excellent constitu-tion, for a *few persons* to steal a corporation upon the town, which is to affect the liberty and property of not less than *eight thousand* of its citizens." "Civis" asserted that a general meeting, unwieldy though it was, should consider the question.[4]

"Civis" was not alone, for on November 15 a meeting of townspeople took place at the Baltimore assembly room. Resolv-ing that a charter "would be BENEFICIAL to this Town," the gath-ering called for a committee to compose the incorporation peti-tion. No one wanted a re-enactment of the previous miscarriage. This time there would be elections to the committee: what better way to ensure unanimity? On November 18 the town's qualified voters elected two committeemen from each of nine districts. These representatives assembled two days later to begin the deli-cate operation of fashioning a charter capable of winning general endorsement. They labored for two weeks. Then on December 2 the committee printed the petition in broadsides and distributed it through the town. It requested a second meeting for December 9 and invited a "full, free and candid discussion of this interesting question."[5]

The discussion was probably more full, free, and candid than the committee had wanted. Like its precursor, the petition died without ever reaching the assembly. "After considerable time spent in the endeavour," "A Baltimorean" wrote in 1791, refer-ring to the committee's efforts, "the scheme was abandoned as impracticable." Noting that "parties had prevailed at that time," he hinted darkly that "as it frequently happens in the concerns of life, the ambition of some, the envy of others, and the sinister views of a few, frustrated a measure which, in all probability, would have redounded to the benefit of the whole." As late as 1808 the incident rankled another townsman, "Aristides," who maintained that the petition had been abandoned amid popular outrage. The townspeople, he said, "took it in their heads that it was an ungenerous and unjust attempt to give a few advantages over many," which so angered them "that for a long time the name of corporation would throw them into a flame." Actually interest in a charter did stir occasionally over the next decade, but "Aristides" had a point: the 1784 proposal had engendered such lasting ill will "that for near a dozen years no one would mention it."[6]

The committee's mistake had been to devise a charter patterned after the conservative Maryland constitution. Maryland had the distinction of adopting the most conservative state constitution of the Revolutionary era, which became the committee's model. The city government would include a bicameral common council—similar to the two-house General Assembly—whose lower chamber, or "First Branch," comprised two representatives from each of nine wards. This First Branch would be a small-scale House of Delegates: in both cases a candidate for office had to own at least £500 in taxable property, and in both cases elections were annual. The upper chamber of the council, or "Second Branch," would function as a miniature state Senate. To shelter the Senate against public opinion and preserve it as a redoubt of conservative strength, the constitutional convention had established an electoral system; two electors from each of Maryland's counties and one each from Annapolis and Baltimore assembled at five-year intervals to pick fifteen senators, nine from the Western Shore and six from the Eastern. The committee wanted to transplant this system in Baltimore. The voters of each ward would choose two electors, who then named one man from each ward to the Second Branch. In two ways, though, the Second Branch was more open than the Senate: the property qualification for office was only £500, half that for the Senate, and the elections occurred every three rather than five years. The voting requirements for the council and assembly elections were the same. One must be a free white male, twenty-one years old, a one-year town resident, and worth £30 on the tax lists. In both elections voting was *viva voce*.[7]

The method for selecting the executive would also follow the example of the state constitution. Maryland's governor was elected by the full assembly. Similarly, the common council would annually select nine aldermen, one from each ward, and together they would choose a mayor. To fulfill the requirement for the mayordom, an individual must possess no less than £2,000, the same as for the governorship. The mayor and aldermen would appoint all local officials from the watchmen to the scavengers. In addition, they would act as justices of the peace and exercise the powers of a county court.[8]

The ill-fated charter proposal was the brainchild of the town's merchants. Of the fourteen men who served on the committee, the occupations of twelve are known. The chairman was merchant Hercules Courtenay, who, according to Baltimore's first city directory published in 1796, became the secretary of the Maryland Insurance Company. Nine of his fellow committeemen were also merchants. Only three fell outside this select circle but not far enough to lose elite status. John Weatherburn had become by 1796 the clerk of the Baltimore branch of the Bank of the United States. William Gibson was the clerk of the Baltimore County Court. Lyde Goodwin was a physician. There were no mechanics on the committee, no ship captains or sailors, no common laborers. If the proposal failed to get an enthusiastic greeting from the "laboring classes," perhaps it is not surprising.[9]

As "Aristides" had said, years passed before anyone resurrected the issue of incorporation. While it slipped from the center of political controversy, the assembly revamped the town's administration. In 1786 it created two new officials: street commissioner and port warden. Every five years the town's voters now elected an elector from each ward, who then chose nine street commissioners and nine port wardens. The property qualification for the first office was £500 and for the second £1,000. The commissioners exercised authority over the surveying, building, and improving of streets and alleys, while the port wardens had jurisdiction over the care of the basin. The old town commissioners remained but their duties were vaguely defined. As a step toward political autonomy, the 1786 measure giving Baltimore its first local elective offices ranks with the 1776 constitution provision allowing representation in the assembly and the 1780 legislation establishing a customs house. But it was a dubious victory. The townspeople had had no hand in drawing up the legislation, except for what influence their two assemblymen might exert. The measure incorporated several features of the rejected charter proposal, including high property qualifications for office holders, an electoral system, and infrequent elections. It was a bad sign. If the assembly would risk defying the townspeople's expressed will in this half-way act, what could Baltimoreans expect when it again considered a bill of incorporation?[10]

In the decade following the 1784 proposal the political context within which the charter was debated changed radically. The French Revolution and the outbreak of war in Europe polarized political allegiances between conservatives who believed they saw democracy running rampant and others who saw republicanism triumphing over monarchy and priestcraft. By the early 1790s the issue of municipal governance actually posed the most fundamental political question of the era: what was "republican" government?

In November, 1793, in this increasingly partisan atmosphere, a number of private citizens laid an incorporation petition before the assembly. Such backdoor tactics were not unprecedented, of course. But this time no one published an announcement in the newspapers, leaving the townspeople to learn about the proposal through hearsay. The petitioners must have calculated that the assembly would respond promptly to their proposal and enact an incorporation law modeled after it. Baltimore would then get its government, though not without causing a public furor. The petition reportedly carried the signatures of leading merchants and lawyers, the same groups responsible for the 1784 proposal.[11]

The conservative position had not stood still over the decade. It had undergone refinements and alterations that the new petition encapsulated. It had grown even more exclusive, more determined to guard wealth and standing against the menace of popular tyranny. On the structure of the city government the proposals of 1784 and 1793 were in substantial agreement: there would be a bicameral city council, with an upper branch chosen by electors, headed by a mayor. There were minor points of departure. The age requirement for the council was raised from twenty-one to twenty-five; the board of aldermen was abandoned; the mayor was selected by the same electors who picked the council's upper branch.

In one area, however, the new petition incorporated several subtle changes that amounted to an entirely different conception of bicameralism. In the 1784 proposal the Second Branch had to meet the same property qualification as the First Branch, and both chambers were elected on a ward basis. Thus the proposal did not explicitly set aside the upper chamber for the propertied classes. As important as wealth was residence: a member of the upper branch must be committed to the interests of his neighbors, and for this reason the proposal required that he own most of his real and personal property in the ward he represented. The 1793 petition, on the other hand, elevated wealth to the sole criterion for the upper chamber. It doubled the property qualification to £1,000 and abolished the residency requirement. Most of the men wealthy enough to serve as upper branch electors lived in the downtown districts along Baltimore Street, not in Fell's Point or Old Town. It could be expected that in a citywide rather than ward-based election the electors would choose their wealthy friends and neighbors, overlooking the less prominent men across Jones' Falls. In sum, the 1793 petition stacked the upper chamber in favor of the downtown wards and the wealthy classes, which really amounted to the same thing.[12]

Anyone familiar with the incorporation movement's stormy history could have anticipated the wails of protest that greeted the charter proposal. But few could have expected the opposition to organize as it did. In 1782 and 1784 the incorporation drive had foundered upon popular opposition but in neither case had the anticonservative charter forces mobilized formally. This is not surprising. The "laboring classes" who seemed at the heart of opposition had no point around which they could easily rally. Not until 1785 did they form the Association of Tradesmen and Manufacturers, and by that time the incorporation controversy had subsided. The situation in 1793 was different. Now the skilled workers could look to an organization for leadership. On December 17, 1793, the Mechanical Society assembled its membership and adopted the following resolution, which appeared in the next day's newspapers: "*Resolved*, That Instructions be given to our Delegates now in the General Assembly, to OPPOSE ANY BILL for INCORPORATING BALTIMORE-TOWN, before such Bill shall be published, and approved of by a Majority of the Citizens." The society was only a year old but it had matured quickly as a political vehicle expressing the mechanics' sentiments. It now stepped forward in a larger role as the spokesman for the townspeople.[13]

Other organizations soon fell in behind the society. In November, 1793, the assembly passed an incorporation measure for consideration at its next session a year later. During the interval four groups joined the Mechanical Society. On January 13, 1794, the citizens of Fell's Point met to deliberate on the proposed legislation, reading the bill "Paragraph by Paragraph." Sometime earlier they, too, had instructed Baltimore's assemblymen to vote against the act, and they now reiterated their opposition. The meeting appointed a committee "to consult with our Fellow-Citizens, and collect their Sense on this important Question; and to adopt such Measures, by Remonstrance or otherwise, as may appear necessary to prevent its Ratification by the Legislature at their next Session." No less fearful of the incorporation act were the inhabitants of the "precincts," the area just beyond the town limits. In August they assembled to devise a strategy for defeating the charter proposal at the coming assembly session. Also resolved to fight the bill was the Carpenters' Society—the oldest, largest, and most influential of the tradesmen's associations. The Baltimore Republican Society, which had been organized recently by merchants, lawyers, and physicians, rounded out the opposition forces.[14]

Cooperation was logical. By the fall of 1794 each of the five groups had appointed committees to collaborate in checking the incorporation petition at the next assembly session. They called themselves the United Committees. The Mechanical Society seems to have been the dominating influence in the coalition. Not only was it the first to declare its opposition to the petition and to instruct Baltimore's delegates to fight it, but it also supplied leadership in three of the other four organizations. Four shipwrights sat on the nine-man committee appointed by the inhabitants of Fell's Point, two of whom rose to become Mechanical Society officers: David Stodder and Joseph Biays. Four members of the Carpenters' Society also served as society officers. Although the principal figures behind the anti-charter movement in the precincts are unknown, it would have been surprising had the master brickmakers, who operated their kilns on the town's outskirts and numbered among the area's wealthiest residents, not been represented. Brickmaker William Krebs lived in the precincts and was an officer in the Mechanical Society.[15]

The only organization in the United Committees over which the Mechanical Society had no direct influence was the Republican Society. Founded in May, 1794, the Republican Society represented the radical faction of the merchant community committed to the cause of France. The preamble to the society's constitution declared: "The flame of liberty must extend or become extinguished: —Patriotism must support, and jealously, the attendant of freedom, guard the altar in which it blazes, with incessant watchfulness. The spirit of domination which has marked the course of the combined tyrants of Europe, excites a well grounded apprehension, that America is implicated in the fate of the French Republic."

The officers of the Republican Society included a president, vice-president, treasurer, six-man standing committee, and four-man corresponding committee. In 1794 and 1795 seventeen men occupied these positions, fourteen merchants, two lawyers, and one manufacturer. None of them served as officers in the Mechanical Society. The United Committees was thus a coalition of two social classes. Through the Mechanical Society and its kindred allies in the United Committees, the skilled workingmen had weight in numbers and initiative. The merchants exerted their influence through the Republican Society. Neither group alone had the resources to build and sustain the movement against the conservative charter; each would make its special contribution.[16]

On September 12 the United Committees published a comprehensive attack on the proposed charter in the newspapers, which expressed an advanced democratic republicanism. Indeed, it could claim credit for Baltimore's most radical vision of republicanism produced before the Age of Jackson. The piece appeared just two months before the scheduled legislative session and three weeks before what promised to be a volatile assembly election. The United Committees catalogued their objections to the charter under twenty-four separate headings. A few of the criticisms dealt with relatively minor points, but most cut away the heart of the would-be government. The committees rejected not merely high property qualifications but all of them: "because wealth ought not to be made a qualification to office; and because no restraint whatever ought to be imposed on the will of the people in their choice of that man, (whether rich or poor) whom they

believe best qualified to serve them." They issued a blanket condemnation of the electoral system for the mayor and upper
branch: "because the people ought to have the right of judging
the qualifications of its own representatives." The committees up-
held the principle of frequent elections, which they charged the
proposed charter with overthrowing. They also struck at *viva
voce* voting: "because this method very much impedes the freedom of elections, and lays the poor and middling class of people
too open to influence from the rich and the great, whom fear or
interest may prompt them not to offend, by giving a vote which
they do not approve."

The charter's provision disfranchising blacks, however much
sanctioned by time and custom, angered the committees because
it ran "contrary to reason and good policy, to the spirit of equal
liberty and our free constitution." The charter also discriminated
against the town's youth by establishing an age qualification of
twenty-five years for service in the First Branch; "merit is not the
exclusive privilege of any particular age," the committees remarked. They questioned the very notion of bicameralism, and
here is perhaps the committees' most radical critique. A two-body
common council created dangerous ties of dependency between
mayor and upper chamber. More fundamentally, it wasn't necessary in a community like Baltimore: "because where unity of interests prevail, (as in the town of Baltimore) unity of sentiment in
legislators is to be expected."[17]

If the United Committees had stopped here, leaving behind
no more than its attack on the charter proposal, it could still take
credit for a remarkable vision of republican government. But it
did not stop at criticism. On September 29 the United Committees offered an alternative to the charter petition in the newspapers, "An ACT respecting the Police of BALTIMORE-TOWN." No
more striking contrast with the conservative incorporation petition could be imagined. The committees eliminated the checks
and balances so carefully constructed in the conservative proposal. Most important, they replaced the two-chamber city council with a unicameral board of commissioners. The city would be
divided into ten districts, rather than the nine wards created under the conservative proposal, each of which elected two commissioners to the board. There was no property qualification. Any

freeman twenty-one years of age who had resided in his district six months, the town a year, and the country two years could run for office. The council elections fell on the first Monday of every October, not at five-year intervals as the conservative proposal had established for the upper chamber. All elections would be by ballot instead of *viva voce*. There would be no executive branch to speak of. The committees' act provided for a president but he was simply a member of the board chosen by a majority of his fellow commissioners. He exercised no special authority beyond presiding over board meetings and convening the commissioners in emergencies.[18]

The remaining provisions of the act stipulated the powers of the board, which included the customary jurisdiction over streets, police, public health, basin, bridges, auctions, markets, pumps, taxes, licenses, and fees. The act prohibited the commissioners from intruding in several areas, which reflected the special interests of mechanics and the Point. The board was not allowed to tax the Point's citizens "for the preservation of the navigation of the bason or docks thereof." Large-draft ships discharged their cargos at the Point; the United Committees would not ask the community to impoverish itself by paying taxes to dredge the basin. In a concession to bakers, the commissioners were permitted to regulate "the assize of bread, but not the price thereof"; both powers were granted to the council in the conservative proposal. Nor would the committees permit the commissioners to set fees for draymen or rates for wharf makers, unlike the conservative proposal that imposed ceilings on the prices charged by these laboring men.[19]

Who in the United Committees conceived the advanced republican ideas in the proposal? Without the proceedings of the organization, it is impossible to answer unequivocally. But one piece of evidence indicates that the Mechanical Society was the first to formulate the basic principle of the act: a unicameral council. On December 17, 1793, the same day that the society's resolution against the conservative proposal appeared in the newspapers, "A Citizen" addressed the mechanics. Where had the Mechanical Society gotten its idea of unicameralism, he asked. How could it expect Baltimore to adopt a mode of government that all the states had rejected in their constitutions? The only model for such an innovation was the Pennsylvania constitution of 1776. But, as "A Citizen" noted, it had been abandoned a year earlier. Thus the Mechanical Society had in mind a unicameral council from the outset, though the idea undoubtedly underwent elaboration and refinement in the United Committees. This was five months before the Republican Society had even organized. On the issue of unicameralism, then, the merchants faced an accomplished fact; they could only accept the position already staked out by the Mechanical Society.[20]

Neither the Mechanical Society nor the United Committees had invented the ideas contained in their act. They were plumbing a radical tradition most clearly embodied in the Pennsylvania constitution, the most radical to emerge from the state conventions. That constitution had also established a unicameral assembly, waived property qualifications for office holding, and instituted annual elections for the legislature. In its determination to maintain the dominance of the legislature, the Pennsylvania convention had created a weak executive arm consisting of a council and president; they could neither prorogue the assembly nor veto its legislation, the two weapons in the arsenal of the colonial governor. The convention had denounced bicameral government as an antirepublican attempt to preserve a privileged upper house for the propertied few. All its vaunted checks and balances notwithstanding, bicameral government was designed to weaken the people's true representatives in the lower house who struggled against the entrenched conservatism of the upper chamber and executive branch. The foes of the Pennsylvania constitution, realizing that the traditional arguments for mixed government were politically inexpedient, revamped their case for bicameralism. They argued that a bicameral system would actually discourage special-interest groups from seeking control over the government and thereby protect the people from their elected representatives. However much the concept of bicameralism changed in the first decades after independence, however much it lost its original conservative character and gained legitimacy from association with the federal Constitution, the suspicion remained that it imposed more checks on the people than on their representatives. When the United Committees revived the notion of unicameralism, they tapped an undercurrent of radical republicanism that had not run out despite the adoption of bicameral legislatures by all of the states as well as the national government.[21]

For a year the debate over incorporation peppered the columns of the press. The advocates of the conservative proposal offered three arguments against the United Committees' act. In the beginning they maintained that the townspeople were incapable of agreeing to an alternative to the conservative charter. "A Citizen" informed the Mechanical Society that it might condemn the proposed charter but "many Men can judge of a Plan, who are not capable to frame one." The conservatives had to drop this tack after September, when the United Committees proposed their own charter. The second argument was that the committees were rejecting constitutional principles that had won near universal endorsement. "Tom the Tinkerer" wrote that the committees were attempting to inflame the townspeople against "our state government and constitution of the United States, which," he added sarcastically, "every fool knows to be absolute tyrannies." Another supporter of the conservative charter reduced the committees' position to what he saw as its logical conclusion: "*abolishing all government.*"

But what most alarmed the conservatives was the United Committees' willingness to purge the municipal government of all checks and balances, in particular the bicameral council. "Do the people of Baltimore differ from all the rest of human species," asked one of them. "Is there no jarring and different interests between different parts of town? Is there a perfect uniformity of opinion and interest so as to render all checks upon a town legislature unnecessary?" This was, of course, the argument James Madison used in defending the federalist constitution. Society was split into antagonistic groups seeking their own ends; government must prevent any one of them from seizing power; only then would the people be protected from their elected servants. While Madison was talking about a nation divided into states and sections, his logic seemed no less applicable to a town with the strong neighborhood loyalties of Baltimore.[22]

The conservative charter drew criticism on many accounts, but perhaps the most frequently voiced objection was that it harmed the workingmen. "If it were only to oppress the poor Draymen and Labourers," wrote "A poor Drayman" about the conservative proposal, "it will, I hope, be sufficient to excite the resentment of all good men." "Rags" claimed that *viva voce* voting would "let the man of *wealth* know, whether the man of *rags* has merited further employment, or another loan, or further indulgence in the time of paying *his* debt; or whether he ought to have *his* little note or bill negociated at the bank: or whether upon occasion, he can be entrusted with any other post than a whipping post." Especially galling to "Rags" was the attempt to regulate the rate of wharfage by "people who never experienced the risk, expence or trouble of making a wharf." "Z." agreed with the United Committees that ballot voting was essential to ensure "the independence of all the middle class and the industry of the lower class of citizens."[23]

On the question of checks and balances the supporters of the United Committees' act had to phrase their position carefully. They refrained from criticizing the state or federal constitution, the latter of which was a sacred cow in Baltimore. They argued that the conditions making a two-house legislature necessary at the state and national levels did not prevail in a local community. In their attack on the conservative charter the United Committees had referred to a "unity of interests" in town. They had condemned the electoral system "because in a situation so limited as Baltimore, every voter may be well acquainted with the character and merits of the several candidates." "Q." expressed his weariness over all the squabbling about "checks and balances"; they were simply a pretext for making the council "independent of the people." Annual elections, he declared, "will forever secure the life, liberty, and property of the people, better than any independent aristocracy that has ever been invented."[24]

The charter controversy spilled into election politics. On October 3, a few days before the assembly elections, the United Committees met at the "Rights of Man" tavern and nominated two candidates as delegates, merchant Alexander McKim and lawyer James Winchester. McKim was the president of the Republican Society, Winchester a member of the corresponding committee. It was logical that the United Committees should turn to the Republican Society for political candidates rather than to the Mechanical Society. A mechanic had never been elected to the assembly, although in 1792 Thomas Coulson, a future vice-president of the Mechanical Society, had made an unsuccessful bid. The committees declared in a public statement that Baltimore needed "characters of firmness, integrity, and ability, well acquainted with the nature of republican government, animated by its spirits and warmly attached to its principles, which alone can preserve the rights of man." When the polls opened on Monday morning, October 6, McKim and Winchester announced that they would not appear at the hustings to solicit votes. They condemned this "antirepublican practice," preferring to stay home and permit the voters "the free unbiased exercise of their own opinions, in supporting those whom they may judge best qualified to discharge a very important delegated trust." At the close of the polls on Thursday, McKim and Winchester were declared winners with 401 and 397 votes respectively. They had apparently run unopposed.[25]

The fate of the charter was now in the assembly. Despite having two representatives committed to its proposal, the United Committees could reasonably expect the conservative legislature to concoct its own incorporation bill and force it on Baltimore. On December 18 their fears were borne out. McKim and Winchester sent a letter to their Baltimore constituents which was printed in the newspapers the following day. They explained that they had proposed the United Committees' bill as instructed, but the assembly attached a crippling amendment: the board of commissioners would exercise its authority only over the residents of Baltimore, not over visitors or people traveling through town. Rather than see their bill emasculated, McKim and Winchester withdrew it from consideration but assured the townspeople that this was only a "temporary inconvenience."[26]

The delegates were too optimistic. The 1794 session passed without an incorporation act, riveting the town's attention on the coming assembly elections in October, 1795. In August McKim announced that he would not seek re-election, citing his "own immediate concerns." By the eve of the contest four others had offered themselves as candidates: the incumbent Winchester, lawyer James Carroll, lawyer David McMechen, and nailmaker Richardson Stewart. The appearance of the latter suggests that the coalition in the United Committees was undergoing strain. In 1794, despite its leading role in opposing the conservative charter and formulating an alternative, the Mechanical Society had rallied around the candidacies of two Republican Society officers, neither of whom was a workingman. But by 1795 the idea had apparently surfaced in the Mechanical Society that it might nominate one of its own officers. Stewart was not only a substantial nailmaker but also a regular member of the Mechanical Society's board of managers. Perhaps the society's decision to strike out independently explains why the United Committees disappeared after October, 1794. The act it had drafted remained the starting point in the movement for a republican charter, but the committee structure seems to have collapsed. Baltimore was not ready for a mechanic delegate: Winchester received 752 votes, McMechen 504, Stewart 263, and Carroll 86.[27]

Once more the assembly failed to enact an incorporation bill, setting the stage in 1796 for another push to secure a charter. As the new assembly elections drew near, Winchester bowed out in favor of merchant Robert Smith, who, along with the incumbent McMechen, won uncontested. But on November 19 Smith resigned his seat to attend to family matters and on December 8 McMechen was informed of his election to the state senate. In the special elections that followed, the old candidates of the United Committees took their seats again: Winchester on December 5, McKim on December 24.[28]

In the meantime, the pro-charter forces were active. On October 19 a notice appeared in the newspapers declaring that a number of citizens intended to petition the assembly for a charter. Prompted by requests that the charter be published for the examination of the townspeople, the petition appeared in the papers on October 24, the United Committees' proposal of two years before. The task of guiding the proposal through the assembly fell to Winchester, who for several critical weeks was Baltimore's sole delegate. He amended the proposal but assured his constituents that the new bill "contained no material alteration from the plan which had been the subject of the deliberation of the citizens at large, for a considerable length of time, and so far as I could judge of their approbation."

This statement was simply untrue. The bill that Winchester had written, presumably in consultation with his fellow delegates, departed radically from the United Committees' act. It provided for a mayor who would exercise the executive authority that the United Committees had denied the board's president in its bill. Above all, he would have a veto power over the council. Only a handful of men would be able to qualify for the office: those who were twenty-five years old, ten-year citizens, five-year town residents, and who were assessed at £1,000. Winchester's bill also instituted the electoral system, with each ward choosing an elector worth at least £500, who in turn voted for the mayor. The city council would consist of twenty members, two from each ward, who had to satisfy a property qualification of £500.

Winchester had surrendered the principles of a weak executive, no property qualifications for office holding, and direct elections. Why? One possible reason was personal. Winchester stood on the brink of a political conversion; he would soon leave the Republican fold and join the Federalists. Another factor may have been the misgivings of the Republican Society over the radical proposals made by the United Committees. In the confusing sequence of elections that finally put him in office, Winchester may have seen an opportunity to blunt the radical edge of the committees' act.[29]

As the delegates were considering Winchester's bill, the advocates of a conservative charter stepped forward. On December 19 Winchester informed his constituents that the bill had been betrayed. "But, to my great disappointment," he wrote in a public letter, "a petition presented from a respectable list of signers, about 140 in number, praying that an incorporation might pass, framed as nearly as might be, after the plan of the federal and state governments, gave rise to an opinion, that the printed system was *not* agreeable to the town." The assembly rewrote the incorporation bill, which, when it finally emerged, bore no resemblance to either the United Committees' act or Winchester's watered-down proposal. In the assembly's version there would be a two-branch city council, of which the upper chamber included five men elected from the city at large. The elections would come every five years. Unicameralism and annual elections, the two features of the committees' bill that Winchester had left intact, were now gone.[30]

Even Winchester could not stomach this mangling of the townspeople's petition. On December 19 he withdrew his bill and persuaded the delegates to postpone consideration of incorporation for another year. He dashed off a letter to Baltimore, explaining what had happened and urging the townspeople to declare their sentiments. If the delegates could be convinced that the conservative petition did not enjoy widespread support, an incorporation bill might yet emerge from the session. On December 22 the townspeople met and expressed their "hearty approbation" of Winchester's bill. With Baltimore facing an unprecedented outbreak of fires and prospects of yellow fever, even Winchester's bill seemed better than none. The chairman of the meeting was merchant James Calhoun, another officer of the Republican Society. The impression is inescapable that these Republican Society leaders—Winchester, McKim, and Calhoun—were retreating from the advanced positions taken by the United Committees. A day after the meeting Winchester shot back a letter from Annapolis saying he would take the matter before the assembly and present the town meeting's resolutions to the delegates. He had hopes for success. On December 29 came the final letter. Winchester had pressed for the original bill but failed to "quiet opposition to the published plan." He therefore exercised the discretion that he believed the situation required and introduced a new compromise measure into the assembly. On December 26 it passed the House of Delegates. As Winchester wrote, the bill was before the Senate. In January, 1797, the bill became law. Baltimore at last had its charter.[31]

But it was not the charter the townspeople had wanted. The final incorporation act was more exclusive than the committee proposal of 1784, petition of 1793, United Committees' act of 1794, and Winchester's bill of 1796. In some respects it went beyond the most conservative of all the schemes devised over the last fifteen years. It established a mayor and bicameral council. The First Branch consisted of sixteen members, two from each ward, elected annually. To qualify for the lower chamber, one had to be twenty-one years old, a three-year town resident, and worth £1,000—double what even the 1793 petition had proposed. The Second Branch was comprised of eight members elected from the city at large. Only those who were twenty-five years old, four-year town residents, and who were assessed at £2,000 could serve in the upper chamber. The mayor, who exercised the power to veto

council legislation as well as appoint most municipal officials, had
to be twenty-five years old, a ten-year citizen, and a five-year resident. Both the mayor and the Second Branch were selected at
two-year intervals by eight electors, one from each ward, who had
to be worth no less than £2,000 apiece.[32]

Was this betrayal? Some citizens thought so. In 1808
"Aristides" remembered bitterly the conservative petition, which
had subverted the bill endorsed by the townspeople. "This petition Mr. Winchester says was signed by such respectable names
that he could not resist them. The assembly was also too weak to
bear up against the weight of respectability; and the cause of the
people was of course weighed down, down." Yet the mechanics
could draw several important lessons from the incorporation
movement. First, the assembly had no compunctions about sad-
dling Baltimore with a measure it had consistently rejected. It
could employ a strategy of delay. By 1796 the townspeople must
have reached a point of exhaustion where any charter seemed desirable if it could settle the fourteen-year controversy. Second, a
relatively small number of "respectable" townsmen were willing
to defy the expressed will of the majority of citizens to secure
their conservative objectives. They found ready allies in the conservative assembly. Third, the political coalition between Baltimore's merchants and lawyers, on the one hand, and mechanics,
on the other, had limits. The role of the Republican Society in the
charter movement is ambiguous. If McKim, Winchester, and Calhoun did not deliberately undermine the United Committees'
act, they were not unshakably devoted to it. Finally, in the battle
for a city government Baltimore's mechanics had learned something about themselves. They had the capacity for producing a
distinctive vision of republicanism.[33]

NOTES

1. Ronald Hoffman, *A Spirit of Dissension: Economics, Politics, and the
Revolution in Maryland* (Baltimore, 1973), pp. 178–84; Paul Kent Walker, "The
Baltimore Community and the American Revolution: A Study in Urban Devel-
opment, 1763–1783" (Ph.D. diss., University of North Carolina at Chapel Hill,

1973), chap. 7; for accounts of city charter controversy, see William Bruce Wheeler, "The Baltimore Jeffersonians, 1788–1800: A Profile of Intra-Factional Conflict," *Maryland Historical Magazine*, 66 (Summer, 1971): 159–63; Whitman H. Ridgway, *Community Leadership in Maryland, 1790–1840: A Comparative Analysis of Power in Society* (Chapel Hill, N.C., 1979), pp. 82–84.

2. Walker, "Baltimore Community," pp. 346–49.

3. *Maryland Gazette* (Baltimore), Oct. 29, 1784; Col. J. Thomas Scharf, *The Chronicles of Baltimore; Being a Complete History of "Baltimore Town" and Baltimore City from the Earliest Period to the Present Time* (Baltimore, 1874), p. 196.

4. *Maryland Gazette*, Oct. 29, Nov. 5, 1784.

5. *Maryland Journal* (Baltimore), Nov. 16, 1784; *Baltimore-Town, Committee-Chamber, December 2, 1784* (Baltimore, 1784), MHS.

6. *Maryland Journal*, Feb. 4, 1785, Nov. 18, 24, 29, 1791, Oct. 12, 1792; *American* (Baltimore), Jan. 30, 1808.

7. *Baltimore-Town, Committee-Chamber*.

8. *Ibid.*

9. *Ibid.*; *Baltimore Town and Fell's Point Directory* (Baltimore, n.d. [1796]).

10. *Baltimore Daily Intelligencer*, Sept. 12, 1794.

11. *Ibid.*

12. *Ibid.*

13. *Maryland Journal*, Dec. 18, 1793.

14. *Ibid.*, Jan. 13, 1794; *Baltimore Daily Intelligencer*, Aug. 7, 1794.

15. *Maryland Journal*, Jan. 13, 1794; *Baltimore Daily Intelligencer*, Sept. 12, 1794.

16. *Baltimore Daily Intelligencer*, May 3, 17, 24, 29, June 3, 1794. For officers, see *ibid.*, June 9, 1794; *Maryland Journal*, July 7, 1795.

17. *Baltimore Daily Intelligencer*, Sept. 12, 1794.

18. *Maryland Journal*, Sept. 29, 1794.

19. *Ibid.*

20. *Edward's Baltimore Daily Advertiser*, Dec. 17, 1793.

21. Francis Newton Thorpe, ed., *The Federal and State Constitutions, Colonial Charters, and Other Organic Laws of the States* (Washington, D.C., 1909), 5:3081–92.

22. *Edward's Baltimore Daily Advertiser*, Dec. 17, 1793; *Federal Intelligencer* (Baltimore), Nov. 18, 1794; *Baltimore Daily Intelligencer*, Feb. 10, 1794; *Maryland Journal*, Oct. 28, 1794.

23. *Maryland Journal*, Jan. 15, Feb. 3, 14, 1794; *Baltimore Daily Intelligencer*, Feb. 8, 11, 1794.

24. *Baltimore Daily Intelligencer*, Sept. 12, 1794; *Federal Intelligencer*, Nov. 13, 19, 1794.

25. *Baltimore Daily Intelligencer*, Oct. 3, 7, 10, 1794; *Maryland Journal*, Oct. 6, 1794.

26. *Federal Intelligencer*, Dec. 19, 1794.

27. *Ibid.*, Aug. 20, Oct. 5, 6, 9, 1795; *Maryland Journal*, Oct. 5, 1795.

28. *Federal Gazette* (Baltimore), Oct. 3, Nov. 23, 26, Dec. 7, 12, 26, 1796.
29. *Ibid.*, Oct. 19, 20, 24, Dec. 13, 22, 1796.
30. *Ibid.*, Dec. 22, 1796.
31. *Ibid.*, Dec. 26, 30, 1796.
32. *Ibid.*, Jan. 14, 1797.
33. *American*, Jan. 30, 1808.

7

REPUBLICANISM AT THE POLLS
AND IN THE STREETS

The French Revolution was perhaps the major event establishing the context within which early American party politics developed. More than the battles over ratification of the Constitution and Alexander Hamilton's economic programs, it posed the issues leading to the creation of the Federalist and Republican parties. As Baltimoreans watched the revolution lift ever more radical spokesmen to prominence, as they watched it spill over its national boundaries to embroil all Europe in war and open the West Indies to "neutral" trade, their political allegiances became more sharply defined.

Through the Mechanical Society and militia the workingmen built themselves into one of the best organized political blocs in Baltimore and the backbone of the emerging Republican party. The politicizing effects of these institutions became apparent in 1794 when David Stodder, a militia captain and Mechanical Society officer, led a series of crowd actions that began by protesting a pro-British ship captain who had insulted the American flag and ended with a challenge to Baltimore's established judicial authorities. The Mechanical Society emerged as the vehicle through which craftsmen voiced their sentiments on Washington's Neutrality Proclamation and Jay's Treaty. In their society and militia units mechanics faithfully supported Congressman Samuel Smith, the architect of the local Republican party, in his political battles after 1795. Indeed, to the extent that a Republican "party" had evolved in Baltimore—with a stable constituency, local leadership, and formal structure—it was based primarily on the mechanic population.

In 1792 the French Revolution crossed its borders. French armies marched against the Austro-Prussian coalition formed to crush the infant republic. Within a year France had declared war on Great Britain, Holland, and Spain. Like most Americans during the early years of the revolution, Baltimore's mechanics rejoiced at the fall of the Bastille and cheered each French victory in the European conflagration. France was a kindred republic, a bastion of liberty—as many Americans saw it—amid the despots of the Continent. It was a welcome ally, for who could be confident that America's infant republic would survive in a world of hostile monarchies? The United States also had diplomatic obligations to France deriving from the 1778 treaties of alliance and commerce. France had pledged in time of war to protect the territorial integrity of the United States. In turn, America promised aid to France's West Indian colonies. The two countries had exchanged the commercial privilege of most-favored-nation status, and in an almost unprecedented abandonment of traditional mercantilist precepts, France granted American merchants the right to trade between the United States and the French West Indies with nominal fiscal encumbrances. On the issue of "neutral" trading rights both France and America agreed that "free ships make free goods."[1]

The international wars of the French Revolution confronted the Mechanical Society with its first major political issue. In April, 1793, President Washington issued a "Neutrality Proclamation" announcing the intention of the United States to hew a nonpartisan line toward the belligerent powers. Although some Americans muttered about reneging on the country's commitments to France, in Baltimore the declaration received warm endorsement. In an address to the president dated May 22, the "Merchants and Traders of the Town of Baltimore" praised the proclamation because it precluded America's entanglement in the European upheaval and guaranteed "the general Prosperity resulting from Peace and the excellent Laws and Constitution of the United States." A few weeks later the Mechanical Society also met to discuss the proclamation and penned its own laudatory message to Washington, which the newspapers published on June 18. The mechanics agreed that neutrality was the only basis on which a thriving national economy could be built; it was the best assurance of "Happiness and Prosperity." The president received the addresses and wrote to each group thanking it for its support and understanding.[2]

The statements on the Neutrality Proclamation marked a significant political juncture in Baltimore. At an earlier time the townspeople would have probably responded to the Neutrality Proclamation by calling a general meeting of all citizens. It was unprecedented that merchants and mechanics should assemble separately to deliberate on the same issue, particularly when they were in substantial agreement. On the other hand, the statements reflected a subtle difference in outlook. The merchants praised the proclamation because it stimulated commerce. While the mechanics acknowledged the proclamation's salutary economic effects, they felt compelled to mention their admiration for the heroic struggle of France: "Being thus exalted to the Possession of civil and religious Liberty, we cannot divest ourselves of Sympathy for all who struggle for the same Blessing." The Mechanical Society expressed the hope that a "generous France" would understand the course America had taken, for neutrality would ultimately serve the best interests of mankind. "Peace will thus be preserved," the society wrote, "the true Interest of our Country promoted, Happiness extended, and an Asylum secured to the Oppressed of every Nation and Country." This was a vision lacking in the merchants' matter-of-fact address.[3]

Declaring neutrality was one thing—enforcing it against the unrivaled British fleet was another. The royal navy claimed the right to remove French property from American vessels, provided just compensation was made. In June, 1793, the British government prohibited American vessels from trading directly between French ports, a trade that France had legalized soon after the outbreak of the war. During the summer and fall, confrontations between American merchantmen and the British navy grew more frequent, which in August prompted Secretary of State Thomas Jefferson to write Baltimore's merchants requesting information on the harassment of their shipping. The merchants appointed a committee that included Baltimore's congressman, Samuel Smith, to report "all unjustifiable Detentions, Spoilations, and Injuries done to the Ships and Property of the Citizens of this State." Then in November the British resolved to make a lightning sweep of American shipping from the Caribbean. New orders-in-council were issued prohibiting all trade with the French colonies. The orders were held secret until late December, giving the navy time to seize several hundred U.S. ships in the West Indies, most of which were condemned and sold. Although the orders were rescinded in January, 1794, the action triggered an outcry in Baltimore and across the nation. "AMERICANS AROUSE!" wrote one Baltimorean, "and no longer suffer yourselves dormant under the base intrigues of the selfish and arrogant tyrant of Great Britain. Your mutilated commerce calls loudly for VENGEANCE!"[4]

The Mechanical Society had been preparing for the crisis through the militia. On August 8 the newspapers printed a call for a meeting the next evening at Starck's tavern of "the Mechanics of Baltimore-Town, who wish to form themselves into a select Company of Militia." The new unit was christened the Baltimore Mechanical Volunteers, perhaps in memory of its Revolutionary precursor that had fought at Germantown and seen its captain die there. A number of old Volunteers still lived in Baltimore and perhaps provided advice and encouragement: the captain of the Revolutionary Volunteers, John McClellan, was an officer of the Mechanical Society, as was its lieutenant, David Poe.

After several months drilling at its chosen parade ground, the Mechanical Volunteers on December 1 joined five other militia units in a review before General Otho H. Williams, a veteran of the Revolution and Baltimore's customs collector. Two days later the militia captains composed a letter expressing their thanks to the general. "Considering a Militia as the proper and best Defence of a free state," they wrote, "we have, in the present eventful and critical Period, without waiting the Command of our Country, assumed the Character of Soldiers." The commanders asked that Williams forbear the imperfections of the parade because "we are not merely Soldiers—we are Citizens, and occupied in Civil Duties." General Williams returned the compliments: "The Manual Exercise, Firings, and Evolutions, were performed, in the general, with Spirit and Precision."[5]

Three of the six captains who paraded before Williams were officers of the Mechanical Society. The captain of the Mechanical Volunteers was Thomas Coulson, who served as vice-president of the Mechanical Society in 1793 and 1794. The captain of the First

Baltimore Company of Light Infantry was John Mackenheimer, a member of the board of managers of the Mechanical Society. The captain of the Fell's Point Volunteers was David Stodder, who also belonged to the board of managers. The occupation of Coulson is unknown. He may have died or moved around 1794, several years before the first city directory appeared, and his occupation does not surface in the town newspapers. Mackenheimer was a carpenter and belonged to the Carpenters' Society until 1795 when he bolted for the newly formed Carpenters' Association. Stodder was a shipwright.[6]

The political principles impelling these prominent mechanics to assume leadership in the militia appear in the public toasts of the Mechanical Volunteers. The Volunteers did not see themselves as merely protecting American commerce or territorial claims; they saw themselves as participating in a worldwide struggle against oppression. In 1794 the unit assembled at Evans's tavern to celebrate Washington's birthday and offered a toast expressing its militant republicanism: "May the Enemies of France be defeated in all their Attempts, and may thinking and brave Men of all other Nations, where Monarchy reigns, follow their example." A year later the Mechanical Volunteers again gathered to honor the president's birthday and their pro-French sympathies had lost none of their intensity: "The French arms—may their successes of '95 exceed those of '94." The Volunteers seemed to see republicanism spreading out of France and liberating the subjugated peoples of Europe. "All our Brethren of Mankind," the unit toasted in an inspired moment, "who wish well to the Cause of Liberty, may they speedily be eased of their oppressive Taxes, which they are obliged to pay to Support a Set of Despots and their Sycophants." Or more succinctly: "May oppression ever meet with effectual resistance."[7]

The mobilization of the militia increased the tense atmosphere that had settled on Baltimore by the spring of 1794. In May the newspapers reported that over 2,000 men had enrolled in the town's four militia regiments: the 39th covered the neighborhood west of Light Street, the 27th between Light and South streets, the 5th between South Street and Jones' Falls, and the 6th east of the Falls. At dusk each day the streets thronged with men heading for their company parade grounds; on Saturdays and holidays hundreds of men turned out for larger regimental or battalion reviews. Those who did not qualify for militia service did their share by organizing work details that marched each morning to Whetstone Point to repair the fort there—young and old, even free blacks were enlisted in the effort. But the mingling of so many people in the streets was itself a source of anxiety. A year earlier an outbreak of yellow fever had devastated Philadelphia, causing a near panic in Baltimore over rumors that the disease was spreading. In 1794 came fresh reports that fever had broken out at the Point. Adding to the tension was a series of clashes that, as we have seen, involved journeymen hatters, shoemakers, and tailors.[8]

The least provocation could ignite this situation, and it came on Thursday, May 1. A Captain Ramsdell, who commanded a vessel anchored at Fell's Point, reversed an American flag and ran it up the masthead of his ship. This was a clearly understood challenge. Just the day before "A native American" had written in the newspapers that "it is incontestibly proven, that British frigates and British privateers have sent into their ports American vessels, with the American flag reversed—this is a *national insult*, not alone committed by privateersmen, but by persons acting under the authority of George the third." Why Ramsdell should seek a confrontation is unclear; some people said he was drunk. The docks were busy with spring shipments arriving; draymen and stevedores were loading and unloading; carpenters and caulkers were outfitting the ships. Soon a large group gathered before Ramsdell's ship. There must have been an exchange of insults. A few "gentlemen" came forward and tried to reason with Ramsdell but he refused to lower the flag. Several of them set out to find Captain David Stodder, the one man who might forestall the violence that seemed close at hand. Stodder hurried down to the docks and warned Ramsdell that his obstinancy was putting his life in danger. But the flag continued to fly, taunting the exasperated on-lookers.[9]

In turning to David Stodder, the gentlemen of Fell's Point acknowledged the prominence attained by the mechanic community's spokesmen. Born in 1749, Stodder had established a shipyard east of the Point where he became one of Baltimore's most respected tradesmen. In 1785 the Association of Tradesmen and

Manufacturers elected Stodder to its standing committee. Three years later the town's ship carpenters chose him to lead the trade in the parade celebrating ratification of the constitution. In December, 1793, he was elected to the board of managers of the Mechanical Society. Despite his vast wealth—in 1804 he ranked in the top 3 percent of the city's property holders—Stodder never wavered in his mechanic identity. Unlike many successful shipwrights who adopted the title "merchant," Stodder continued to list himself as a "ship builder" in the city directories from 1796 until his death nine years later. In 1797, when the Adams administration decided to build five frigates for the navy, it assigned one to Baltimore's David Stodder. His thirty-eight-gun *Constellation* can be seen in the Baltimore harbor today and testifies to the skill, wealth, and confidence of the man who constructed it. When the ship was completed, Stodder notified the Secretary of War but did not forget to acknowledge his workingmen: "I am under the greatest obligations to the carpenters that assisted, for their readiness in obeying my orders, as well as their activity in executing them at the instant dictated."

Stodder's influence extended to the black community. In 1800 he owned seventeen slaves, making him the second largest slaveholder in town. Stodder also employed free blacks at his yard as caulkers, draymen, and laborers. A few weeks after the Ramsdell incident a seemingly unimportant event revealed the influence Stodder held among blacks. In May the newspapers announced that free blacks would be mobilized in work crews to repair the fort guarding the basin. But there were misgivings. Fearful of mobilizing blacks in light of the St. Domingue revolution, the town authorities sought somebody who could ensure their proper conduct. They chose Captain Stodder, who assembled the free blacks at his Fell's Point home, equipped them with tools, and marched them to the fort.[10]

Ramsdell was seized from his ship. A crowd that one observer estimated at *"thousands of republicans"* drove the ship captain up Bond Street toward Old Town. The police were too busy helping the rioters to resist. Robert Townsend, one of three captains of the Fell's Point night watch, marched at the head of the crowd carrying the maligned American flag. Stodder later said that he and several friends trailed behind, waiting for an opportunity to rescue Ramsdell. But before they could intervene, someone cried out that Ramsdell was "in the service of England," which proved to be the signal many had been awaiting. Captain Ramsdell was tarred and feathered, the first such incident since 1773. The procession continued up Bond Street until Stodder and his associates finally secured Ramsdell's release and escorted him back to his ship. The next day tempers were still hot. Apparently a young sailor named Senton spoke up for Ramsdell or was suspected of privateering for Great Britain, and he too received a tarring and feathering. Stodder again found himself in the middle of the disturbance.[11]

Not everyone considered Stodder as blameless as he claimed. One man who suspected him of instigating the riots was Samuel Chase, the old Revolutionary hotspur who had recently undergone a conservative conversion as chief judge of the Baltimore County criminal and civil courts. On Saturday afternoon Judge Chase issued arrest warrants for Captain Stodder, John Steele, Christopher Raborg, and Captain William Reeves, requiring each of them to post recognizances. All of them pleaded their innocence. Captain Stodder took his case directly before the public by publishing an account of his actions in the newspapers. He said he had tried to stop the crowd from seizing Ramsdell; later he had tried to persuade the crowd to release him; the following day he had tried to protect Senton, who had formerly been his apprentice. Stodder called him "a grand villain," who had "stole money from me to a considerable amount before I found him out." "Had I been seen doing anything against him," Stodder explained, "people might have said I owed him some grudge."

On Saturday afternoon the four accused men met Judge Chase at the court house. They all declared that they would go to prison before posting security. Chase had a difficult decision to make. Overnight Stodder had become a local hero, a symbol of republicanism. Hundreds of townspeople had followed him from the Point to the court house, where they now awaited Chase's decision. Should the judge risk another confrontation by jailing Stodder and the others? As he pondered this dilemma, Judge Chase later claimed to overhear Captain Reeves addressing the crowd outside the court house, saying that "I (calling me by my name) countenanced and advocated a person (meaning capt.

Ramsdell,) who had insulted the American flag; and also an American Pirate (meaning one Sinton, who was tarred and feathered on Friday last) and that I threatened to commit to gaol the friends of America." Even more alarming, Chase claimed to hear "several persons declare, that if I committed Capt. Stodder, the Gaol should be pulled down, and not one stone left on another."[12]

Captain Stodder seemed to enjoy his notoriety. As he and Judge Chase conferred inside the court house, both men could hear the people outside cheering their hero. Chase claimed: "*Great Numbers of People, then in the Court House*, cried out repeatedly—'A Stodder—A Stodder,' and huzaad, as if at an Election." Stodder explained to Chase that he was bound by the will of his fellow citizens, for he believed "there were near two thousand people in Baltimore Town, who said I ought not to enter into recognizance." How could the captain defy these thousands? Judge Chase resolved to solicit advice from "Citizens of the first reputation and knowledge," who agreed that arresting Stodder in front of the hundreds of citizens gathered around the court house might incite another riot. The judge therefore decided to delay a final decision until the next morning when he scheduled another meeting with Stodder.[13]

First thing Sunday morning, before the appointed time, Stodder called on Chase at his home, but neither man was prepared to back down. The judge later reported that Stodder wanted to post security but feared that the Point's inhabitants would "destroy his property" if he did. Aiming to discredit Stodder, Chase published this account in the newspapers and forced the captain to print a denial. In the meantime, the citizens of Fell's Point had held a meeting where they resolved to demolish Chase's home if Stodder was imprisoned. Judge Chase arrived at the court house at eight o'clock in the morning and waited for several hours with no sign of Stodder. He finally returned home just a few moments before Stodder marched up to the court house leading "a *great number* of Inhabitants of Fell's Point." Their rallying cry was: "A Stodder—A Stodder; and *no security*." The judge delayed ordering Stodder's arrest because, as he later explained to the governor, it would provoke greater disturbances. By Sunday night Fell's Point had witnessed further defiance of the law. After discovering his role in the Thursday tarring and feathering of Ramsdell, Judge Chase removed Townsend from the watch force. As the night watch prepared for their rounds on Sunday, a group coverged on the watch house and demanded that Townsend be reinstated. Led by Thomas Trimble, Morris Job, and John Weaver, they declared that "Townsend was put in by the Citizens of Fell's Point, and they were the citizens, and he should not be broke for the conduct for which he was broke." Townsend, who had come along, resumed his duties.[14]

On Monday morning Captain Stodder entered security and the others followed suit. In his public statement the captain maintained that "the Desire of the Town" was that he post recognizance. Several days later Judge Chase discovered how deeply dissension had seeped into the militia, the only force that could have resisted a riot. Several companies, perhaps those led by Stodder and Reeves, had denounced the judge and pledged to defy any order to suppress rioting. Chase's problems were not yet over. In August he presided over a grand jury of townsmen who found the accused rioters innocent of all charges. Chase was outraged. Several of the jurymen, he claimed, had participated in the rioting themselves. He reproved the sheriff "for having summoned so BAD a Jury." In turn, the jury condemned Chase for the remark and accused him of plural office holding in simultaneously serving on the civil and criminal courts. "A judge in exercising his legal discretion," Chase replied in the supercilious manner that would continue to rankle Republicans, "is only answerable to God and his conscience, and is above all human tribunal, unless he acts from corrupt motives."[15]

The Ramsdell-Senton riots had elevated the officers of the Mechanical Society to the level of heroes, personifications of patriotic republicanism. Judge Chase identified seven men as ringleaders in the rioting. The occupations of six are known: Stodder and Steele were shipbuilders, Raborg a coppersmith, Weaver a blacksmith, and Job a blockmaker; the only nonmechanic was Reeves, a ship captain. Three of the six mechanics were officers of the Mechanical Society.[16]

The controversy surrounding the riots ebbed after the August trials, but Baltimore's resentment against British policies continued to be the focus of political debate. In 1794 John Jay negotiated a peace treaty with Great Britain, and by the next year it

was ready for President Washington's signature. When Baltimoreans first received a copy of the treaty in June, 1795, many
concluded that America had conceded to Britain on nearly all
substantive points. Appealing directly to the president, they
urged Washington to kill the measure by witholding his signature.
On July 8 "A Citizen" called for a meeting of townspeople to convey the "general dissatisfaction" with Jay's Treaty. Two weeks
later "A.B." declared that "the town of Baltimore will not be back-
ward in testifying their dislike and disapprobation at this alarming
crisis." On July 24 "Boethius" exhorted his fellow citizens to in-
voke their right of petition "to crush this monster in its infancy." [17]

On July 27 a meeting of townspeople at the court house lis-
tened to an address and appointed a committee to collect signatures, which would then be forwarded to the president. The next
day the memorial was placed at the town's exchange for signatures; two days later it was on its way to Philadelphia. The address
contained a comprehensive attack on the treaty. First, the townspeople bristled at the provision returning the western forts to
American control by 1796, "an unnecessary distant period" considering that they already belonged to the United States under
the terms of the 1783 treaty. Second, the treaty failed to compensate the southern states for the slaves that the British confiscated
during the Revolutionary War. Third, it said nothing about the
infamous practice of impressment and thus left American sailors
at the mercy of the British navy. Fourth, the provisions pertaining to ships unlawfully seized by the British and condemned in
January, 1794, were cumbersome and vague; only after protracted
legal proceedings could American merchants recover damages.
What was to assure them that such confiscations would not occur
again?

Finally, the most objectionable sections of the document
pertained to America's neutral trade. The treaty recognized the
right of the British navy and privateers to remove enemy property from American vessels, thus abandoning the principle that
"free ships make free goods," which the republic had officially endorsed since independence. "This is a cession of vast importance
to America as a trading nation," the address read. "Situate as she
is, remote from the powers of Europe; pacific in the temper and
disposition of her government; she is not likely to be embroiled in

wars. The advantages, then, that would result from her being the carriers of property for the contending nations are too evident to require elucidation, and too important to be given up without an equivalent." None of the so-called concessions that the British had made constituted an "equivalent" offsetting the surrender of America's neutral rights.[18]

The opposition to Jay's Treaty revived the coalition of the Mechanical and Republican societies that had originally been forged in the United Committees over the city charter. The seven-man committee appointed at the July 27 meeting embodied this alliance. It included Alexander McKim, the president of the Republican Society and United Committees' candidate for the assembly in 1794; Adam Fonerden, the president of the Mechanical Society; Solomon Etting, a merchant who had served on the Republican Society's standing committee; James A. Buchanan, another merchant who belonged to the Republican Society's corresponding committee; and the ubiquitous David Stodder, now a popular hero. The two remaining committeemen were David Mc-Mechen, who was probably included because he was Baltimore's delegate to the assembly, and John Steel, who may have been either the merchant or shipwright of that name.

Both associations had compelling reasons for seeking cooperation. The Mechanical Society had much to gain; it was a mark of political legitimacy to be dealing with the merchants on equal terms. A coalition also deflected the criticism that would have arisen had either organization opposed the treaty alone, namely, that the protest reflected selfish interests. The Republican Society needed political allies. For the past several months, ever since President Washington had leveled a widely circulated denunciation of the "democratic societies" he feared were producing anarchy, Baltimore's Republican Society had been under heavy attack in the press. The membership undoubtedly felt vulnerable and hesitant about opposing Jay's Treaty, the cornerstone of the president's foreign policy, without backing from other sources.[19]

In August Washington signed the treaty. The debate now shifted to the House of Representatives. In March, 1796, Edward Livingston of New York introduced a resolution demanding that the president relinquish the documents exchanged during the treaty negotiations. He argued that the Constitution, which granted the representatives the power to fund treaties, also gave them the right to review their contents. Baltimore's congressman, Samuel Smith, spoke in favor of the resolution. He refrained, though, from indicating how he would vote when the funding bill came before the House. President Washington refused to hand the papers over to Congress, challenging the representatives to withhold the appropriations and setting the stage for a major constitutional battle.[20]

Meanwhile, Baltimore's conservative merchants had been active mobilizing support for the appropriations bill. On April 12 Secretary of War James McHenry, formerly a Baltimore assemblyman and favorite of the Association of Tradesmen and Manufacturers, warned merchant Robert Oliver about Smith's inclination to oppose appropriations. He advised Oliver and other merchants to pressure Smith into supporting the funding measure. A committee was quickly formed, consisting of merchants Thorowgood Smith and Nicholas Rogers and lawyer James Winchester. It drew up a set of "instructions" to Congressman Smith, directing him to vote for the bill. On April 18 the committee placed the instructions at the offices of two insurance companies and solicited the signatures of the townspeople. At the end of the day it sent the package containing 501 names to Smith.

The following day three of Baltimore's wealthiest merchants— Robert Gilmor, Archibald Campbell, and William Patterson—received a letter from a corresponding committee of the Philadelphia merchants. The northern merchants apparently suggested combining forces against Smith. On April 20 Gilmor, Campbell, and Patterson called a meeting of their fellow "Merchants and Traders" to discuss the letter. The meeting chose a new committee comprised of Campbell, Patterson, T. Smith, and Jesse Hollingsworth—all top merchants—to compose a memorial urging the House of Representatives to fund Jay's Treaty. Soon afterward the instructions that the Baltimore merchants had presented to Congressman Smith appeared in the Philadelphia newspapers.[21]

The merchants had challenged the Mechanical Society. First, there was the question of the appropriation itself. It is impossible to assess the mechanics' opinion on funding the treaty. While Jay's Treaty had been severely criticized, many individuals believed that Congress was duty-bound to implement it once President

Washington had signed the document. Furthermore, certain segments of the mechanic community that depended on active commerce—the shipbuilding trades, for instance—thought the treaty
indispensable to their livelihoods. The best that can be said is that
the mechanic community, though it generally disliked the treaty,
was divided over the issue of appropriations.

More important was the question of the merchants' "instructions." On this issue all mechanics could reach consensus,
regardless of their opinion on the treaty or appropriations. To the
Mechanical Society, the merchants had attempted to dictate to
Baltimore's congressman how he should vote without consulting
the workingmen. It seemed to epitomize the arrogance against
which the mechanics had been struggling, and it could not pass
without protest. On April 21 the board of managers of the Mechanical Society, angered at the "*partial* Notice" that the merchants had issued before their meeting, called an assembly of "all
the Manufacturers and Mechanics of the Town, Fell's Point, and
Precincts."[22]

The gathering took place at Peter Wyant's tavern and was reported to be "a more numerous meeting of the Mechanics and
Manufacturers of Baltimore-Town, precincts, and Fell's Point,
that, was ever known on any occasion." There was a dispute over
the exact attendance. "Candor" claimed only 300 persons attended, nearly all of whom had already signed the merchants' instructions. "Real Candor" rejoined that hundreds of mechanics
who had attended opposed funding. "A Mechanic," who estimated nearly a thousand, captured the indignation that permeated the meeting. "I beg to inform 'Candor,'" he wrote,

> that the mechanic or manufacturer are as much and *more* inter-
> ested in the welfare of this country than any *importing* merchant
> whatsoever. The mechanic depends on his daily exertions for sup-
> port, and any little he lays by to purchase some spot of ground for
> the ease and comfort of his family:—The merchant does all in his
> power to import the manufactured goods, so as to undersell the
> American manufacturer; and by that means he is injuring the cause
> of the country, which, when in danger, his *purse* sends some per-
> haps honest mechanic, whose necessity induced him to come for-
> ward in its defence.

The meeting drew up addresses to the House of Representatives and Congressman Smith, expressing its confidence in their actions. The statements did not, however, attempt to bind them to one position or another on the funding bill; the careful wording bespoke the desire not to alienate those who supported appropriations but resented the instructions. The memorial to the House condemned the merchants' instructions, which seemed "calculated to have an improper influence on the representatives of the people"; it took a swipe at the treaty, "in many respects highly injurious to the interest and honor of the people of the United States"; and it proclaimed "ENTIRE CONFIDENCE" that the representatives would "adopt such measures as will be most conducive to the prosperity of the United States." In a separate letter to Smith the meeting praised his efforts "to preserve the constitution inviolate in the late discussion in the house of representatives."[23]

On April 24 Congressman Smith wrote both groups of constituents. He was effusive in his thanks to the Mechanical Society, "a society at once so numerous and respectable; a society who have always been the supporters of order and good government." He recalled warmly the critical period in 1794 when insurgents in western Pennsylvania rebelled against the excise tax on whiskey and fifty members of the Mechanical Society "did accompany me to quiet the discontents." The merchants received a cool reply. Smith informed them that their worries were unjustified because he had already decided to support the appropriations bill. He then lectured them on the potential abuses of instructions, pointing out that his other constituents in the town and county might become apprehensive about this undue "mercantile influence." The argument between Smith and the merchants dragged on for several weeks, as they disagreed over the exact number of persons who had signed the instructions. On May 1 Congressman Smith lived up to his word and cast his vote in favor of the funding bill, which narrowly passed by fifty votes to forty-eight.[24]

The controversy over Jay's Treaty and appropriation marked a critical turning point in the development of the Republican party in Baltimore. Congressman Smith had solidified his support among the workingmen and the Mechanical Society while estranging a powerful segment of the merchant community. The merchants who had drafted the instructions expected deferential treatment from their representative, not the cavalier handling they had received from Smith. But in 1796 this disgruntled Federalist elite of merchants and lawyers lacked a popular base of support. Thus in October, 1796, Smith easily won re-election to a third term in Congress. The Federalists apparently did not bother fielding a candidate. A month later Baltimore cast nearly 70 percent of its votes for the presidential elector George Duval, a supporter of Thomas Jefferson. To the Federalists Smith seemed to be shepherding Baltimore into the Republican fold while they watched helplessly.

Within a year and a half, however, the political scenario had been reversed. The Federalists seemed to have found the issue to revive their party: the mounting hostility between America and France. In April, 1798, Congress discovered that the French foreign minister Talleyrand through his agents "X, Y, and Z" had demanded a "bribe" from the envoys whom President Adams had sent to negotiate a treaty. The anti-French outpouring that followed the disclosure threatened to ruin the political fortunes of many Republican congressmen, Samuel Smith among them. The Republicans had consistently striven to avoid confrontation with France; they had even accused the president of trying to provoke one to save his faltering party. Now Adams and the Federalists seemed vindicated and the Republicans tainted with disloyalty. In Baltimore, with a congressional election approaching in October, the Federalists looked forward to settling accounts with Smith.[25]

Who would be their standard bearer? The Federalists needed someone who enjoyed widespread appeal, someone who could attract the voters who had traditionally supported Smith. The merchants with whom Smith had clashed were well-known Federalists, which diminished whatever credibility they had among the predominantly Republican voters of Baltimore. Nor were the arch-conservative legalists Luther Martin and Samuel Chase any better choices. In August and September the anti-Smith coalition emerged around the candidacy of James Winchester, one of Baltimore's rising young lawyers. Unlike most of his conservative adherents, Winchester could claim republican credentials: he had been a member of the Republican Society in 1794 and 1795, a representative to the assembly from 1794 to 1796, and an elector to the state senate in 1796. The Smith party called Winchester a political renegade, and there is no doubt that his views, reflected in his actions in the assembly over the incorporation question, had grown more conservative. But the Smith men taxed credibility by calling him a "tory." With Winchester as their man the Federalist elite could assume the mantle of "true patriots" and "true republicans." They could appeal to the voter who had always considered himself a republican, who had supported the Constitution and opposed Jay's Treaty, who had even admired Congressman Smith, but who nonetheless believed that the French depredations on American shipping called for sterner retaliation than their representative seemed prepared to back.[26]

Hotly contested elections had never been gentlemanly in Baltimore. Most townspeople could still remember the fisticuffs in the 1788 election between Chase and McHenry. But the campaign waged by Winchester established a new low in scurrility and abuse. On August 9 Winchester announced his candidacy and declared that he would focus on the issues, not personalities. Under the pen name "A Republican" he maintained that Smith's voting record aligned him with the "enemies of the administration"—Jefferson, Madison, Gallatin, Livingston. He accused Smith of voting against all measures to resist French highhandedness. Even after the disclosures of the XYZ affair, Winchester said, Smith continued to befriend France and opposed a bill that would have abrogated America's treaties with that country. Smith had also voted against the Sedition Act, which Winchester called a "wholesome law."

It soon became clear that Winchester's assault on the public record of his opponent was a prelude to an attack on his character. In August Maryland Senator John Eager Howard disclosed that Smith, while dining at the table of President Adams, had remarked that the American envoys should have paid the bribe, which after all was cheaper than war. "The president answered," according to Howard's account, "that he would not *give* the value of the duty *on a pound of tea!*" The story was published in the newspapers just as Winchester announced his intention to run for office. For the next two months the Smith and Winchester parties printed various accounts of the conversation. Indeed, this single alleged comment became the central issue of the campaign. The final verdict came from Delaware Federalist James A. Bayard, who recalled Smith making some such remark but in jest. Before the campaign had finished, Winchester had also accused Smith of secretly colluding with the French government to obtain special protection for his ships, which turned out to be a flagrant misrepresentation.[27]

Congressman Smith called upon the political allies he had made during the Jay's Treaty controversy. His first appeal to the mechanics came through the militia, for Smith was brigadier general of the Third Maryland Division covering Washington, Frederick, and Baltimore counties in addition to Baltimore City. On August 1 he exhorted Baltimore's militia officers to redouble their efforts to meet enlistment quotas. The timing of the announcement in the newspapers was not fortuitous, nor was the significance of his statement: "let us regard as unworthy, that man, who, at this momentous juncture of our affairs, shall attempt to disseminate the seeds of discord and disunion among a people, who, united, are fully able to repel the attacks of any enemy who may dare to invade their territory."

General Smith trekked back and forth across Baltimore City and County, summoning the troops under his command, reviewing them at regimental and battalion parades, haranguing them with the same message: beware of "discord and disunion." His political ties to the militia became visible in a series of demonstrations before his home. On August 3 Captain Thomas McElderry marched his Republican Company to General Smith's townhouse and dismissed them "as a mark of their approbation of his political conduct, and to shew their attachment to their commander." Three days later the general was treated to a larger show of support. Captain Philip Mosher assembled his Mechanical Volunteers before Smith's home, as did Captain John Chalmers his Friendship Volunteers and Captain James Biays his Fell's Point Troop of Light Dragoons. "This is true Federalism," exclaimed printer Thomas Dobbin of the Republican *Baltimore Telegraphe*: "Men with arms in their hands, against unwarrantable demands of France or any other nation, seeking to unite and to form one solid body in defence of their Independence, rise superior to those, who, by their imprudent conduct, attempt to sow the seeds of discord and disunion among our citizens." General Smith offered his loyal troops cold water which, as one of the privates later admitted, was laced with brandy.[28]

Mechanics had been largely responsible for the militia demonstrations. They commanded three of the four units: Mosher was a blacksmith, Chalmers a ropemaker, Biays a shipbuilder. McElderry was a sugar refiner. Mechanics probably made up most of the troops as well. The Mechanical Volunteers had been organized specifically for skilled workingmen. Founded in 1798, the Friendship Volunteers consisted chiefly of Methodists who were heavily laboring class in composition. Chalmers himself was a Methodist minister and accepted the captaincy only after consulting his fellow churchmen. The Fell's Point Troop of Light Dragoons came from a plebeian section of town, although its exact composition is unknown. These mechanic militiamen were fiercely independent and bridled at attempts to influence their political sentiments. They supported General Smith because he had proven himself a worthy republican, both in his actions during the Revolutionary War and as Baltimore's delegate to the state assembly and to the House of Representatives.

A few days after the militia units had gathered at Smith's house a Winchester supporter asserted in the newspapers that "for militia captains to attempt to turn their companies into political engines to suit their own private views, ought to meet with the detestation of every friend to the community." The following day McElderry, Biays, and Mosher issued a joint rebuttal in the papers: "We declare that the motives that induced us thereto, are with us the free exercise of our own and respectable companies choice, for which we hold ourselves not accountable to any man or set of men." The fiery Chalmers said he would give personal satisfaction to any man who dared challenge him openly. The attack offended the troops as well as the captains. "A Militia Man" wrote: "It is due to the men who compose those companies, to declare to the public, that they are justly classed among our most respectable citizens—that they are, as is the case with all our militia, as independent in their circumstances and in their opinions as their officers—and that the officers would not do any act which to them would not be perfectly agreeable."[29]

The problem facing Winchester was how to weaken Smith's influence among the militia and mechanics. On August 16 he is-

sued a statement in the press attempting to sully the general's
name in the eyes of his troops. In 1794 farmers in western Pennsylvania had rebelled against the "whiskey tax." As commander of
the Third Brigade, General Smith had called for 300 volunteers to
march to Frederick Town to guard the federal arsenal there. Although the turn-out far exceeded Smith's expectations, it became
clear that the militia troops had been unprepared. In early 1795
Smith delivered a speech before the House citing the weaknesses
of the southern militia and urging the adoption of a new national
militia law. Quoting Smith out of context, Winchester attempted
to demonstrate that the general opposed the militia as such. He
accused Smith of charging the troops with cowardice. He even
suggested that the general's speech had the effect of inviting a
"French invasion," overlooking the fact, as Smith pointed out,
that in 1795 America was on the brink of war with England, not
France.

   In reply to Winchester's attack Smith asked why his opponent should suddenly rise to the defense of the militia when he
had never served a day of military duty in his life. Ten militia officers rose in support of their slandered commander, all of whom
had served under Smith in the Frederick Town expedition. Not
only had the general's conduct been exemplary, they said, but the
troops had indeed been "wholly unfit." Once again it was the mechanics who rallied behind the general: of the eight officers whose
occupations are known, John Mackenheimer was a carpenter,
John Weaver a blacksmith, John Allbright and Henry Nagle brickmakers, William Jackson a carter, and John Shrim a cooper. Mackenheimer, Weaver, Nagle, and Shrim were officers of the Mechanical Society.[30]

   As the election approached, the Smith party appealed openly
for mechanic support. On September 25 the newspapers announced a meeting for the following day of "the free, independent
Mechanics and Manufacturers." The statement claimed that "unwarrantable and degrading means" had been used to manipulate
the mechanics' vote, that these "base designs" must be frustrated,
and that the mechanics "have and will maintain an opinion of our
own." The main culprit was evidently merchant John O'Donnell,
a Federalist supporter of Winchester and lieutenant colonel of the
6th Regiment. He had allegedly refused employment to any me-

chanic voting for Smith. The Smith party had a special grievance with O'Donnell. In an effort to paint Smith as a French partisan, O'Donnell testified that in 1795 he had heard the general comment that if "the French were in consequence to invade or land in this country as enemies, he would not oppose, but receive them as friends." Now the Smith men turned O'Donnell's smear tactics against him. O'Donnell denied the charges and printed lists of thirteen mechanics and six tenants who certified that they had never been coerced. The Smith party responded with their own list of four mechanics who swore that O'Donnell had threatened them.

In the pro-Winchester *Federal Gazette* "Impartial" decried the attempt "to excite jealousy and disunion between the merchants and mechanics," whose interests "if not altogether reciprocal, are at least so interwoven, that the one can scarcely do without the support of the other." In the same issue "Mentor" reasoned that Winchester should not be held accountable for the indiscretions committed by his overzealous supporters, but then he committed one of his own by defending the employer's right to hire and fire whomever he pleased. Taking a more politic approach, "A Baltimorean" published a certificate in which shoemaker William Belton testified that Smith had refused him employment ten years before for voting against his wishes. "General Smith," he concluded, "certainly considers the mechanical interest in this city as either devoted blindly to his interest, or as too ignorant to penetrate his absurd schemes for inveigling them."[31]

The mechanics' meeting took place on Wednesday evening, September 26, at the Circus near Philpot's bridge crossing the Falls. Even the pro-Winchester press acknowledged that it was "perhaps, the most numerous ever witnessed in this city." Captain James Biays was elected chairman; William Harris, who a year later was chosen to the board of managers of the Mechanical Society, served as secretary. The meeting issued a statement in the newspapers the next day. Over the previous fifteen years there had been some blunt calls for mechanic unity, but none could match this one in sheer forcefulness. The statement began by asserting the "right of suffrage" that each citizen enjoyed under the constitution. It noted the attempts of "some persons" to subvert the "constitutional right" of the "mechanics." It declared that "the preservation of this privilege inviolate, is the best security to liberty and the surest barrier against the encroachments of aristocracy." The meeting then agreed on three resolutions. First, the mechanics must protest such intimidation because the precedent "will in the course of time grow into practice, and will ultimately convert the laboring part of the community into mere instruments in the hands of the rich, to be used and applied at pleasure at every election." Second, each mechanic must join his brethren in resisting this coercion to save "himself and his posterity the miseries that inevitably spring from an uncontroled and corrupted aristocracy." Finally, the mechanics announced that they would vote for that candidate whom they should "deem most capable to serve us." Never had the mechanics been so unequivocal in their call for "independence" or their denunciation of "aristocracy."[32]

The mechanics defended their independence in the streets as well as the meeting halls. On Thursday evening, September 27, both parties held parades for their candidates. When their paths intersected, the Smith men charged into the ranks of their opponents and dispersed them. General Smith, the opposition newspaper reported, had refused to restrain his partisans. The next day the ever-present Captain Biays led a Smith parade through Fell's Point. A rumor had been circulating that Winchester's supporters included British sailors whose ship was in the basin. When Biays's group came upon a group of sailors, the captain stopped and bellowed: "Stop, gentlemen, the BRITISH SAILORS ARE PASSING." A few Federalist onlookers protested; Biays acted *"very rude and insolent"* toward them. Some of Smith's supporters went beyond rudeness and broke into a private home, scattering a Federalist meeting there. In sum, when the polls opened on Monday morning, October 1, it promised to be a stormy election. There was the inevitable jostling for control of the hustings. The Smith men wore a badge "Smith and liberty" while Winchester's supporters tied a white ribbon around their hats. General Smith, his adversaries claimed, hired the town's chief tavernkeepers to *"keep open house"* for his supporters. The final vote count showed that Smith had defeated Winchester 2,610 to 1,911. He had won 59 percent of the city's 2,223 ballots and 56 percent of the county's 2,298.[33]

It is possible to reconstruct partially the constituencies of each man. Although the polling records are gone, there is a list of 46 men who on September 27 declared themselves for Winchester and another of 394 voters who on November 1 congratulated Smith on his victory. With the exception of ten men including planter Charles Ridgely, all of the Winchester supporters lived in the city. On the other hand, 219 names on the Smith list fail to appear in the city directory of 1798 because they apparently resided in the county. Another 31 Smith men were listed in the directory without occupations, leaving a total of 144 signatures. Thus it is possible to identify 3 percent of the townsmen who voted for Winchester and 11 percent of those who voted for Smith. Presumably these were the voters most committed to their candidates; they at least thought it sufficiently important to sign a statement endorsing them. They were also the ones deemed important enough to be asked to sign; practically no laborers appear on either list. Thus the two lists are far from a representative sampling, but they do seem roughly comparable.[34]

The composition of the parties differed strikingly. Of 35 Winchester supporters who could be identified in the city directories, 63 percent were merchants, 14 percent magistrates, and 11 percent lawyers. The list included only one mechanic, shoemaker William Gibson. Where, then, did Winchester's mass following come from? He had received 901 votes in the city; they could not have all been merchants and lawyers because there weren't that many. A plausible answer was provided by a correspondent who analyzed the constituencies of each party in the newspapers. He claimed that Winchester's supporters were "principally of the great body of mercantile characters, and that part of the mechanical interest connected with commerce, as shipbuilders, &c. and but a very small proportion of other mechanics." Thus Winchester attracted a following among mechanics in the maritime industries who identified their interests with unrestrained commerce and perceived France as a threat to it. Navigation acts encouraging American shipping would provide jobs for ship carpenters, riggers, caulkers, sailmakers, block makers, ship chandlers, and all the tradesmen whose livelihoods depended on these activities.

As for the Smith following, the newspaper correspondent wrote: "In the city the great support of gen. Smith consisted of

mechanics, who are very numerous, and from being united in societies, act systematically." In other words, the mechanics had
provided not just votes but organization as well. An analysis of the
Smith list confirms this impression. Merchants constituted only
29 percent of Smith's supporters; innkeepers, storekeepers, and
grocers 15 percent; physicians, public officials, and other professionals 8 percent; pilots, sea captains, and sailors 5 percent; unskilled laborers 2 percent. The bulk of the votes, 51 percent, came
from mechanics. There were nine shipbuilders, seven carpenters,
six tailors, six blacksmiths, six shoemakers, five hatters, four cabinet makers, three tobacconists, and three saddlers; the remaining
twenty-four voters belonged to nineteen different trades.[35]

Baltimore's mechanics were the backbone of the Republican
party and the leaders of the street politics that emerged in the
1790s. In 1793 the Mechanical Society took a decisive step in establishing itself as the political spokesman for the city's workingmen by issuing a public statement praising the Neutrality Proclamation of President Washington. Within a year a new international
crisis called forth a second vehicle of mechanic political power,
the militia. The intimate links between these two bodies became
evident in May, 1794, when shipbuilder David Stodder, a captain
in the militia and officer of the Mechanical Society, led a series of
crowd actions that escalated into a full-scale confrontation with
the city's judicial authorities. After 1795 the militia and Mechanical Society continued to provide vital support for Congressman
Samuel Smith, the architect of the local Republican party, as he
aligned himself with the opponents of the Washington and Adams
administrations. The mechanics clashed head on with conservative merchants over the questions of funding Jay's Treaty and
"instructing" Congressman Smith. The final contest came in 1798
when Federalists mounted a determined effort to oust Smith from
the office he had held for six years. They failed, thanks largely to
Smith's support among the workingmen. Without the institutional foundation that workingmen established in the militia and
Mechanical Society, Congressman Smith would have been a man
without a party.

NOTES

1. Samuel Flagg Bemis, *Jay's Treaty: A Study in Commerce and Diplomacy*, 2nd ed. (New Haven, Conn., 1962), pp. 28–31; for a good discussion of party development see Frank A. Cassell, "The Structure of Baltimore's Politics in the Age of Jefferson, 1795–1812," in Aubrey C. Land, Lois Green Carr, and Edward C. Papenfuse, eds., *Law, Society, and Politics in Early Maryland* (Baltimore, 1977), pp. 277–96.

2. *Maryland Journal* (Baltimore), May 31, June 18, 1793.

3. *Ibid.*, June 18, 1793.

4. *Ibid.*, Sept. 3, 6, 1793; *Baltimore Daily Repository*, Sept. 4, 1793; *Baltimore Daily Intelligencer*, Apr. 26, May 1, 1794.

5. *Baltimore Daily Repository*, Aug. 8, 1793; *Maryland Journal*, Nov. 8, Dec. 7, 1793, June 27, 1794.

6. *Maryland Journal*, Dec. 7, 1793.

7. *Ibid.*, Feb. 24, 1794; *Federal Intelligencer* (Baltimore), Feb. 24, 1795.

8. *Maryland Journal*, Mar. 19, May 21, 1794; *Edward's Baltimore Daily Advertiser*, July 3, 1794.

9. *Baltimore Daily Intelligencer*, Apr. 30, May 2, 1794; *Maryland Journal*, May 7, 1794.

10. *Maryland Journal*, Mar. 27, May 1, 1788, July 5, 1791; *American* (Baltimore), June 23, 1806; *Baltimore Daily Intelligencer*, Dec. 13, 1793, May 28, 1794; *Federal Gazette* (Baltimore), Sept. 19, 1797; Second Census of the United States, 1800, Baltimore City; Alphabetical Lists of Assessed Persons, 1804, Baltimore County Commissioners, MHR.

11. *Maryland Journal*, May 7, 1794; Report of Samuel Chase to Gov. Thomas Lee, May 6, 1794, Emmet Collection, New York Public Library.

12. Report of Samuel Chase; Samuel Chase, *To the Citizens of Baltimore-Town, May 4, 1794* (Baltimore, 1794), MHS.

13. Report of Samuel Chase.

14. *Ibid.*

15. *Baltimore Daily Intelligencer*, Aug. 26, 1794.

16. Report of Samuel Chase; *Maryland Journal*, Feb. 12, Dec. 13, 1793.

17. *Federal Intelligencer*, July 8, 1795; *Maryland Journal*, July 21, 24, 1795.

18. *Federal Intelligencer*, July 25, 28, Aug. 6, 1795.

19. *Ibid.*, July 28, 1795; *Maryland Journal*, June 9, 1794, Jan. 9, July 7, 1795.

20. Frank A. Cassell, *Merchant Congressman in the Young Republic: Samuel Smith of Maryland, 1752–1839* (Madison, Wis., 1971), pp. 64–66.

21. *Ibid.*, p. 67; *Federal Gazette* (Baltimore), Apr. 18, 20, 22, 1796.

22. *Ibid.*, Apr. 21, May 5, 1796.

23. *Ibid.*, Apr. 22, 23, 25, 27, 1796; *Maryland Journal*, Apr. 25, 1796.

24. Cassell, *Merchant Congressman*, pp. 67–72; *Federal Gazette*, Apr. 28, May 4, 5, 1796.

25. Cassell, *Merchant Congressman*, chap. 6; *Federal Gazette*, Oct. 6, Nov. 14, 1798.

26. *Federal Gazette*, June 29, Sept. 7, 1796; *Maryland Journal*, June 9, 1794, July 7, 1795.

27. *Federal Gazette*, Aug. 9, 24, Sept. 4, 5, 1798. For controversy over alleged comment, see *ibid.*, Aug. 1, 2, 3, 4, 24, Sept. 4, 5, 1798.

28. *Ibid.*, Aug. 1, 1798; *Baltimore Telegraphe*, Aug. 8, 1798.

29. *Baltimore Telegraphe*, July 9, 1798; *Federal Gazette*, Aug. 7, 8, 1798.

30. *Federal Gazette*, Aug. 16, 17, 18, 20, 1798; *Baltimore Daily Intelligencer*, Sept. 15, 22, 23, 25, 1794.

31. *Federal Gazette*, Sept. 8, 25, 26, 29, 1798; *Baltimore Telegraphe*, Sept. 28, 1798.

32. *Federal Gazette*, Sept. 27, 1798.

33. *Ibid.*, Sept. 28, 29, Oct. 1, 2, 3, 1798.

34. *Ibid.*, Sept. 28, Nov. 1, 1798.

35. *Ibid.*, Oct. 5, 1798.

PART THREE

THE CRISIS OF
THE MECHANIC COMMUNITY,
1800–1812

8

PUTTING MECHANICS IN OFFICE

From 1763 to 1800 Baltimore's tradesmen had developed into a cohesive political force through the Mechanical Company, Mechanical Fire Company, Mechanical Volunteers, Whig Club, Association of Tradesmen and Manufacturers, Mechanical Society, and organizations of the carpenters, hatters, shoemakers, and tailors. Their awakening political consciousness was a crucial factor shaping the major events of the period. Mechanics had organized in support of the independence struggle, provided critical support for the Constitution, launched a successful drive for a national protective tariff, spearheaded the movement for a republican city charter, and formed the lifeblood of the Republican party.

After the turn of the century, however, mechanics seemed to lose direction. The clearest reflection of the change was the disappearance of the Mechanical Society, the workingmen's most ambitious institutional experiment in the generation following the Revolution. For the first time since 1785—save for a few years after 1789—mechanics lacked a representative organization cutting across craft lines and citywide in scope. Although workingmen still exerted political power, it became localized in neighborhoods where they predominated. Ward 7 became the mechanics' stronghold, encompassing the lower half of Old Town and the upper half of Fell's Point. From 1797 to 1812 virtually all of the ward's councilmen in the First Branch were mechanics; after 1808, when property qualifications were reduced, mechanics broke into the exclusive Second Branch as well. The first mechanic was elected to the assembly in 1806 and re-elected two times. Not surprisingly, stone cutter Robert Steuart drew most of his support from Ward 7 where he lived. Finally, the city's mechanics sent one of their own to the House of Representatives. In

1810 they helped elect Peter Little, a watch and clock maker, to Congress from the 12th District covering Baltimore City and County. Thus, even as the citywide mechanic movement fragmented and grew more localized after 1800, workingmen exploited their strength in Ward 7 to put fellow tradesmen in office.

In 1800 the Mechanical Society quietly dissolved. No longer did the newspapers print its annual list of officers, announcements of quarterly meetings, appeals for arrears—the bits and pieces of evidence that had illuminated its activities since 1792. No one even noted that the society had gone, much less asked why. In February, 1800, the papers carried a call for a meeting of the prospective members of the "Baltimore Mechanical Commercial Company," where "the constitution prepared by the committee, will be laid before them." This new organization was never heard from again; perhaps it was a last-ditch effort to salvage something from the society.[1]

What happened to the Mechanical Society? The fact is, we don't know. The society left no records, aside from what occasionally surfaced in the newspapers. All we can do is guess at the reasons behind the society's demise, but two guesses seem plausible. First, the crisis in foreign affairs that had been one of the factors precipitating the formation of the Mechanical Society had passed by the turn of the century. The prospect of another war with Great Britain ebbed after Jay's Treaty went into effect, while the undeclared naval war against France was over by 1800. With Jefferson's ascendancy to the presidency, the signing of a new treaty with France, and a truce between the major warring powers, America seemed on the threshold of a new era of diplomatic tranquility. Born in war, the Mechanical Society died in peace.

Second, the gloomy economic environment that had encouraged mechanics to organize for mutual assistance had brightened by 1800. It is no coincidence that the Mechanical Society appeared at the same time as the associations of carpenters, hatters, shoemakers, and tailors. With prices rising rapidly craftsmen needed help, which the benefit funds of these associations were designed to provide. Nor is it a coincidence that the Mechanical Society was most active during the era of the first journeymen strikes for higher wages. In the half-decade after 1800 there were no strikes. Only one new tradesmen's association formed. In other words, things were looking better at home and abroad; the Mechanical Society probably disbanded in 1800 because it had little to do.

The end of the Mechanical Society did not signal the collapse of the mechanics as a political force. On the contrary. Their political base shifted to those parts of the city where mechanics enjoyed the advantage of numbers. Baltimore was divided into eight wards of roughly equal populations. Wards 1 through 5 covered the heart of the city west of Jones' Falls; here was the largest concentration of wealthy merchants, lawyers, and professionals. Ward 6 encompassed the northern part of Old Town above York Street, a largely mechanic community. Ward 7 included the southern half of Old Town and Fell's· Point north of Allisanna Street, attracting the greatest concentration of craftsmen. Ward 8 covered the waterfront of Fell's Point south of Allisanna, the home of the shipbuilders and workingmen in the maritime trades. Mechanic candidates for office could always count on the solid backing of Ward 7, a good showing in Ward 6, and occasional support from Ward 8. On the other hand, Wards 1 through 5 were in the hands of merchants.

The wards developed distinctive styles of local leadership reflected in the First Branch of the city council. In October every year the qualified voters in each ward chose two representatives to the First Branch, who had to meet a property qualification of $1,000 from 1797 to 1808 and $300 afterwards. From 1797 to 1812 ninety-one men served in the First Branch. The average term in office was two and a half years. Typically, about ten of the sixteen councilmen elected each October had served the year before; the most turnover came in 1803 when thirteen new men were elected, the least in 1809 when only two new faces appeared in the First Branch. Ward 1 was most apt to put a new man in office, electing a total of fifteen different representatives to the First Branch. Wards 5 and 6 exhibited the greatest continuity, as each returned only eight individuals to the council. Eight terms was the most any single man served; merchants James Carey of Ward 2, William Lorman of Ward 3, and Thomas Kell of Ward 4 shared that honor. By contrast, the heavily mechanic Ward 7 did not let anyone stay in power over five years, less than any of the other wards. Mechanics seem to have been expressing their distrust for permanent office holding, a major theme of their own defeated charter proposal.[2]

Leadership mirrored the wards' social composition. In Wards 1, 2, and 3 merchants dominated the First Branch while occasionally making room for such prominent mechanics as nailmaker Richardson Stewart, brickmaker Benjamin Berry, and tailor John McCannon (see Table 16). Merchants and professionals also held most of the positions in Wards 4, 5, and 6, although mechanics took more than a third. One of the favorites of Ward 5 was cooper John Shrim, who served six terms along with merchant Baltzer Schaeffer. Another popular mechanic representative from Ward 6 was carpenter John Mackenheimer, who sat in the council five years. In Ward 7 mechanics practically monopolized office. Indeed, the only nonmechanics to win elections there were clerk John Rutter and merchant Philip Moore, neither of whom served more than one term. The leading office holders were stone cutter Robert Steuart (five terms), brushmaker Frederick Shaeffer (five), stone cutter William Steuart (four), and carpenter Joshua Ennis (four). In Ward 8 the composition of the First Branch reflected the presence of a powerful shipbuilding community, which supplied the largest single group of representatives. Most of the mechanics elected to the First Branch were familiar figures: fourteen of the forty who had served as officers of the Mechanical Society from 1793 to 1800 won seats in the council. In Ward 7 the former officers accounted for four of the twelve councilmen and thirteen of the thirty terms.

The mechanics were Republican party stalwarts before 1800 and remained so afterward. Ward 7 was synonymous with Republicanism. After 1800, when the city newspapers began publishing voting returns on a ward-by-ward basis, the clearest indicators of party strength were presidential and congressional elections. In these high-level contests Republicans held about a three-to-one advantage over their rival. In 1800 they ran George Duval as presidential elector against the Federalists' Jeremiah T. Chase and won 77 percent of the city's votes. Duval routed Chase east of the Falls, drawing his greatest support from the heavily mechanic Ward 6 with 89 percent and Ward 7 with 90 percent. He also ran strongly in Ward 5, just across the Falls in Baltimore, with 83 percent and

TABLE 16
COMPOSITION OF FIRST BRANCH OF CITY COUNCIL
(in terms): 1797–1811

Ward	Mechanics	Merchants	Professionals	Shipbuilders
1	4	26		
2	3	26	1	
3	3	25	2	
4	10	10	10	
5	13	17		
6	11	19		
7	28	1	1	
8	9	6	4	11

SOURCES: *Federal Gazette* (Baltimore), Feb. 21, 1797, Oct. 2, 1798, Oct. 8, 1799, Oct. 7, 1800, Oct. 6, 1801, Oct. 5, 1802, Oct. 4, 1803, Oct. 2, 1804, Oct. 6, 1807, Oct. 4, 1809, Oct. 3, 1810; *Baltimore American*, Oct. 8, 1805, Oct. 7, 1806, Oct. 7, 1808, Oct. 8, 1811. For occupations, see the various city directories published from 1797 to 1815.

in Ward 8 with 84 percent. Duval's showing fell off markedly in the merchant-dominated neighborhoods: 66 percent in Ward 1, 73 percent in Ward 2, 50 percent in Ward 3 (losing by one vote), and 68 percent in Ward 4.

It is not possible to analyze the 1804 and 1808 presidential elections because Federalists did not run a candidate. The congressional elections, though, reveal a similar pattern. Only once from 1800 to 1812 did Federalists attempt to unseat the two Republican congressmen representing Baltimore City and County. In 1808 they backed William H. Winder against the Republican incumbents, Alexander McKim and Nicholas R. Moore. The Republicans triumphed with 3,500 votes each to their opponent's 814. They did best in the mechanic wards. Winder was 439 votes behind the second-place finisher in Ward 6, 671 in Ward 7, and 575 in Ward 8. He also lost the downtown wards but by smaller margins: 382 in Ward 1, 188 in Ward 2, 88 in Ward 3, 171 in Ward 4, and 215 in Ward 5.[3]

Their support in the mechanic wards was crucial to the Republicans in the more evenly balanced state assembly and senate elections. The sectional voting pattern resulting from strong neighborhood loyalties became evident in two canvasses taken by the Federalist *Federal Gazette*. In May, 1802, the editors asked townsmen how they had voted in the October assembly elections.

Their figures, though unofficial for Wards 5 and 6, could "be relied on as correct within a few votes either way." The Federalists had a 70-vote advantage in Ward 1, 157 in Ward 2, 156 in Ward 3, and 3 in Ward 4; the Republicans controlled Ward 5 by 150 votes, Ward 6 by 500, and Ward 7 by 440. The *Gazette* did not offer an estimate for Ward 8. Four years later the paper published the results of a second canvass, noting that it was not "official." The Federalists had preserved a 295-vote lead in Ward 1, 245 in Ward 2, and 145 in Ward 3. They had lost Ward 4 by 64 votes. Republican voters outnumbered Federalists in Ward 5 by 332, Ward 6 by 207, and Ward 7 by 401. One estimate gave the Republicans a 170-vote edge in Ward 8, another 55.

Whatever the exact vote count, which fluctuated from election to election, the canvasses underlined the sectional political alignment that had developed in assembly elections by the early nineteenth century. The same held true for the state senate elections. In 1806 the Republicans backed Alexander McKim as elector of the senate against Federalist John Hillen. McKim won the election with 60 percent of the city's votes but lost most of the downtown wards. He received only 40 percent of the votes in Ward 1, 37 percent in Ward 2, 37 percent in Ward 3, and 50 percent in Ward 5 (losing by a vote). He took Ward 4 with 55 percent. The eastern half of the city saved McKim from defeat, giving him 63 percent in Ward 6, 92 percent in Ward 7, and 88 percent in Ward 8. In short, on the key Old Town and Fell's Point wards hinged the Republicans' control of the assembly and senate delegation.[4]

Ward 7 mechanics were more than Republicans; they were "independent" Republicans. After 1800 the Republican party splintered as the different interests it embraced sought to divide the spoils of victory. In Baltimore this factionalization was not a fight between elites; it resulted largely from the determination of Ward 7 mechanics to elect brother workmen as assemblymen and later as congressmen. In the fall of 1804 the city's mechanics drew up a petition to the assembly. What the petition said is unclear. In any case the mechanics convinced two assembly candidates to endorse the measure: Andrew Ellicott and Jesse Hollingsworth. Ellicott owned large flour milling operations outside the city, which made him sympathetic with Baltimore's manufacturing interests. Hollingsworth was a merchant specializing in the grain trade. Both men were moderate Federalists. Many mechanics were ready to overlook their politics, however, because none of the regular party nominees—merchants Thomas Dixon and Cumberland Dugan and lawyer John Stephen—would apparently endorse the petition.

On September 15 "A Mechanic" wrote in the Federalist newspapers urging all townspeople to elect Ellicott and Hollingsworth, "who will support the petition of the mechanics." The same day in the Republican press "A Carpenter, A Blacksmith, A Stone-Cutter, A Mason" also declared their support for Hollingsworth. "We are informed," they said, "he is favorable to a petition of the Mechanics which will be brought before the legislature at their next session, and we believe him as competent to represent this city as any man in it." On September 17 the *American* printed a piece by "A native Mechanic" recommending the candidacies of Ellicott and Hollingsworth, "who will support the view of the Mechanics." A week later "Anvil" agreed that mechanics should nominate their own candidates. "The mechanics intend to make a bold push," he wrote, "for some member this year to advocate their petitions." But "Anvil" feared that the politics of Ellicott and Hollingsworth might estrange too many Republican workmen. He therefore nominated mechanic Jacob Small, whose candidacy never got off the ground.[5]

The 1804 assembly election posed the gravest threat to Republican unity since the 1798 congressional election. The Republican press warned the mechanics about the dangers of breaking ranks. "Why have the republicans struggled so long to turn out the federalists from power," asked "Mediator," "if they are immediately to quarrel with each other about the division of it." "Manlius Curius" predicted dire consequences if Federalists should "worm themselves into our state legislature" by using "the specious pretext of supporting a popular measure." On the day before the election another plea came from "None of your WHITE RIBBAND Gentry." "The known attachment of the Mechanic interest of this city," he declared, "to our worthy president Jefferson, will, it is presumed, not suffer a single vote to be given to any man inimical to his government."

The Republican leaders—especially William Pechin, editor

of the *American* and a future assemblyman himself—did not stop
at rhetoric. They attempted to erect local machinery that could
guarantee party unity while undercutting the mechanics' independent behavior. On September 13 he proposed "a systematized
plan, which would secure a *satisfactory* chance of pointing out
such candidates as would be generally pleasing, and of course
more unanimously supported." He suggested that the "democratic republicans" hold meetings in each of the wards. These
gatherings would appoint two "conferees" to a citywide meeting.
There the assembled conferees would nominate two official Republican candidates for the assembly. On September 24, a week
before the polls opened, ward meetings took place across the city.
Although they failed to reach complete agreement, scattering
their nominations among Stephen, Dixon, and Dugan, they did
reject the candidacy of Ellicott. Hollingsworth decided to withdraw from the race. The citywide convention never materialized.[6]

Ignoring the Republican injunctions and official nominations, Ward 7 gave the election to Ellicott. The final results were
close: Stephen 1,542, Ellicott, 1,192, Dixon 1,001, and Dugan
336. Not surprisingly, Ellicott ran well where the Federalists had
traditionally been strong. In Wards 2 and 3 he placed first among
the four candidates; in Wards 1, 4, and 5 he placed second. Also
in keeping with traditional voting patterns, Ellicott did badly in
the Republican strongholds of Wards 6 and 8, where he placed a
distant third. This left Ward 7. If the ward's mechanics had followed normal voting behavior, Ellicott would probably have lost
the election to Dixon. But Ward 7 broke from custom. It gave
Ellicott 174 votes, second only to Stephen's 209 and ahead of
Dixon's 142 and Dugan's 110. Ellicott's success is more remarkable because on September 24 the Ward 7 "democratic republicans" had nominated Dixon and Dugan, the two candidates who
came in last. The Republican leadership had tried and failed to
stop Ward 7's mechanics from bolting.

Both the Federalist editor Mathew Brown of the *Gazette* and
Pechin of the *American* were partially correct in their assessments of the election. "Mr. Ellicott," Brown noted, "was not
chosen because he is called a *federalist*; nor Mr. Stephen, entirely, for being called a *republican*; but because, for good reasons, they were thought most fit." Pechin wrote that Ellicott "is

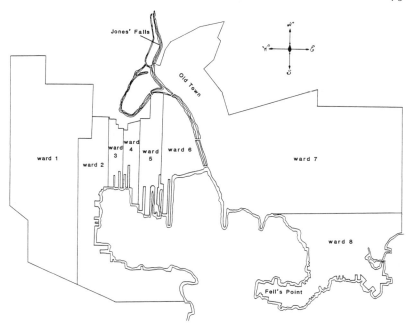

Baltimore City Wards.

said 'of no party, and not brought forward by a party'—but be this as it may, it is certain he owes his election, in a great measure, to the republican party!" Both editors failed to note that Ellicott's victory stemmed chiefly from the resolve of Ward 7 and mechanics to pursue their own interests even in defiance of the established Republican leadership.[7]

The Republican disunity exposed in Ellicott's election only deepened as Ward 7's mechanics continued to assert their political independence. In 1805 they nominated a fellow mechanic to the assembly, stone cutter Robert Steuart. Born in Scotland in 1745, Steuart arrived in America at the age of twenty-three. He and his brother, Hugh, had contracted to cut stone at Nottingham Iron Works close to Baltimore town. They each received an annual payment to keep the works in good order and were free to take other jobs in their spare time. After the war Steuart established a stone cutting business in Baltimore. By 1791 he was bragging in the local newspapers that his quarry was "of the finest Quality of Freestone, and his Work on the most reduced Prices— cheaper than any on the Continent." Steuart even published a list of prices, an uncommonly bold practice in eighteenth-century advertising. He invited orders from all the neighboring states. In 1815 Steuart's estate was assessed at $1,160, placing him in the top 20 percent of the city's property holders. Like many successful mechanics in the construction trades, he eventually rose to the status of a professional contractor and builder. In the 1824 city directory Steuart called himself an "architect" after twenty-eight years of listing himself a "stone cutter." After he died in 1826 his son, Robert Jr., apparently carried on the family business.[8]

By the eve of the 1805 election Robert Steuart had become Ward 7's leading spokesman. His political career encapsulated a generation of change in the mechanic community. He got his first taste of public life in the mechanic associations. In the 1790s he was an officer of the Mechanical Society, first as a manager and later as vice-president. During the same years he served as a staff man in the Mechanical Fire Company. Finally, in 1806 Steuart was elected to the first board of directors of the Mechanics' Bank, a position he filled regularly thereafter. Steuart's career also illustrated the political links between mechanics and Ward 7. From the mid-1790s until his death Steuart lived on Duke Street, in the heart of Ward 7. At a time of great residential mobility Steuart chose to stay put. It was a politically significant ploy, for he was proving his loyalty to Ward 7. Steuart became a familiar face in the neighborhood. From 1797 to 1805 Steuart was elected to the First Branch five times; no other individual from Ward 7 could match this record. In 1805 he was named the ward's collector of poor relief, which acquainted him with the indigent families of the neighborhood. In the same year Steuart received an appointment to collect subscriptions in Ward 7 for the newly organized School of Industry, a project to employ the city's destitute women and children. As was natural for a Ward 7 mechanic, Steuart rose in the Republican party. In 1807 he won election as Sachem of Jersey for the Tammany Society, an organization with strong ties to the Republican party.[9]

The mechanics had found a good candidate in Robert Steuart. He was sixty years old, a proven mechanic spokesman, a leader of Ward 7, and an unequivocal Republican. But past experience underscored the difficulties in electing a mechanic to the assembly. From 1776 to 1805 twenty-eight assembly elections had been held in Baltimore; merchants, lawyers, and physicians had won them all. Twenty-eight men in all had represented the city in the assembly. Their term in office was usually brief: fifteen had served one term, nine two, and three three. Only lawyer David McMechen could be said to have made a career in the assembly, sitting in the House of Delegates for fourteen years. Periodically mechanics had attempted to break this monopoly but without success. In 1792 mechanic Thomas Coulson lost a bid for an assembly seat as did nail maker Richardson Stewart three years later. In 1797 card maker Adam Fonerden actually won in a four-man race, but for unknown reasons the assembly overturned the election and issued a warrant for a new one. In the meantime Fonerden decided to withdraw from the new race because his wife had died, which enabled lawyer Walter Dorsey to take the seat he had lost to Fonerden a few months before. Whether these three mechanics appealed directy to skilled workingmen by claiming to represent their interests is unclear. That each of them was an officer in the Mechanical Society suggests as much: Fonerden was a president, Coulson a vice-president, Stewart a manager.[10]

In some respects Steuart's candidacy posed a more difficult dilemma for the Republican leadership than Ellicott's had. At least Ellicott could be attacked as a Federalist; Steuart obviously could not be. The Republicans revived the ward meetings devised a year earlier to forge party discipline. A few days before the election Ward 7's Republicans nominated Steuart to the assembly and also appointed a committee to confer with other ward representatives "in order to form a unanimity of sentiment throughout the city, with respect to assemblymen." "A Mechanic" writing in the *American* suggested that workingmen and merchants, the two major groups in the Republican party, split the assembly ticket. He hoped that "every mechanic will step forward at the next election and support Robert Steuart, and some worthy merchant in whom we may confide—a true republican, of as good sound principles as the worthy Steuart."

This compromise presupposed a greater degree of unity than the Republicans could summon. By election day six men in addition to the two incumbents had declared their candidacies. A number of Republicans accused Steuart of endangering the party's chances to oust Federalist Ellicott by pursuing his own selfish goals. "Though he might have held his pretensions as good or better than others," wrote a correspondent in the *American* about the stone cutter, "yet whoever was most actuated by a regard to public good, would have sacrificed his personal claims, even to those who were less wise, less furnished with legislative knowledge, if no doubt of principle existed, rather than to bear a part in defeating the true friends of equal liberty." But what the writer found more alarming was the thought that mechanics were striking out on their own and forming a separate "interest." He attacked a nomination that

> calls on the mechanics of Baltimore, to set up a separate interest from their fellow-citizens; to unite for that purpose in opposition to others and send a member to the legislature on their own behalf. Has any one class of citizens such a privilege? are we not all involved in one interest? or has any body of men so narrow a view of a legislator's function as to think of sending a man with a mind confined to the interest of a part?[11]

With eight men campaigning for the same votes, the Republicans could reach no agreement on candidates. To the chagrin of the Republican leadership, Ellicott not only won re-election with Stephen, but placed first. In general the voting pattern fell along predictable lines. Ellicott again based his support in the downtown wards, running ahead of the pack in Wards 1 and 2 while placing second in Wards 3, 4, and 5. The key realignment occurred in Ward 7. There Steuart won an overwhelming victory with 258 votes. On the other hand, Ward 7 gave only 53 votes to Ellicott, whose victory a year before had stemmed largely from its support. Out of every five votes cast for Steuart, two came from Ward 7 (see Table 17). Republican factionalism had once again produced a Federalist victory. Even editor Brown admitted that the election results flowed from "*divisions* among *democratic republicans.*"[12]

In 1806 Robert Steuart was back in the race. The mechanics had not been discouraged by the preceding year's defeat but, rather, redoubled their efforts to put their man in office. On August 22, several weeks before the other candidates stepped forward, the *Gazette* printed an announcement of Steuart's intention to renew his bid for an assembly seat. Eight days later the

TABLE 17
WARD SUPPORT OF ROBERT STEUART: 1805–10

Ward	1805	1806	1807	1808	1809	1810
1	4%	17%	10%	16%	14%	13%
2	4	11	11	10	11	11
3	4	7	5	8	11	7
4	5	8	7	6	9	4
5	9	9	9	8	8	9
6	22	21	19	14	17	13
7	39	21	32	21	23	30
8	13	6	7	17	7	13
Total	100%	100%	100%	100%	100%	100%
Votes	654	1,170	633	3,317	2,075	1,455

SOURCES: *Baltimore American*, Oct. 8, 1805, Oct. 7, 1806, Oct. 6, 1807, Oct. 3, 1809, Oct. 2, 1810; *Federal Gazette* (Baltimore), Oct. 4, 1808.

American printed a similar statement: "it is hoped that the republicans in general, and the mechanics of Baltimore, in particular, will keep in view ROBERT STEWART, as a candidate for a representative in the legislature of the State."

Steuart came under attack from two directions. First, his opponents questioned his integrity. It was rumored that during the Revolution Steuart had refused to swear a loyalty oath to the new government, choosing instead to pay the "treble tax" on non-associators. The facts of the case were disputed because a fire had since destroyed the relevant state records. Steuart insisted that he had taken the oath. He cited as evidence his patriotic service as a militia ensign in the Gunpowder Company during the war. Furthermore, he challenged the motives of his chief accuser, William C. Gouldsmith, who had belonged to the same Gunpowder Company. Gouldsmith had run for the position of ensign and lost. Immediately afterward he accused Steuart of toryism. Steuart had demanded a court-martial to clear his name, which unanimously exonerated him of the charges. But the questions about his wartime behavior never completely died down. As late as 1810 Steuart was still defending his actions. He admitted to having known several fellow Scotchmen who refused to swear the oath; he might even have signed a petition praying that they be relieved of the treble tax. But Steuart reiterated: "I was on the side of the whigs then; and I trust I am a whig still."[13]

Steuart also received criticism for overstepping the bounds of a mechanic. Like nearly all workingmen, he did not have a formal education. Some elitists argued that Steuart lacked the refinement necessary for the legislature. Such was the argument of "W.," who on August 30 published an attack on Steuart that by implication questioned the ability of any mechanic to hold political office. His description of the ideal legislator left little doubt that he had a lawyer in mind: "Men, sir, of experience and reading in such cases should be called upon to conduct the affairs of state.—Men, sir, who have spent their earlier and juvenile years in diving into [the law's] mysteries." To "W.," Steuart not only wanted education; he also lacked detachment and disinterestedness. "Why degrade our political reputation," he asked, "and put in the power of artful designing delegates to act as to them shall seem most and most conducive to their own interests."[14]

Such sentiments provoked mechanics to justify their demands for political representation. On September 26 "A Rough Mechanic" declared that his fellow workingmen had the same right to nominate candidates "as the *learned* and mercantile part." He believed that the opinions of "W." threatened the mechanics' "prerogative of freemen, a right to equal representation." He claimed that the mechanic might lack a refined upbringing, but that did not prevent him from proving his courage at arms "whilst the *well-born* gentry would be too much engaged in expounding the law, and filling their coffers from the public distress, to take the smallest share of the danger." "The sons of labour," concluded "A Rough Mechanic," "will never shrink from danger in the field of battle, nor will I suppose them capable of dereliction of republican principle." The *American* printed a few lines of verse aimed at "W.":

> So would a royal monarch scorn
> Any but those that's nobly born . . .
> Them few rash lines shall d—— thy name,
> And blast thy hopes of future fame—
>   With the Plebeians.

But the piece that best illuminated the values of the "*Plebeians*" came from the pen of "Q in the Corner." He emphasized the unique attributes that belonged to the mechanics, none of which could be bought with a formal education or large fortune.

> Robt. Stewart, a mechanic, and one who believes, as every real republican ought to believe—that high birth does not give talents; that the son of a king may be a fool and the son of a blacksmith a man of sense—that a mechanic possesses as much discernment as a lawyer and is as competent to know the real interests of his country.
>
> Robert Stewart is a man who by honest industry has accumulated an independence, who wants neither *place*, office nor patronage from the governor, and wishes nothing more than the prosperity of this city, and the mechanic interest particularly.[15]

Once again the Republicans struggled in vain to agree on candidates. As early as June Pechin had refused to publish nominations that did not identify party affiliation, hoping thereby to prevent Federalists from concealing their politics. Pechin emerged as the leading spokesman for the conferee system, which he seems to have envisioned as a means to undermine the candidacy of independents like Steuart. On September 18 the "democratic republicans" of Wards 7 and 8 held meetings nominating a pair of lawyers, W. G. D. Worthington and Elias Glenn. The secretary of the meeting was Leonard Frailey, Pechin's partner and co-editor of the *American*. The meeting's chairman was Joseph Allender, a prominent physician and councilman from Fell's Point. By contrast, the ward meeting which a year before had nominated Steuart was chaired by brushmaker Frederick Shaeffer with carpenter Ludwig Herring as secretary.

The nomination of Worthington and Glenn was evidently unacceptable because a week later Republicans were still arguing about candidates. On September 25 they held a citywide meeting. According to a Federalist observer who attended, five candidates were considered: Steuart, Glenn, Worthington, Edward Aisquith, and Joel Munson. Nothing was decided; only Glenn and Munson had appeared. Pechin objected to this abandonment of the conferee system, reasoning that "it must be evident, that in such a promiscuous meeting as must necessarily take place, a number of hostile or clashing interests will almost preclude the chance of giving decision or force to any nomination which can be made."

A few days later a second citywide meeting took place, from

which Federalists were barred. The Republican *Telegraphe* reported that while a "considerable majority appeared to be in favor of ELIAS GLENN and THEODORIC BLAND, Esq's," the party members decided to stage ward meetings on October 2. Bland was yet another lawyer. The wards appointed conferees who a few days later nominated Glenn and Bland. According to "Peeping Tom," the conferees "consisted of feds, quids, and a few democratic republicans." The vote was Glenn twenty-one, Bland fourteen, Fonerden twelve, and Steuart nine; Aisquith, surprisingly, was passed over completely. Conferees were still a new device in Baltimore and not entirely accepted by either Federalists, who feared Republican organization of any sort, or many Republicans, who distrusted the formalized and centralized power the conferee system implied. On October 6 a broadside circulated through the city, addressed "To the INDEPENDENT Voters of Baltimore," conveying a resentment against the innovation that crossed party lines: "Call them *Conferees, Electors*, or what you will, they are DICTATORS in essence: and however modestly they may christen their assembly, their views are dangerous, and their system destructive to Freedom."[16]

Thus two groups had aligned themselves against the mechanics' candidate: the Federalists, from whom the Republican Steuart could expect little support, and the Republican conferees, who had rejected the upstart candidate. Yet Steuart won with 1,170 votes, and Aisquith with 1,430. The Republican conferees had once again failed to generate much enthusiasm for their nominees: of the eight candidates, Glenn placed fourth with 884 votes and Bland sixth with 439. For three consecutive years they had been rebuffed by Republican voters, suggesting how divided the party leadership and rank-and-file had become. But this same disunity was key to Steuart's victory. Eight men had entered the race, nearly all of whom had Republican credentials. They split the vote, enabling Steuart to win with only 20 percent of the city's ballots. No less important in the stone cutter's successful campaign was his Ward 7 constituency. In only two wards did Steuart run ahead of his opponents: Wards 6 and 7, which together gave him 40 percent of his total vote (see Table 17). [17]

These two factors—party factionalism and Ward 7 support—

accounted for Steuart's re-election to the assembly in 1807 and 1808. Republican leadership could not limit the number of candidates, nine of whom campaigned in 1807 and five in 1808. In 1807 Steuart won with a mere 15 percent of the city vote, although the figure rose to 41 percent a year later. Ward 7 consistently gave him the necessary votes to win, despite his poor showing in the downtown wards. By 1809 Steuart was ready to retire from office and offered to step down if another mechanic candidate would declare himself. None did and Steuart returned to the hustings. But the special circumstances contributing to his victories from 1806 through 1808 had dissolved; the Republicans had finally succeeded in narrowing the field to two candidates, Bland and Worthington. Steuart still had his Ward 7 backing, but no longer could he count on Republicans elsewhere splitting the vote. Thus, although he received 29 percent of the vote in 1809, he lost the election. Steuart tried again the next year but again the Republican party had rallied around two candidates. He lost with 26 percent of the vote. Perhaps the blow of the defeat was softened by the fact that the two victors included James Martin, a tailor, who carried on the mechanics' representation in the assembly. By any standard Steuart's career in the assembly was impressive. Of the thirty-three assemblymen who represented Baltimore from 1777 through 1810, only four could match Steuart's three terms in office and only one could exceed it.[18]

In 1810 the mechanics culminated the drive to open the doors that had kept them from political office. In that year Peter Little, a watch maker and silversmith who resided on the city's outskirts, declared he would seek election to Congress from the 12th Maryland District, which covered the city and county. Born in Pennsylvania in 1775, Little had migrated to Baltimore at the age of fourteen. In 1806 he was elected to the assembly from Baltimore County. His campaign had revealed the outlines of a political coalition that would resurface in 1810. Little first announced his intention to fight for legislation that would benefit the precincts, whose inhabitants believed they paid the costs of city government without enjoying the advantages. He also wooed the mechanics' vote. Writing in the *American*, "Sincerity" assured workingmen that they could trust a brother like Little: "the industrious habits of his life insure his regard for the conveniences of that class of the community who most deserve legislative attention and protection."

Four years later Little was again profiting from the alliance of the precincts and mechanics. The two incumbents, Alexander McKim and Nicholas R. Moore, were under fire as "submission men" because they had voted to abrogate the Embargo Act. Many mechanics believed the act, or something like it, would protect them against competition from British imports. At a meeting of the candidates on September 12, Little emphasized his commitment to American manufacturing and "condemned in general terms the conduct of the 10th and 11th Congress for want of energy and professed himself an advocate of stronger measures." Several weeks earlier "A Mechanic *of Baltimore*" wrote of Little:

> It is true he is a mechanic: the interests of the class of citizens now struggling for a competition with the mammoth of England, as well as the manufacturers, appear to have been lost sight of in the zeal for the commercial, although believed they are inseparably connected with our independence. . . . Amongst the citizens of Baltimore I feel no wish to draw a line of distinction, yet it has not unfrequently been made an objection, (*upon the nomination of one*) "why he's a mechanic," as carrying with it something degrading; such conduct should not be: are not mechanics as worthy members in society as others? It is true, few are born great men, or receive the advantages of a liberal education; yet many possess abilities in an eminent degree.

"A Mechanic" was battling against the same prejudices that had hampered Steuart in his first campaigns. "I know that it may be considered as mortifying by many lofty heads," wrote "One of the People," "that a man from his humble sphere of life should be named as a representative to the general government, but it is a feeling of which the great body of the people by no means partake and one that is unworthy of comment."[19]

Little won the election along with another critic of the "submission men," ship captain Joshua Barney. The voting returns highlighted the mechanic-precinct coalition. Little and Barney carried Ward 1 by large majorities. This ward abutted the western precincts and shared many of its concerns; that Little resided in the area and had represented its interests in the state legislature solidified his support there. Little's second base of support was Ward 7, where he received 415 votes, more than any candidate in any ward. His call for stronger measures against Great Britain, his commitment to American manufacturing, and his status as a mechanic contributed to his overwhelming victory in the workingmen's ward. Together, Wards 1 and 7 gave Little 45 percent of the votes he garnered in the city. Without that backing he might have been defeated. In Wards 2, 3, and 4 he placed last among the candidates; although he ranked among the leaders in Wards 5, 6, and 8, he did not gather enough votes to offset the losses downtown.[20]

The nineteenth century brought great changes for the mechanics of Baltimore. As the European upheaval that had convulsed American politics during the 1790s subsided and the economic insecurity facing many workingmen diminished, the mechanics abandoned their greatest institutional innovation of the early national era. The dissolution of the Mechanical Society in 1800 left workingmen without a common point around which to organize citywide. Their political power receded into the heavily mechanic neighborhoods, Ward 7 above all, from which workingmen mobilized to elect their brethren to office. They turned first to the local level and from 1797 to 1812 filled the First Branch of the city council with mechanics. Next they leveled their sights on the state assembly. After several unsuccessful attempts to place a mechanic in the legislature, the workingmen finally elected stone cutter Robert Steuart to the assembly. From 1806 through 1808 Steuart owed his assembly seat to friends, neighbors, and mechanics in Ward 7. By 1810 mechanics were prepared to make a bid for national office. Forging a political alliance between Ward 7's mechanics and the inhabitants of the precincts outside the city, watch maker and silversmith Peter Little campaigned successfully for a seat in Congress by advocating stronger measures in defense of America's manufacturing interests. After 1800 Ward 7 inherited the leadership once held by the Association of Tradesmen and Manufacturers and the Mechanical Society. Lacking the citywide base of those organizations, it nonetheless did what they had been unable to do: put mechanics in office.

NOTES

1. *Federal Gazette* (Baltimore) Feb. 12, 1800.

2. For residential patterns, see chap. 1. In his analysis of the First Branch, Gary Lawson Browne finds that between 1797 and 1815, 10 of 66 members (15 percent) were "manufacturers." My own figures indicate that from 1797 through 1811, 240 terms were served on the First Branch, 81 (34 percent) by mechanics. See *Baltimore in the New Nation, 1789–1861* (Chapel Hill, N.C., 1980), pp. 42–46.

3. *Federal Gazette*, Nov. 11, 1800, Oct. 4, 1808; *American* (Baltimore), July 14, 1808.

4. *Federal Gazette*, May 2, 1803, May 5, 1807, Sept. 2, 1806.

5. *Ibid.*, Sept. 15, 1804; *American*, Sept. 15, 17, 24, 1804. For a different interpretation of political developments, see Frank A. Cassell, "The Structure of Baltimore's Politics in the Age of Jefferson, 1795–1812," in Aubrey C. Land, Lois Green Carr, and Edward C. Papenfuse eds., *Law, Society, and Politics in Early Maryland* (Baltimore, 1977), pp. 277–96.

6. *American*, Sept. 13, 21, Oct. 1, 2, 1804; *Federal Gazette*, Oct. 2, 1804.

7. *American*, Oct. 2, 1804; *Federal Gazette*, Oct. 2, 1804.

8. *Maryland Journal* (Baltimore), Feb. 15, 1791; *American*, Oct. 6, 1806, Nov. 3, 1826; Baltimore Assessment Record Book, MS. 55, MHS.

9. *American*, Dec. 13, 1793, Dec. 5, 1799, Jan. 9, Nov. 27, 1805, June 10, 1806, May 23, 1807; *Maryland Journal*, Mar. 21, 1794.

10. The names of assemblymen were published in the newspapers in early October each year. For delegates from 1778 through 1796, see *Maryland Journal*. For 1797 through 1811, see *Federal Gazette*.

11. *American*, Oct. 4, 12, 14, 1805.

12. *Ibid.*, Oct. 8, 1805; *Federal Gazette*, Oct. 8, 1805.

13. *Federal Gazette*, Aug. 22, 1806; *American*, Aug. 30, Sept. 26, Oct. 6, 31, 1806.

14. *American*, Aug. 30, 1806.

15. *Ibid.*, Sept. 1, 2, 26, 1806.

16. *Ibid.*, June 9, Sept. 23, 25, 30, Oct. 2, 1806; *Federal Gazette*, Sept. 26, 1806; *Baltimore Telegraphe*, Oct. 1, 1806; *To the Independent Voters of Baltimore* (Baltimore, 1806), MHS.

17. *American*, Oct. 7, 1806.

18. *Ibid.*, Oct. 6, 1807, Sept. 30, Oct. 3, 1809, Oct. 2, 1810; *Federal Gazette*, Oct. 4, 1808.

19. *American*, Sept. 16, 1806, Aug. 29, Sept. 4, 14, 1810; Edward T. Schultz, *History of Freemasonry in Maryland* (Baltimore, 1885), pp. 335–36.

20. *American*, Oct. 2, 1810.

9

THE MECHANIC INTEREST DIVIDES:
BANKS AND CHARTER REFORM

By the early nineteenth century Baltimoreans often talked about the "mechanic interest." It was a term that expressed a relatively new political reality, referring to the attitudes, values, and interests around which mechanics had organized since 1763. As "Another Mechanic" put it in 1805: "It is well known that the mechanic interest has always been able to elect whom they please, and consequently sought for by those who wished to be exalted to places of honor, and sometimes offices of profit." What the author failed to note was that after 1800 the mechanic interest was torn in several directions. While the top master craftsmen were showing signs of growing conservatism and an inclination to retreat from the advanced political positions of the 1790s, a new group of lesser-known mechanics arose to challenge the traditional leadership of the mechanic community and carry forward the principles of democratic republicanism.[1]

These shifts in the mechanic interest became apparent in the movement for a mechanics' bank and the battle for charter reform. In 1806 a number of master craftsmen resolved to establish their own bank, but immediately split into two factions. One faction, consisting of well-known mechanics, framed a constitution that seemed to surrender financial control to merchants. Another group of relative unknowns, calling itself the Phalanx Society, drafted a constitution designed to ensure that the mechanics would be in command. The conservative faction prevailed but paid a high price in producing a major schism within the mechanic interest. At the same time the conservative features of Baltimore's city charters were coming under attack. The movement for reform gathered momentum for five years until finally in 1808 a special city convention met and ratified amendments to the charter. For mechanics it was an ambiguous victory. The master tradesmen who had been officials of the Mechanical Society and led the fight for a republican charter in the 1790s divided over the issue of reform. Though it withdrew from the most radical positions of the United Committees, the convention revived the principles of democratic republicanism that had been temporarily eclipsed by the 1797 charter.

In the spring of 1806 a number of mechanics were toying with the idea of a bank. The idea had been simmering for years. Although the city already had three banks—the Bank of Maryland, Bank of Baltimore, and Union Bank of Maryland—mechanics had complained for over a decade that these institutions ignored their needs while pampering the merchant community. Nobody doubted that merchants controlled the banks. Only the moderately affluent could afford to pay $250 for a share of bank stock, which entitled its holder to vote for the board of directors. These were the men who decided who got loans and discounts and who didn't. Not surprisingly, no mechanic ever sat on one of the banks' board of directors. In 1805 "Another Mechanic" captured the frustration and antagonism that workingmen felt toward the banks:

> Much of late has also been said about the banks and their directors, to influence the minds of the public. What, in the name of common sense, have we to do with them or their directors? for *we* get no discounts, though we may have often tried, and upon as *good* paper, (as they style it) as the city can afford. Perhaps some who have commenced a *mercantile* business, may now and then be favored, but I never knew, no not even *one* solitary instance of a mechanic's obtaining a discount if he followed his branch of business; then I ask again, what possible interest can we have in them?

To mechanics the banks were symbols of financial chicanery and social elitism. A year later "Justice" put it succinctly: "all the Banks at present in operation in Baltimore are sources of great grievance and machines of oppression to mechanics."[2]

In early May a "meeting of Mechanics and other Citizens" appointed eighteen individuals as commissioners to frame "articles of association" and collect subscriptions for a mechanics' bank. The commissioners assigned the task to a smaller committee of five. A lawyer was hired to steer the mechanics through the legal details. Still, drafting the document did not go smoothly and the commissioners soon split into two factions. Some of them—apparently those who had originally conceived the idea of a bank—became suspicious of the committee's intentions while it deliberated over the constitution. According to "A Friend to Union" who sympathized with the committee, "it should seem that the fears of a few, otherwise worthy characters, were somehow excited, apprehending thro' an overzeal perhaps, that the Mechanics' interest and influence, was not properly attended to in the committee." In other words, the committee was plotting to sell out the mechanics to the merchants. Robert and William Edwards were two mechanics who feared betrayal. In a public statement in the *Evening Post* they explained that a number of new commissioners, who had been appointed after the bank's overall structure was determined, expressed "sentiments in some respects subversive of those principles which we thought indispensably necessary for the perfection of the institution and security of the Mechanics' interest." The original commissioners succeeded in forcing some of the "subversives" to withdraw. But a few remained. To prevent them from undermining the institution, the original commissioners demanded that everyone on the committee sign "*a paper* binding each of them *to adhere* to those identical fundamental principles in *favor of mechanics*, which all of them *professed to espouse*." Some of them signed; some didn't.[3]

The original commissioners now suspected that the committee of five would produce an anti-mechanic constitution. Thus they rushed into print a draft of their own that became known as the "First Set" of bank articles. It appeared on May 14 in the *Evening Post* under the signature of "the PHALANX SOCIETY, or Association of Sincere and True Principled Friends of Mechanics, and the Middling and Poorer Classes of the Community generally." The constitution established a "Mechanics' Bank of Baltimore." It consisted of twenty-eight articles, most of which were designed to guarantee a bank by and for mechanics. It set the capital stock at a million dollars, subscribed in shares of $25 each, a tenth of what a share cost at the other banks.

Several of the articles promised to be controversial. Article IV stipulated the qualifications of bank directors. On the first Mon-

day in June each year the subscribers would elect eighteen directors. They had to live in Baltimore or within two miles of it, they
had to be U.S. citizens, and they had to own at least twenty shares
of stock each. In addition, no fewer than twelve of the directors
had to be "practical mechanics, artificers or handicraftsmen, for
and during the term of two years next preceding their election."
For ordinary business transactions eight directors and the president constituted a quorum; for loans and discounts over $15,000
ten directors were required. In both cases the majority had to be
"practical mechanics." The president also had to be a mechanic,
whom the directors would choose from their own body. The
board would then pick another "practical mechanic" to fill the va-
cancy left by the president, which preserved the mechanics' two-
to-one majority. Each year half of the directorships would become
vacant, to be filled by general election; the constitution required
that six of the nine new officers be "practical mechanics." Article V
established the manner of electing directors. Subscribers who
owned fewer than 51 shares had one vote each; 51 to 100 shares,
five votes; 101 to 150 shares, ten votes; 151 to 200 shares, fifteen
votes; and over 200 shares, twenty votes.

Article XV made explicit the assumptions that underlay the
constitution: "All practical mechanics, artificers, and handicraftsmen, and the middling and poorer classes of the community, not
being stockholders, shall be accommodated with discounts or
loans in preference to all other descriptions of persons whom-
soever not being stockholders, and their applications shall be
selected, considered and determined on, in the first instance ac-
cordingly." The Phalanx Society was making sure this was a Mechanics' Bank in fact as well as name.[4]

In the meantime the committee of five continued to hammer
out its own constitution. On May 31 it appeared in the *Federal Gazette*, which was surprising because mechanics ordinarily
avoided the Federalist press. The "Second Set" coincided with
the "First Set" on a number of points. Both established a million
dollar capital stock and pegged the price of a share at $25. Both
reserved a portion of the shares for the state legislature should it
decide to incorporate the bank and invest in it. The major differences between the two sets were over the qualifications for
bank directors and the procedures for electing officers. Article II

of the Second Set provided for fifteen directors, "nine of which directors shall be practical mechanics or manufacturers." The directors would select a president. Eight directors constituted a quorum "for transacting the business of the company," five for "Ordinary discounts." The Second Set proposed a more complicated formula for determing the voting power of shareholders, which allowed a maximum of thirty votes reached at 100 shares. It established annual elections on the first Monday in June, although the initial one would be scheduled for August 25, 1806.[5]

Despite the surface similarities, these were fundamentally different constitutions. The First Set established provisions maintaining the predominance of mechanics that were either absent or attenuated in the Second Set. Under the First Set the board of directors was stacked two-to-one in favor of "practical mechanics"; under the Second Set, three-to-two. The First but not the Second Set required the bank president to be a mechanic. According to the First Set, mechanics must constitute a majority of the board of directors at all business meetings. The Second Set said nothing about the composition of the directors who made up a quorum; conceivably, the six nonmechanic directors could transact ordinary business by themselves. The First Set required that the bank directors extend preferential treatment to nonstockholders who were either mechanics or belonged to the "middling or poorer classes." The Second Set was silent here. Under the First Set small stockholders had considerable voting power; the maximum number of votes per stockholder was twenty. The Second Set permitted greater concentration of voting power in the hands of large stockholders, setting the maximum at thirty votes. For example, a man who held fifty shares under the First Set would have one vote, under the Second Set fifteen votes. Finally, the First Set explicitly stipulated who fell under the workingman heading—"a practical mechanic, artificer, or handicraftsman." The Second Set adopted a broader term—"practical mechanics or manufacturers." In the First Set alone a mechanic director had to have practiced his craft for two years. Under the Second Set it was possible for a mechanic to have given up his trade years, even decades, earlier and still qualify as a mechanic.

For a month the newspapers carried a running debate over the merits of the two constitutions, which delineated growing class distinctions in the producing classes. The most important piece came from "An Examiner." A self-professed mechanic, the author attacked the Second Set for prostituting the bank to non-workingmen. He argued that the term "practical mechanics and manufacturers" was too inclusive. It embraced men who had little interest or sympathy with mechanics. What were the differences between "mechanic" and "manufacturer" that the Second Set had conflated? "An Examiner" answered: "The shoe-maker is a manu-facturer; the brush-maker is a manufacturer, and the rope-maker is a manufacturer: but all these and many other classes of working people are *improperly* called manufacturers—their proper title is *handicraftsmen*, and they are generally of *middling* circum-stances—and what is more, they are people of discernment."

Having drawn this distinction, the writer listed a few exam-ples of real manufacturers: "Flour manufacturers, sugar manufac-turers, gun-powder manufacturers, &c." These men employed large work forces, they invested big capital, they produced man-ufactured goods—but they were hardly "mechanics." Unlike me-chanics, the manufacturers had close ties to merchants. Perhaps they themselves were merchants who invested in manufacturing on the side. They might be financial manipulators—"shavers"—"many of whom are *fondly* interested in the *other* Banks." "An Examiner" identified what he believed to be the fundamental dif-ference between the two groups:

> In short, the DICTIONARY definition and distinction between man-ufacturer and handicraftsman amounts to this: that although the *handicraftsman* is sometimes called a manufacturer, yet his work is actually *fashioned or performed by the hand*; but the manufac-turer, *properly so called*, does not employ his *hands* in his work, other than in *removing* his materials from one place to another, in barrels, bags, coups, &c.

He objected to the Second Set's failure to put a limitation on the number of manufacturers elected to the board. What was to prevent all nine of the directorships reserved for "practical me-chanics and manufacturers" from going to the latter? Where would the mechanics be? The remaining six directorships be-longed to "rich men of other classes." The Second Set did not stipulate how long a "practical mechanic" had to practice his trade, "whether for two years or for *two hours*." What about the mechanic who had left his trade years ago to pursue another business? The Second Set said nothing about the level of skill a "practical mechanic" should have attained to qualify as such, "whether he shall have built a ship, or merely *screwed on a closet lock*." "An Examiner" exclaimed that everyone seemed to profit from the Second Set except "the poor *artificer*, who is left out of the JUNTO altogether."[6]

By blurring the distinction between "mechanic" and "manufacturer," the Second Set represented a throwback to an earlier era. In semantic terms the Association of Tradesmen and Manufacturers had been a step forward because it separated the skilled from the unskilled worker. Such terms as tradesman, manufacturer, mechanic, handicraftsman, artificer, artist, and artisan shared one thing in common: they alluded to working people above the level of "common laborers," "laboring poor," "poorer classes." The Mechanical Society had gone even further in this regard, for it distinguished the small-scale craftsman who worked at the bench from the big-time manufacturer who might never have undergone an apprenticeship much less worked with his hands. Thus when the authors of the Second Set combined "practical mechanics and manufacturers," they resurrected the semantic fuzziness that the Mechanical Society had striven to clarify. Having struggled hard to become a self-conscious entity, the mechanics, in "An Examiner"'s opinion, were being lumped together with classes whose interests they did not share. He was not alone. In June the newspapers advertised the publication of a new pamphlet, which seems to have disappeared since: "The Mechanics' Monitor or ALARM BELL; On a very important occasion, and interesting particularly to all Mechanics and generally to the middling as well as the poorer classes of all occupations; for a poor man may yet be favored with riches, and so may his children after him." Written by "A Workman," the pamphlet attacked "the *Spurious*" Second Set and professed to contain "some secrets concerning the destruction of the Mechanics' best interests on that subject, through the conduct of persons *Not Mechanics*."[7]

The argument over words concealed a deeper division. The authors of the First Set were virtually unknown. Five days after the publication of their constitution, the Phalanx Society issued the names of commissioners delegated to collect subscriptions. Not a single one had served as a Mechanical Society officer or in the city council. Several correspondents asked who these men were. "I have lived in this city twelve years," wrote "T. B.," "and know but one of them, and many of my neighbors are in the same situation." On the other hand, the authors of the Second Set had no problems being recognized. Five of them were former Mechanical Society officers: William Jessop, Chrisotpher Raborg, James Mosher, Adam Fonerden, and Robert Steuart. Eight had won election to the council: the above five plus Owen Dorsey, George Decker, and Adam Welsh. The two groups of commissioners differed in other ways. Seven of the thirteen Phalanx Society men lived at Fell's Point, compared to one of fourteen of the established group.[8]

The Phalanx Society seems to have embodied the ambitions of a new generation of master mechanics, who had earned neither the reputation nor the wealth of the older group. Consider the following attack on the Second Set and its authors, published on June 18: "Can any mechanic be weak enough to believe this institution intended for his benefit? Well; but there are '*Christopher Raborg, James Mosher, Adam Fonerden*, &c. &c. all mechanics,' you will say. But are they not *rich* mechanics? And *rich men*, be they mechanics, merchants, or whatever you please, are fond of speculating. The *poor* mechanic will not be benefited by it." The Phalanx Society marked the entry into city politics of several less prominent mechanics. Three months after the controversy Joshua Ennis of the Phalanx Society won election to the First Branch of the city council from Ward 7. He served four terms. Two other members of the Phalanx Society also rose in political office after the bank debate: Nathaniel Hynson sat in the First Branch from Ward 7 in 1810 and 1811, Thomas Sheppard from Ward 8 between 1808 and 1811.[9]

The Second Set eventually prevailed. The two sides may have settled their differences through compromise, for each had expressed an interest in conciliation. The Phalanx Society had been the underdog from the outset, pitted against the city's top mechanics. The success of a bank hinged in large part on the reputations of its directors, and the Phalanx Society did not have the big names. On June 23 the commissioners of the Mechanics' Bank

opened their books to receive subscriptions. On that one day
they sold 22,500 of the 36,000 shares available to the public.
Elections to the board were scheduled for July 14. The campaigning was unprecedented. Exclaimed editor William Pechin: "Bank
nominations, like a flood, overwhelm our office." The mechanics
urged their brethren to elect strong-willed workingmen to the
board. On July 11 "Many Stockholders of the Eastern District"
nominated Thomas Sheppard, a member of the Phalanx Society.
"We all know," they wrote,

> commercial men have greater opportunities of acquiring knowl-
> edge of the general form and method of doing business than most
> mechanics, and if we send men who will *only* merely say *yea* or
> *nay*, that the whole business must naturally fall on the commercial
> men, and they as an equivalent for their services will expect the
> whole direction of the institution—But, to prevent this, let us send
> men who are in every shape their equals; *men*, who will be useful
> to mechanics, and who will support their interests.

"Justice" said he would support genuine mechanics only, "those
who have borne the fatigue and drudgery of the day." [10]

To many mechanics "shavers" posed the greatest danger to
their bank. They were speculators, usurers, who demanded exorbitant interest on loans. They did not work; they used money to
make money. The stockholders who nominated Sheppard carefully noted that he was "a gentleman in very independent circumstances, acquired by his own indefatigable industry, and not on
borrowed capital." Mechanics thought the distinction was crucial.
Wealth in itself was not bad, provided that it resulted from honest
labor and not parasitic finance. If "shavers" and "razor blades" in-
fested the board of directors, the philanthropic intentions of the
Mechanics' Bank would be lost. According to one writer, money
would remain "confined in the hands of the directors and their
friends, shavers, and speculators, to the great injury of the middling and lower class of society, and contrary to the wish and intention of a large majority of stockholders."

Another correspondent, "Anti-Shaver," foretold how shavers
could destroy the bank. He offered the hypothetical case of two
mechanics, both of whom earned the same amount over a year.
One was a "regular" mechanic whose business activities were

spread evenly over the year. The other was an "irregular" mechanic in a trade that required large capital investments during the busy months. A shaver on the board of directors would extend a loan to the regular mechanic. If he did not, the mechanic could either borrow what he needed from a friend or tighten his belt for a few weeks. He was not in the shaver's mercy. But the same director might reject the request of the irregular mechanic for a loan. Because the irregular mechanic needed money fast, he would have no choice but to seek out loan sharks, perhaps the very director who had denied his request. "As for my own part," wrote "Barlow," "I will not vote for any man as director, be he who he may, who was ever known to profit on the distresses of his neighbours, and I hope at least my brother mechanics, who are stockholders will join me."[11]

The authors of the Second Set won most of the directorships. Of the fifteen men elected to the board, ten had been commissioners under the Second Set. Only one representative from the Phalanx Society received a seat: Thomas Sheppard. Given their standing in the community, the Second Set men probably expected to win. But they seem to have been stung by the Phalanx Society's criticism. In issuing their constitution, they had presented themselves as true spokesmen for the mechanics. The document, they claimed, rested "upon liberal principles, yet effectually preserving the preponderance of the Mechanics' interest." During the campaigning the Second Set forces played on this theme. On June 30 "Justice" nominated fifteen men to the board, all of whom had been Second Set commissioners. He praised them in terms the Phalanx Society had itself employed a month before:

> Be not satisfied with merely knowing the candidates are Mechanics or manufacturers, but investigate the character and principles of the man—enquire whether he wishes to see all mechanics prosper, as if he alone would possess the "loaves and the fishes," and instead of lending a helping hand to his fellow mechanics, would he oppress & grind them, that he may be tryumphant; this be assured, (with same be it spoken) is the disposition of many, although mechanics!

A year later at the bank's second election the board of directors belatedly adopted a tighter definition of mechanic urged by the

Phalanx Society. Although they still left the door open to "manu-facturers," the directors required that "practical mechanics" must have practiced their trade for three years and at least one year prior to the election. The debate over the Mechanics' Bank had exposed the growing tension within the mechanic interest, as a new generation of master craftsmen fought for recognition and at-tacked the increasing conservatism of the established leaders.[12]

The second movement that revealed the rift in mechanic leadership as well as the triumph of democratic republicanism was for charter reform. The 1797 charter had represented a bitter disappointment for the Mechanical Society and all those favoring the incorporation proposal of the United Committees. Not sur-prisingly, soon after its adoption the conservative charter was fo-menting discontent among the townspeople. After 1800 they delivered petitions to the assembly requesting that the most ex-clusionary provisions of the charter be amended. In 1803 the leg-islature passed an act, contingent upon the approval of the First Branch of the city council, that instituted major charter reforms. It cut the property qualifications for office holding, implemented ballot voting, abolished indirect elections, and required rotation in office for the mayor. In March, 1803, the First Branch consid-ered the amendments and rejected them "unanimously," offering as explanation that "the present charter of incorporation meets with the approbation of a large majority of the citizens of Balti-more." Three years later "Andrew Marvel," writing in the *Ameri-can*, was still fuming over the council's decision:

> Such an united opposition was made by all the members and de-pendents on the present system; such a temper was worked up among a number of house owners, who now hold all the places in the councils, and of course the power of taxation upon every inhab-itant of the city, as well as the pleasure of ruling all; that the act was rejected and every imperfection of the charter preserved to the great pleasure and profit of those who ruled above or under, as well as of all those who hate equal rights, and abhor the people's power.

In addition to killing the amendments, the council expressed the opinion that it should exercise sole power in petitioning the as-sembly on charter reform.[13]

The action of the council signaled a political shift within the mechanic leadership. The reforms offered by the assembly embodied the same political principles that the Mechanical Society had espoused a decade before, principles contained in the United Committees' charter proposal. Four of the sixteen councilmen who deliberated over the amendments in March, 1803, had been society officers: William Jessop of Ward 1, Christopher Raborg of Ward 4, John Shrim of Ward 5, and John Mackenheimer of Ward 6. They finally had a chance to enact those same republican principles they had so recently advocated. But they did not; they rejected the amendments "unanimously." The four were then serving their first terms in office. They had just arrived politically; their motives, the mechanic councilmen were renouncing ideals that had been central to the political vision of the Mechanical Society.[14]

The 1803 setback did not halt the reform movement. In September, 1804, a month before the city council and state assembly elections, a new petition to amend the charter circulated through town. Its authors proposed to submit it to the legislature at its November session. The document called for all the familiar changes: ballot for voice voting, direct elections for the mayor and Second Branch, restricting the mayor's term in office to three out of five years, a $500 property qualification for the First Branch and $1,000 for the Second, no plural office holding, greater authority to the council in appointing municipal workers. The petition appeared in the *American* on September 20; the editor called for a citywide meeting two days later "where the citizens will have an opportunity of hearing the same better elucidated than through the channel of paper."

The charter question sent shock waves into the council elections scheduled for the first Monday in October. The residents of Ward 6 assembled a week before the polls opened and nominated Peter Bond and Aquila Miles to the First Branch, "as persons favorable to said amendments." Later a wardsman said:

> Thus, citizens, it is hoped you will give your suffrages to those candidates alone who are decided friends to the amendment—that you will blast and wither this fruitful source of aristocracy forever—that you will shew yourselves ready to embrace the most patriotic, the most interesting recognition of your rights, ever pre-

sented to your choice in your corporate capactiy—The cavils of dogmatism; the sneers of federalism and aristocracy; the bickerings of ignorance, or the domineering contumely of purse-proud wealth to the contrary NOTWITHSTANDING.

Not everyone in Ward 6 accepted this assessment of the reforms. A few days after the meeting "A Republican Of the Sixth Ward" condemned the amendments and nominated the incumbents, John Mackenheimer and John Miller, to the council. Both had agreed to fight the reforms.[15]

Ward 6 was doing the unprecedented. Never before had city council elections been embroiled in political controversy. In theory and largely in fact a man's neighbors elected him to the council for his integrity and experience, not his view on a particular issue or party affiliation. Judging from the election results, the townsmen were not ready for a politicized council. In Ward 6 the incumbents beat the challengers in a close race, 121 and 129 votes to 113 and 118. The outcome probably resulted less from the candidates' position on reform than the fact that Mackenheimer and Miller were incumbents, having represented the ward since 1802. Discarding a faithful public servant for his views on a local question may have seemed dishonorable. Ten of the sixteen councilmen elected in October, 1804, were incumbents; two of the remaining six did not run for re-election. Thus only four councilmen were voted out of office. The reform advocates suffered a handicap because the amendments did not pose a clear "party" issue. Federalists generally opposed charter reform, but so did a considerable number of Republicans. Pechin argued that the Republicans' split over the amendments issue was so deep that it enabled Andrew Ellicott to win the assembly election. Many Republicans, he claimed, had voted for the Federalist candidate and against their own party because he had opposed charter reform.[16]

In February, 1805, the newly elected city council again rejected the reform measure. Jessop, Shrim, and Mackenheimer cast their votes against it; Raborg had been defeated for re-election. Also opposing reform was Frederick Shaeffer, another former Mechanical Society officer, who had been elected from Ward 7. But the council was more conciliatory than it had been earlier. According to "Andrew Marvel," the First Branch feared that the townspeople might bring another petition before the assembly if it failed to make some concession. Thus while the council spurned the entire reform act, it petitioned the assembly for the passage of several amendments: reduced property qualifications for office holding and ballot voting in city elections. The council's petition was laid before the assembly in November. The senate approved the compromise but the delegates rejected the piecemeal approach and sent the whole reform package back to Baltimore. The Federalist press accused the assembly of making charter reform "a party question against the city of Baltimore," exclaiming that "it cannot be reasonably supposed that the legislature will be able to force upon us a charter which all good men must oppose, and all men of property must reprobate."

For a second time, then, the city council elections in October, 1806, centered on the questions of the amendments. What most distressed "Civis," writing in the *Gazette*, was the proposal to eliminate the electoral system and open the city's highest offices to popular elections. "The inquiry into the integrity and moral character of a candidate for public office," he maintained, "requires deliberation, which is not always observed in popular elections, and thus we sometimes find, that men void of even the semblance of morality, who impudently, shamelessly and notoriously contemn good morals, are elected to high and honourable stations, to which they could never be appointed, if they were candidates in an election by electors." "Pericles" in the *American* agreed: "Is there no door open in this case for intrigue, for bribery or for servility courting popularity by disgraceful arts?" Once again the voters balked at turning out their familiar representatives. Thirteen of the officials elected in October, 1806, had belonged to the council two years before; the remaining three had not run for office. Shrim, Mackenheimer, and Shaeffer were reelected; Jessop did not campaign. The results were predictable. In February, 1807, the council killed the reform measure for a third time.[17]

The final push for reform came in late 1807. On November 17 a meeting of townspeople composed a new petition, claiming that "the existing act of incorporation of the City of Baltimore, is considered by your petitioners to be utterly irreconcileable with some of the noblest principles of our constitution, and absolutely hostile to many of the most acknowledged rights of the citizen." The *Gazette* suggested that the friends of the charter submit to the assembly a "counter-memorial" praising the present frame of government. The assembly threw its support, as it had since 1803, on the side of reform. It adopted a new comprehensive reform measure that in most respects resembled its predecessors. The act kept the electoral system for mayoral elections but reduced the elector's property qualification from $1,000 to $300. It also slashed the First Branch's qualification to $300 and the Second Branch's to $500.[18]

The measure stood a better chance of enactment than at any time previously. Unexpected events had suddenly put the charter in a menacing light. On November 3 the townspeople witnessed a huge protest against Aaron Burr, recently acquitted of treason, and the prominent Federalist lawyer Luther Martin, who had spent the last three months defending him. Gathering at the Point, the crowd marched across town to Federal Hill where it destroyed effigies of Burr and co-defendant Harman Blennerhassett, Chief Justice John Marshall, and Martin. The procession paused at Martin's home, which the lawyer and several dozen Federalist friends had occupied with arms, and threatened to attack. Mayor Thorowgood Smith, a moderate Federalist, panicked and ordered the militia to suppress the crowd if necessary. No violence occurred, but news of the mayor's actions unleashed a torrent of criticism. The mayor had showed his true Federalist colors, said Republicans; he had betrayed himself as an enemy of the people. The incident seemed to confirm what advocates of charter reform had said all along: the conservative charter created a city government insensitive to the public will. Thus the November 17 meeting that drafted the petition for charter reform saved its harshest words for the indirect mayoral elections:

> Where there is no common sentiment between a people and a chief municipal officer, who is not the immediate object of their choice, where an absolute indifference to their feelings and sentiments must frequently arise from a remote responsibility in this officer, where an absurd analogy between the affairs of an empire and the concerns of a corporation, and where a pernicious distinction between the different classes of society, throws the moderately wealthy into an odious disqualification to serve the people, it be-

comes time seriously to expostulate, and ask redress where it is never refused to a just complaint.[19]

The assembly instituted a new prodecure for submitting the amendments to the townspeople, which strengthened the reform forces. There was little doubt that the act would meet another defeat in the council. Of the sixteen councilmen elected in 1807, fifteen had served the previous year. The legislature provided that the act would be judged by a special convention to be elected February 14, 1808, including two representatives from each ward. During the campaign both friends and enemies of reform summarized the positions that had been staked out for five years. Writing in the Federalist press, "A Moderate Republican" insisted that men of both parties supported the existing charter. He claimed that the document itself was the creation of the "'Republican Mechanical' and of 'the Democratic' Societies of Baltimore town," which bent the truth considerably. The anti-reform group attempted to dissuade the laboring poor from supporting the amendments. "An old Baltimorean" addressed "THE INDUSTRIOUS POOR OF BALTIMORE" and explained that they should have no grievance with the charter because the council included "some from every ward, from the Hill, from the Point, from Old Town, from new Town; some merchants, some mechanics, some descendents of Germans, some descendents of Irishmen." Protesting that reform advocates had duped draymen into believing that they paid exorbitant fees under the charter, "Truth" countered that the tax of six or seven dollars a year was reasonable.

On the other side, Pechin of the American railed against "the most aristocratic features in the present charter" that included high property qualifications for office holding. "A Plebeian" added his agreement:

Surely it must be very grating to the feelings of every enlightened citizen, but more particularly to the worthy mechanic, to find that he is disqualified from holding a seat in the first and second branches of the city council, merely because he does not stand assessed on the assessor's books for the first branch of the city council at one thousand dollars, and for the second branch at two thousand dollars. The fact is this, (with the exception of some worthy charac-

ters) that the great ones of the earth cannot bear to be put on a
level equal with the middling class of mankind.[20]

By late January both sides had formed tickets. Thus for the
first time a local political issue had become the overwhelming
consideration in a city-level election. The two tickets underlined
the breakdown in the cohesiveness of the mechanic leadership.
On the anti-reform side stood two former Mechanical Society officers: Richardson Stewart of Ward 2 and Christopher Raborg of
Ward 4. Undoubtedly, Shrim, Mackenheimer, and Shaeffer would
also have run for the convention if their membership in the council had not disqualified them. On the pro-reform ticket were William Wilson and James Mosher of Ward 3 and David Shields of
Ward 5, all one-time Mechanical Society officers. Seven of the
sixteen men on the anti-reform ticket were mechanics, eight on
the pro-reform.[21]

The reform ticket won the election. A week later they "unanimously ratified and adopted the amendments to the city charter." The election results revealed the same sectional voting pattern that had characterized assembly, senate, congressional, and
presidential elections. They demonstrated that the principles of
democratic republicanism embodied in the reforms received their
greatest support from the mechanic neighborhoods. The heavily
mechanic Wards 6, 7, and 8 cast 82 percent of their votes for the
reform ticket. Not surprisingly, the reformers ran best in Ward 7
with 83 percent of the vote.[22]

The issues of a Mechanics' Bank and charter reform brought
to the surface tensions within the mechanic interest that had
been developing since 1800. First, they revealed a tendency
among prominent master craftsmen to abandon the republican
principles they had propounded in the 1790s. In 1806 former officers of the Mechanical Society drafted a bank constitution that
failed to guarantee the predominance of workingmen. From 1803
to 1808 a number of them opposed charter reform, although they
had espoused the proposed amendments a decade before. Furthermore, the bank and charter controversies showed that a new
generation of mechanics was ready to challenge the traditional

leadership and uphold the principles of democratic republican-ism. These were the men who formed the Phalanx Society and composed a bank charter ensuring that mechanics would be in control. They were the mechanics who, in the 1808 city conven-tion, voted for reform. Finally, the resolution of these two issues represented a triumph for democratic republicanism. Although the Mechanics' Bank was shaped in accordance with the conser-vative constitution, the directors eventually adopted several of the reforms that the Phalanx Society had insisted upon. The movement for charter reform also succeeded in 1808 when the city convention ratified amendments, many of which had been originally proposed by the Mechanical Society and the United Committees in the 1790s.

NOTES

1. *American* (Baltimore), Oct. 5, 1805.

2. *Ibid.*, June 30, July 10, 1806.

3. *Ibid.*, May 20, 27, 1806; *Baltimore Evening Post*, May 24, 1806.

4. *Baltimore Evening Post*, May 14, 1806.

5. *Federal Gazette* (Baltimore), May 31, 1806.

6. *Baltimore Evening Post*, June 6, 1806.

7. Although I was not able to find the original pamphlet, an advertisement for it appeared in the *American*, June 21, 1806.

8. *Baltimore Evening Post*, May 16, 18, 20, 31, 1806; *Federal Gazette*, May 31, 1806.

9. *Baltimore Telegraphe*, June 18, 1806.

10. *American*, July 10, 11, 1806; *Federal Gazette*, June 19, 23, 1806.

11. *Baltimore Evening Post*, June 28, July 1, 1806; *American*, July 11, 1806.

12. *American*, May 23, June 30, 1806; *Federal Gazette*, July 15, 1806.

13. *American*, Sept. 28, 1804, Oct. 2, 3, 1806; *Federal Gazette*, Dec. 6, 1805.

14. *Federal Gazette*, Oct. 5, 1802.

15. *American*, Sept. 20, 26, 28, 29, 1804.

16. *Ibid.*, Oct. 26, 1804; *Federal Gazette*, Oct. 2, 1804.

17. *American*, Sept. 20, Oct. 2, 3, 1806, Feb. 28, 1807; *Federal Gazette*, Jan. 22, Oct. 3, 1806.

18. *American*, Nov. 30, 1807, Jan. 19, 1808.

19. *Ibid.*, Nov. 30, 1807.

20. *Ibid.*, Jan. 29, Feb. 1, 1808; *Federal Gazette*, Jan. 27, 28, 1808.

21. *American*, Jan. 26, 27, 29, 1808.

22. *Ibid.*, Feb. 3, 9, 1808; *Federal Gazette*, Feb. 2, 1808.

10

MILITANT JOURNEYMEN

The years that witnessed mounting tensions within the mechanic interest coincided with a new wave of journeymen militancy. From 1800 to 1805 the only new trade associations to appear were the Baltimore Typographical Society for journeymen and the Baltimore Ship-Wrights for masters, and neither reflected disaffection between employers and workmen. But in 1805 the quiescence ended. For the next seven years Baltimore saw the rise of a journeymen movement that in scope and intensity exceeded the labor clashes of the 1790s.

In a number of respects militant journeymen broke from the past. First, there were more strikes than ever before. The tailors turned out in 1808 and possibly in 1805, the shoemakers in 1809 and 1810, and the printers possibly in 1810. Second, the tactics of the masters and journeymen betrayed attitudes of bitterness and intransigence that had been absent earlier. Blacklists and lockouts became increasingly commonplace. Third, the journeymen dissension spread to trades that had been traditionally free from strife. While shoemaking and tailoring continued to be the storm centers of militancy, the journeymen carpenters organized their own society in 1806 and the journeymen printers pressed for higher wages four years later. Fourth, the actions of the journeymen associations for the first time became politicized. In 1808 several members of the shoemakers' society tarred and feathered their Anglophile shop foreman, provoking a clash between Federalists who condemned the action and Republicans who sympathized with it. Finally, a journeymen association was dragged into the courts on charges of conspiracy. In 1809 the Baltimore County Criminal Court fell into line with the judicial authorities in Philadelphia and New York by handing down indictments against the

Union Society of Journeymen Cordwainers, which led to one of
the conspiracy trials well known to historians.

The most important tradesmen's society founded in the period 1800 to 1805 was the Baltimore Typographical Society. In
December, 1800, the journeymen printers met "to sign a memorial from the 'Asylum Company of Journeymen Printers,' to the
congress of the United States, praying that an additional duty may
be laid on books imported into this country—those for the use of
public libraries excepted." The Asylum Company may have been
a precursor to the Baltimore Typographical Society, which as
early as 1803 was corresponding with the journeymen printers of
Philadelphia. The printers' association differed from the journeymen societies of the 1790s. Unlike the United Journeymen Cordwainers and Journeymen Tailors' Society, it did not arise from a
strife-ridden trade. The Typographical Society was not organized
to challenge employers on the issues of wages or apprenticeship,
as were the associations of journeymen shoemakers and tailors.

Printers occupied a special place in the mechanic community
that explains the peculiarities of their society. The nature of their
work led to a conversance with the latest trends of thought, latest
news from Europe and America, latest developments among their
fellow printers throughout the republic. The printing shops nour-
ished political discourse and speculation; note that the Asylum
Company exempted public libraries from the tariff duties it had
proposed on books. They were schools producing many self-made
intellectuals of the artisan community. Thus printers enjoyed a
sense of craft solidarity that unified masters and journeymen, encouraging both to think of themselves as guardians of learning and
culture. Consider the toast offered by the Typographical Society
in celebration of Independence Day 1805: "'Printing, the art pre-
servative of all arts'—May its proper application make good *impressions*, and may it never be slurred by *imperfect* workmen."[1]

The printers' society seems to have maintained good relationships with employers. The strong bonds between journeymen
and masters are revealed in another of the Typographical Society's
Independence Day toasts: "Employers and employed, the two
great parties of the world.—May a constant reciprocity of good
offices, *bind* fast the chords of mutual friendship, each bearing in

mind this solemn truth, that all power founded on injustice is *imposition*." Three years later in 1808 the society proposed a toast echoing these sentiments: "Our professional brethren throughout the Union—when their country calls, May they be found in the foremost *columns* with their *shooting-sticks* and *balls* in good order."

One of the most important services provided by the Typographical Society was burying its members. The ceremony assumed significance in the eyes of journeymen because many members could not afford a proper burial. On these occasions the president called upon the membership to form a special procession accompanying the dead man's friends and family to the graveyard. On September 26, 1809, the society attended the funeral of printer Justus Brown, who had died "at a very advanced age." Its eulogy contained an attack on economic injustice as well as a statement of what constituted a virtuous workingman:

> His excellent qualities and amiable manners, had secured to him the friendship & esteem of every person who knew him. A humble christian, a zealous patriot and a worthy citizen, had his fortunes been as prosperous as his virtues were numerous, he would not have remained a striking example of the fact, that even in our favored country, rigid honesty, warm benevolence, and unremitted industry, some times go without merited reward.

The society wore black arm bands for a month to commemorate the passing of one of its members. This honor was extended to employers as well as journeymen. In 1808 master printer Thomas Dobbin died, a faithful Republican and editor of the *Baltimore Telegraphe*. The Typographical Society attended his funeral and donned their arm bands for two months as a special token of respect. Dobbin's son, George, took over the shop. When in January, 1809, the printing office partially burned down, the Typographical Society again stepped forward with support. Dobbin wrote that his presses were able to continue operating "through the generous and friendly offers of our brother printers in Baltimore to whom we can make no adequate returns for such kindness."[2]

Few tradesmen's associations could rival the Typographical Society in longevity or organization. Although the society adopted a new constitution in February, 1808, it seems to have functioned without interruption to 1812 and beyond. On May 2, 1812, a meeting took place of the "Baltimore Typographical Association," but its relationship to the original society is unknown. Only the Carpenters' Society, which probably operated continuously from 1791 to 1806, could better the record of the printers. The United Journeymen Cordwainers had existed from 1792 through 1794 but had disbanded by 1806. The Journeymen Tailors' Society seems to have been organized and reorganized several times between 1794 and 1799. The employers' associations of hatters, shoemakers, and tailors were even shorter-lived. The Association of Master Hatters appeared once in the newspapers in 1792 but never again. The Master Tailors' Society surfaced during the 1794 strike and disappeared afterward. The United Master Shoemakers, organized in 1810, also seems to have been a temporary response to striking journeymen. The printers sustained their society through tight organization. The backbone of the Typographical Society was a standing committee that met every Saturday evening, handled daily business, and prepared the agenda for the general assemblies. The rank-and-file met once a month, more than any other tradesmen's association.[3]

A second organization appearing in the early nineteenth century was the Baltimore Ship-Wrights. Founded in July, 1804, the Ship-Wrights brought together a number of master shipbuilders and carpenters. The organization elected James Cordery as president and James Wheeden and William Drummond as superintendents. It maintained an office at the Point and kept a stock of spars and "seasoned stuff for the building of several vessels." The Baltimore Ship-Wrights seem to have represented the middle ranks of the trade. Neither Cordery, Wheeden, nor Drummond were as wealthy or owned as many slaves as the top shipwrights like David Stodder, Joseph Despeaux, or James Biays. But they occasionally did business with them: Cordery, for example, hired the slave caulkers of Despeaux. Perhaps the smaller shipbuilders had decided to pool their capital to compete with the giants of the trade, for the Ship-Wrights stressed "that all the persons forming this association are masters of their business, and as they intend themselves, principally, to give their personal application in executing work for their employers, it is fondly hoped, that on this score they will claim a preference from those who make it an object to have things done in a masterly manner."[4]

The Typographical Society and the Ship-Wrights did not upset the quiet that had settled upon the workshops after 1800, but within five years there were signs of renewed journeymen militancy reminiscent of the mid-1790s. One of the first signals came from the tailors. In the summer of 1794 the journeymen tailors had struck successfully for 7s. 6d. a job. Five years later they turned out again for higher wages but were defeated. Thus in October, 1805, when the pay scale had remained unchanged for over a decade, the journeymen threatened to strike for 8s. 9d. a job. Our knowledge of this incident comes from a statement of the master tailors a few years later, who claimed that their workers had "formed a combination to make us comply, promising at the same time not to require any further augmentation—business being then brisk we thought it advisable to accede to their terms." The journeymen had won the new wage rate of 8s. 9d., although it is not clear whether they went on strike. Nor do we know if the old Journeymen Tailors' Society led the action.[5]

Soon the journeymen carpenters were also expressing dissatisfaction. Since 1791, as we have seen, the Carpenters' Society had worked effectively at mediating disputes between employers and workmen. Admittedly, there had been cases of dissension. In 1795 Frederick Haifligh and several others bolted the society to establish their own Baltimore Carpenters' Association, but this new organization did not embody journeymen protest. Rather it reflected the resentment of some master carpenters who accused their colleagues of violating the established price list. When on February 27, 1806, the journeymen carpenters called a special meeting, they were striking out in a new direction. Several days later they appointed a committee to draft a constitution. By the second week of March the committee had completed the task and submitted the document to the membership. Two months later, in May, the newspapers printed a notice for a general assembly of the "Baltimore Carpenters' Society." This was a new journeymen organization, not the old one. The secretary was James Mowton. Meanwhile, at its last annual meeting in July, 1805, the old Carpenters' Society of Baltimore had chosen John Ready as secretary.

Faced with the journeymen challenge, the old society apparently disbanded. It issued no calls for meetings after 1806. Three years later seventeen prominent master carpenters, many of whom had belonged to the Carpenters' Society of Baltimore, recommended that the public patronize the new firm of Adam Denmead and George Wall, who had "associated themselves for the purpose of Measuring and Valuing House Carpenter's and Joiner's Work." This task had once been undertaken by the Carpenters' Society of Baltimore.[6]

The most important indication of the changing mood among journeymen came in the shoemaking trade. The shoemakers had formed the earliest of Baltimore's journeymen associations in 1792, the United Journeymen Cordwainers. The society functioned for two years but whether it survived the 1794 strike is unclear. There is no evidence of its activities after the strike. Nor does it appear that shoemakers clashed with their employers in the decade following the turn-out. In 1806 the shoemakers reorganized as the Union Society of Journeymen Cordwainers. They wrote a constitution and set of bylaws, the only ones to survive. On the third Monday of each month the society held a general meeting where it transacted the most pressing business concerning the whole membership. In adopting monthly meetings the shoemakers may have been emulating the Typographical Society. As the society's strength depended on these regular meetings, the constitution contained a provision expelling any member who missed four without a good excuse. The officers of the Union Society consisted of a president, secretary, treasurer, and standing committee of seven. To prevent the president from acquiring undue power, the bylaws provided for his election every three months. The standing committee, which was responsible for most of the society's financial concerns, gathered on the second Monday of the month to prepare its report for the general assembly.[7]

If the society's bylaws are read at face value, the general meetings were models of decorum and adhered to parliamentary procedure and orderly debate. Between the lines, though, we catch glimpses of an embattled leadership trying to anticipate potential disciplinary problems that could ruin the society. One group that posed a threat to order consisted of nonmembers who attended the meetings. They might claim to be prospective applicants when in fact they were spies that the employers hired to disrupt the proceedings. To weed out such "strangers" before they could do harm, the society appointed a doorkeeper who stood guard and checked the credentials of each individual entering the hall. Another possible troublemaker was the shoemaker who had previously belonged to a journeymen association elsewhere but who had earned a reputation as a "bad member." The society excluded these journeymen altogether, although it is unclear how it handled traveling journeymen. Perhaps to police the workmen who moved up and down the Atlantic seaboard in search of jobs, the society in September, 1807, wrote to the Philadelphia journeymen shoemakers and suggested a regular correspondence. It was also possible that dissension might arise within the membership of the society itself. To check internal fights and bickerings, the constitution prohibited "gaming of any kind," "disputing," "quarreling," "obsene discourse," and "Oaths or Drunkeness" during the meetings.[8]

The basic task of the society was collecting and distributing dues. The constitution established a dues structure within reach of the journeymen's modest finances: an entrance fee of 50¢ and monthly payments of 25¢. When the benefit fund reached $100, the president and committee were empowered to advise the membership on ways the money might be invested. With the consent of the standing committee, the president could draw on the fund to meet daily expenses so long as he spent no more than $10. The society's operating costs could not have been large. Only the secretary received a salary, of $1 a month. To qualify for benefit payments, the constitution stipulated that a journeyman must be a dues-paying member for at least a year and "sick or disabled through no fault of his own." If he met these conditions, the treasurer was directed to pay him $3 a week for the first six months and $1 a week afterward. Considering that in 1811 a journeyman shoemaker who labored six days a week earned about $8.50, the society's benefit payments represented the minimum for survival. Disabled workingmen, especially with families to support, would have to supplement their incomes elsewhere.[9]

The society naturally kept a close eye on its benefit fund. It not only covered payments to the disabled but also financed funeral expenses, the salary of the secretary, everyday bills, and unforeseen legal costs. The constitution set out in detail the procedures for burials, revealing the same preoccupation with a proper funeral as the printers did. Journeymen shoemakers were always traveling. The unpredictability of employment necessitated a willingness to move, as did the general preference for a well-traveled journeyman who was acquainted with the latest fashions. Not surprisingly, journeymen worried about dying alone in a strange town. To allay such fears, the society allocated $20 to cover the costs of a member's funeral and required that all his brethren join the funeral procession. Like the printers, the shoemakers wore black arm bands, while officers had white sashes. Another outlay that journeymen could not ignore was possible legal fees. "If any member of this Society," the bylaws stated, "shall be prosecuted for performing any duties required by the articles of this Society he shall be indemnified for all expenses in defending such prosecution if in such defence he acts conformable to the instructions of this Society." In other words, the society would pay legal fees if the prosecuted journeyman did not betray the secrets of his brethren.[10]

The constitution also laid down rules governing working conditions. Like all tradesmen's associations, the Union Society drew up a list of prices below which its members refused to work. Any member who did not honor the list faced expulsion. Nor did the society permit its members to work at a shop where another journeyman violated the price list, unless he received a special dispensation from the officers. The constitution also provided that no member could work for an employer who hired nonsociety journeymen. Child labor posed perhaps the gravest threat to journeymen because it provided their employers with a source of "cheap" labor. In 1794 the United Journeymen Cordwainers had refused to instruct more than two apprentices per employer. As the masters grew increasingly dependent on apprenticeship, the journeymen had to take a tougher stand. According to the constitution, no member was permitted to "teach or instruct any apprentice for any employer in the City or precincts there off under penalty of being excluded." If the master was forced to expend the time and effort training an apprentice himself, the society hoped he might find it more economical to hire a skilled journeyman.[11]

For the first three years the Union Society managed to avoid a large-scale confrontation with the employers. It took action against members who refused to abide by the regulations in the constitution and bylaws, but such incidents were isolated. On June 8, 1807, the masters agreed to raise wages on boots with leather bindings by 25¢ a pair. No strike had taken place, but there may have been one threatened. A limited boycott was usually effective in dealing with recalcitrant employers. For example, it appears that master shoemaker Jacob Wynard ignored the new prices on leather boots. He was a big shoemaker who, at his retirement in 1809, employed no fewer than six apprentices. For seven months the Union Society boycotted Wynard's shop and demanded that he "give the established wages and discharge the present scabs." In January, 1808, Wynard proposed a compromise. He would agree to the society's conditions provided that he be permitted to employ inmates at the city jail to make cheap shoes. The society agreed and on January 11, 1808, lifted the boycott.[12]

In the meantime the journeymen tailors had been active. They resorted to two strategies in demanding higher wages after the victory of 1805. The first was to revise the rating system for clothing. Each article of clothing received a rating in jobs, with each job, according to the journeymen, requiring about a day's labor. The tailors succeeded in increasing their pay by forcing the employers to assign higher ratings to some pieces of clothing. Looking back over the period 1805 to 1808, the master tailors complained that an article of clothing rated at four jobs in the beginning had risen to eight jobs three years later. The second way journeymen boosted their wages was more direct. After the *Chesapeake* affair of June, 1807, with war imminent and the Baltimore militia mobilizing, there was a sudden demand for all varieties of military equipment, including uniforms. The tailors took advantage of the new market for uniforms by raising their wages from $7 a week to $8 or $9.[13]

Within a year the journeymen created a political issue. On October 18, 1808, several members of the Union Society of Journeymen Cordwainers and a few other mechanics tarred and feathered Robert Beatty, their shop foreman. Beatty was born in England. Before coming to the United States, he had worked in

Bermuda as a shoemaker. By the summer of 1808 he had arrived in Baltimore and gotten a job as shoe foreman for James Lambie, who had recently opened a boot factory on South Street. From all accounts Beatty was an irrepressible Anglophile. In the aftermath of the *Chesapeake* incident his pro-British opinions were especially unpalatable. Beatty seems to have pushed his shopmates too far. According to one first-hand account, he cursed "all Americans indiscriminantly as a pack of rebels to their king, and rascals to each other—and hoped to see the day when one of his majesty's sons would obtain his just rights over these states and be their king. He damned the President & government in the most bitter manner, and hoped when the British came here, as he intended to join them, to have the pleasure of shooting the President."

Beatty did not like Irish Catholics either and boasted to John Giddleman, a journeyman shoemaker who probably worked at Lambie's, that "he himself could beat all Ireland with two hogsheads of whiskey." Giddleman belonged to the Union Society, and he may have passed the word along to several fellow journeymen: George Wooleslager, Barney Jordan, and others. Wooleslager must have bridled at hearing Beatty's anti-Irish pronouncements. Four years later, upon being committed to the city jail, he cursed the watchmen who arrested him as "damn'd orangemen."[14]

Beatty's shopmates soon had enough of their exasperating foreman. On Tuesday afternoon at four o'clock the journeymen dragged Beatty out of the shop and tarred and feathered him. They then put him on public display. They tossed him into the back of a cart, tied a halter around his neck, and drove him from Baltimore across town to the Point. Along the way the shoemakers attracted a large crowd of onlookers that included the mayor, Thorowgood Smith. Despite his pleas, the mayor was powerless to stop the journeymen. He was a Federalist, which did not endear him to the Republican shoemakers. Furthermore, Smith was in no position to test his authority. A year before he had panicked and called out the militia during a riotous disturbance, which brought an avalanche of criticism down on him. The mayor did not want to make the same mistake twice.[15]

The tarring and feathering of Robert Beatty threw the Union Society of Journeymen Cordwainers into the public limelight. A day after the incident the influential *Baltimore Evening Post* carried an article accusing the Union Society of masterminding the assault. There was circumstantial evidence to support the allegation. The day before the attack the society had held its monthly meeting. Overnight, the officers of the Union Society found themselves the objects of condemnation. They were understandably alarmed because the society's legal status was problematic. The last thing the Union Society needed was a confrontation with a hostile court. On the same day that the *Post* article appeared the president of the society called a special meeting of the membership. At this gathering the society ordered its secretary to write a denial of the charges and see it into print. The piece, which appeared nine days later, stated that the Union Society "utterly denounce all such proceedings as anti-republican, and contrary to the letter and spirit of our law and constitution, and as repugnant to their ideas of a free government." The statement carried the signatures of the president, secretary, and committeemen. The society's leadership had no choice but to repudiate those responsible for the act. To the officers of the Union Society who had struggled to maintain discipline among the membership, Jordan, Wooleslager, and Giddleman must have seemed like the hotheads whose irresponsible actions threatened the existence of the society.[16]

Robert Beatty became a political symbol that both Federalist and Republican parties tried to twist to their own ends. With the passage of Jefferson's controversial Embargo Act in late 1807, Federalists across the nation saw an opportunity to recoup their party's dwindling fortunes. In this context Baltimore's Federalists seized upon the tarring and feathering as the logical culmination of the Republicans' unthinking opposition to Great Britain. A day after the incident the Federalist press issued a call for a town meeting. On October 21 the self-styled "friends of order" composed a resolution stating that "we will, at the hazard of our lives, aid the civil authority in arresting and dispersing all mobs which may invade the personal rights and property of our fellow citizens, or disturb the quiet of the city." As if to underline the political loyalties of the "friends of order," the meeting elected Federalist Samuel Sterett to the chair.

The Republicans scorned the meeting as a Federalist trick. William Pechin called it an "electioneering artifice." He said that if the meeting had been properly publicized and widely attended, the unpopular Sterett would never have been called to the chair. Baptiste Irvine, editor of the more radical Republican *Whig*, sarcastically advised the "friends of order" to adopt a resolution against journeymen shoemakers, "a stubborn jacobin race, supplied with knives and lapstones." According to one observer, the Federalists tried to provoke a fight with Republicans. They "paraded about with pistols, threatening & insulting the people; who, however, could not be forced to violence which these champions of good government strove to produce." The Federalists even collected a fund for Robert Beatty, who a few months later opened his own shop.[17]

The Republicans took up the cause of the journeymen. While disapproving of the journeymen's violent methods, they asked what true patriot could not help but sympathize with their indignation. With leading Republicans expressing their support for the journeymen, the Union Society suddenly found that the event which had at first boded ill now was working in its favor. A remarkable piece defending the shoemakers came from the pen of "A Journeyman Cordwainer." Weren't the shoemakers merely following the illustrious example of their Revolutionary forefathers, who likewise tarred and feathered tories? How, the author continued, could formal laws cover all the crimes committed against the community? Sometimes the people could not permit justice to be stymied in the courts; they had to take matters into their own hands. They would seize an easily abused power but, "A Journeyman Cordwainer" said in words familiar to Americans steeped in Whig tradition, "better to trust to the discretion of a multitude than to the caprice of a despot." "I am serious," he concluded, "I think the discretionary law of tarring, &c. is a happy general supplement to particular law, providing for heinous offences which would otherwise escape punishment."[18]

In January, 1809, the eight assailants were brought before the Baltimore County Criminal Court. In anticipation of the trial the Union Society had called a general meeting and allocated $5 for a lawyer to defend their accused members. The indictments did not name the Union Society specifically, but the officers feared "that there might be some very impropper questions that would implicate themselves or the Society generally." The shoemakers

were found guilty of assaulting Beatty and on January 25 were
committed to the city jail. The sentences were harsh. Seven of
the defendants received three-month jail sentences and $50 fines
while one got off with a month and a $20 fine. At the end of their
jail term each of the mechanics was required to post a $500 recog-
nizance for a year's good behavior, a sum clearly out of their reach.
The Republicans had not abandoned the shoemakers. After three
days in jail they received a visit from the city's "Republican Gentlemen" who treated them to dinner. Later the same day Governor
Nathaniel Wright, bristling at Beatty's anti-Americanism, pardoned the shoemakers. In early February Beatty was tried for
perjury and acquitted.[19]

While the shoemakers were gaining notoriety in the political
arena, the tailors continued their fight for better pay. In the fall of
1808 they declared that 8s. 9d. a job, the rate of the past three
years, was "scarcely adequate to support a single man, much
more a family, as many of us have." The tailors demanded 10s. per
job, which would bring their weekly earnings from an estimated
$7 to $9. On November 7 the journeymen delivered their ultimatum to the employers, who rejected it. The masters took issue
with the estimates of their working men, contending that on some
articles of clothing the proposed wage increase would actually
amount to 13s. 1d. a job. They also published an account of their
financial predicament, which purported to show that the proposed rate would bankrupt the ordinary master tailor. The average employer sold a thousand suits of clothes a year for a total of
$7,000. From this figure came certain fixed expenses: $832 for the
salaries of a clerk and foreman, $500 for rent, $464 for employing
a tailor on alterations, and $70 for candles and firewood. If on top
of these costs the journeymen heaped the proposed 10s. per job
pay rate, the master stood to lose $199.33 a year.[20]

The masters locked the journeymen out of the shops and declared that any workman who refused to join the society they had
recently formed would be blacklisted. According to some accounts, the employers intended to roll back the journeyman's
earnings from $7 a week to $6. The journeymen appealed to the
public and stated that the masters "give work to their apprentice
boys and women, who scarcely know any thing about the business, rather than give us reasonable wages; and at the same time

they charge their customers the same price as if they were getting their work done by mechanics." It was therefore in the public's best interest to support the journeymen. Fortunately for the striking workmen, the employers could not hold ranks. Although thirty masters had joined in blacklisting the journeymen, seven others conceded the new pay rates. The employers lashed out at these renegades who had abandoned their society and who "by uniting with the journeymen have been the primary cause of prices being raised to what they are, and if patronized by the public, they may calculate on the present prices being in a few years doubled." Whether the remaining thirty employers ultimately granted 10s. per job is unknown.[21]

Six months after the tailors' strike the Union Society of Journeymen Cordwainers called its first turn-out. Defended by the city's leading Republicans at the Beatty trial and pardoned by the governor, the shoemakers were flushed with popularity. Perhaps this favorable climate of opinion encouraged them to challenge the employers. The shoemakers' strike in June, 1809, revolved around the issue of the closed shop rather than wages. Moreover, it was a limited action aimed at two employers who persisted in using nonsociety workmen. Master shoemaker James Sloan employed three journeymen in his manufactory who did not belong to the Union Society, while Angello Atkinson hired one. Both men ranked among the largest of Baltimore's shoemakers. From 1794 to 1815 Sloan acquired eleven apprentices at the orphans court and Atkinson eight. Politics may have exacerbated tensions in the shops, for Sloan was a well-known Federalist and member of the conservative Washington Benevolent Society. On June 26 Allen Sergeant, the Union Society's secretary, delivered a message to Sloan demanding that he discharge John Davidson and the other nonsociety employees. Davidson brought his case before the Baltimore County Criminal Court, which at its July session issued thirty-seven indictments against the Union Society for conspiracy "to prevent a Journeyman, who had been excluded from their Society, from obtaining employment from a Master Cordwainer."[22]

Never before had the courts taken such action. Fearing the court might confiscate its funds, the society held a general meeting and ordered its savings withdrawn from the bank. The president and committeemen then appointed several trustees who placed the money in new accounts under their own names. They hired attorney Luther Martin to defend the society, a surprising choice at first glance because Martin was an outspoken Federalist and enemy of the Jefferson and Madison administrations. But Martin was widely acknowledged by friends and foes to possess one of the nation's sharpest legal minds. The society might also have calculated that a Federalist lawyer would allay the suspicions of a conservative judge and jury. The trial began on August 11. George Powly, the president of the society, was the only journeyman to actually stand trial. Ten days later at three o'clock in the afternoon the jury adjourned. The verdict came on Tuesday morning, August 22—guilty. Three days later Davidson printed a statement in the newspapers denying that Sloan had advised him to prosecute the society. The Union Society of Journeymen Cordwainers, at least formally, appears to have disbanded. It is difficult to assess the Republican party's attitudes in the case. Although Republican editors had occasionally expressed sympathy with journeymen in other cities, they were conspicuously silent over the Union Society case.[23]

The defeat of the shoemakers did not prevent other journeymen from continuing to press for better pay and working conditions. By the fall of 1810 an impasse had evidently developed in the printing trade, which so far had escaped the unrest of the journeymen shoemakers and tailors. On September 26 the newspapers printed a notice to the journeymen printers about "the intention of our brethren in Philadelphia, to alter the present regulation of their Prices." A meeting was called of the Typographical Society and "others, disposed to co-operate with them." What this cooperation entailed is unclear. The Baltimore printers may have promised their Philadelphia brethren that they would not scab their jobs. It is also possible that they joined in demanding the new prices themselves. Three days later the society's corresponding committee requested a second meeting. Then on October 9 the following advertisement appeared:

20 JOURNEYMEN PRINTERS *Want Employment.*
A line addressed to A. B. at this office, will be duly attended to.
No application need be made but by those disposed to give the
NEWLY ESTABLISHED PRICES.

From this notice it appears that the Typographical Society, emboldened by the example of the Philadelphia printers, had demanded higher wages. Some of the printing offices, though, refused to pay the "newly established prices." The twenty journeymen who worked at these shops walked out. Whether they succeeded in pressuring their employers to pay the new prices or found work elsewhere is unknown. The Typographical Society held another special meeting on December 1 on "business of importance," but the nature of that business is also uncertain.[24]

At the same time that printers were altering their prices, the shoemakers closed down the shops again. While the Union Society of Journeymen Cordwainers had probably dissolved itself, the shoemakers quickly reorganized in the Union Philanthropic Society of Journeymen Cordwainers. Adding the word "philanthropic" to its title did not soften the society's fighting spirit. On November 3, 1810, the society demanded a raise of 25¢ on each pair of "Cossack" boots. To justify its proposed prices, the society published a detailed account of shoemakers' earnings in the newspapers. According to its figures, employers paid their journeymen $3 for each pair of boots. An ordinary shoemaker who worked fourteen hours a day could make three pairs a week. After deducting 50¢ for the materials that the journeyman had to supply, the typical shoemaker earned only $8.50 a week. Under the new wages his earnings would increase to $9.25 a week. Echoing the earlier protests against child labor, the society said the masters were "imposing the work of apprentices and *market work* upon the public" while charging the same as for custom work. On December 13 the Union Philanthropic Society urged the public to patronize the shops of Hugh Keys and Arthur Miller, two masters who had agreed to the new rates. By January 1, 1811, it had added seven new names to the list.[25]

The master shoemakers retaliated with a stick and a carrot. Forty-six employers leagued together in the new United Master Shoemakers. The society blacklisted members of the Union Philanthropic Society, which protested that the action drove "from the city of Baltimore a number of useful and experienced workmen, to the great injury of the citizens in general." The masters then issued a call for new workmen, promising "to give to any number of Journeymen Boot & Shoemakers, who will come to the

city of Baltimore, and commence in our employ the most profit-
able work, constant employment, and punctual payment." The
advertisement appeared in the newspapers of Philadelphia and
Lancaster, Pennsylvania; Hagerstown and Easton, Maryland; and
Washington, D.C. It apparently worked. As early as December
17 master Benjamin Walters assured the townspeople that "he is
not in the least injured by [the strike], having at this time as good
workmen as ever as he could wish." To break the strike, the master shoemakers had to win the loyalties of their new scab work
force. By October, 1811, the United Master Shoemakers had established a benefit fund for its journeymen members. "We wish to
apprize you," the employers notified their workmen, "that our
funds are ample to the support of the needy and afflicted, and
shall at all times cheerfully contribute when applied to for assistance." At the same time they assured the newly hired journeymen of their continued employment, denying a rumor that they
had reached settlement with the Union Philanthropic Society that
called for the firing of all scabs.[26]

As the months passed, the unity that had initially characterized the employers' actions started to crumble. In December,
1810, forty-six employers signed a statement refusing work to
striking journeymen, but when a similar declaration appeared ten
months later only thirty reiterated their position. Tempers flared
as some masters broke rank, especially the less established employers who lacked the economic resources to withstand a prolonged strike. According to the Union Philanthropic Society, the
masters who had agreed to the new prices were "young men who
have lately commenced in the boot and shoe making business."
The records of the orphans court bear out the statement. From
1794 to 1815 only four of the nine "young men" who paid the new
wages acquired an apprentice at the orphans court. On the other
hand, of the forty-six members of the United Master Shoemakers,
forty had apprentices. The mean apprentice holding of the "young
men" was three, compared to six for the United Master Shoemakers. The top apprentice holder among the "young men" had five,
the leader among the United Master Shoemakers had seventeen.[27]

In its own terms the journeymen movement was a success.
In October, 1805, the tailors demanded a pay raise from 7s. 6d. a

job to 8s. 9d., and got it. For the next three years they overhauled the rating system so that by 1808, according to disgruntled employers, they were receiving double what they had traditionally made on certain articles of clothing. In June, 1807, the journeymen tailors boosted their weekly earnings from $7 to between $8 and $9 by driving up the wages for uniforms. In November, 1808, at least seven of the thirty master tailors who locked their striking workmen out of the shops eventually agreed to the new pay rate of 10s. a job. The shoemakers had a similar experience. In June, 1807, masters conceded a pay hike of 25¢ a pair for boots with leather bindings. In late 1810 and early 1811 no fewer than sixteen of the original forty-six master shoemakers who had originally refused the journeymen's demands for a 25¢ raise on "Cossack boots" ultimately acquiesced, in addition to the nine who had gone along from the beginning. Finally, consider the case of the printers: in October, 1810, they probably closed down a few shops for higher wages, which suggests that some employers were willing to grant the new prices without a strike. The only clear defeat suffered by the journeymen concerned the issue of the closed shop rather than wages, and it took the intervention of the courts to break the shoemakers' strike of June, 1809.

The journeymen achieved more than higher wages. Their organizations exhibited greater strength and resilience than those of the 1790s. The United Journeymen Cordwainers probably lasted only a few years after its founding in 1792. The Union Society of Journeymen Cordwainers operated continuously from 1806 to 1812, although after the 1809 strike it prudently inserted "philanthropic" in its title. The Baltimore Typographical Society also functioned without interruption from at least 1803 to 1812. Perhaps most important, the journeymen won political legitimacy through their organized activities, most clearly in the Robert Beatty affair in October, 1808, when suddenly members of the Union Society became defenders of democratic republicanism, lionized by Republican party leaders at the city and state levels.

NOTES

1. *American* (Baltimore), Dec. 10, July 6, 1805; *Federal Gazette* (Baltimore), Dec. 11, 1800; George E. Barnett, "The Printers: A Study in American

Trade Unionism," *American Economic Association Quarterly*, 3rd ser., 10 (Oct., 1909):4.

2. *American*, July 6, 1805, Feb. 16, May 30, 1808, Sept. 26, 1809.

3. *Ibid.*, May 1, 1812, June 25, 1808; *Federal Gazette*, Feb. 26, 1808; *Whig* (Baltimore), June 1, 1808.

4. *American*, July 7, 1804.

5. *Baltimore Daily Intelligencer*, June 10, 20, 1794; *American*, June 5, 8, 1799, Nov. 16, 1808.

6. *American*, Feb. 25, Mar. 12, Aug. 30, 1806; *Federal Gazette*, May 30, Aug. 30, 1806, Apr. 18, 1809.

7. *Edward's Baltimore Daily Advertiser*, July 3, 1794; *Maryland Journal* (Baltimore), July 9, 1794; Constitution and Bye Laws of the Union Society of Journeymen Cordwainers of the City and Precincts of Baltimore, Baltimore County Commissioners, Private Commissioners, MHR.

8. *Ibid.*, articles 1, 2, 5.

9. *Ibid.*, articles 7, 8, 4, 3, 25; *American*, Jan. 1, 1811.

10. Constitution and Bye Laws, articles 28, 25, 21, Apr. 15, 1807.

11. *Ibid.*, articles 16, 22.

12. *Ibid.*, June 8, Dec. 14, 1807, Jan. 11, 1808. For Wynard's apprentice holdings, see Petition Docket, Jan., 1809, Session, pp. 14, 16, 17, 21, Criminal Court of Oyer and Terminer, Baltimore City Criminal Court, MHR.

13. *American*, Nov. 16, 1808.

14. *Federal Gazette*, Oct. 22, 28, 1808; *Whig*, Nov. 26, Dec. 8, 1808; *American*, Sept. 8, Oct. 20, 27, 1808; *Report of the Committee of Grievances and Courts of Justice of the House of Delegates of Maryland, on the Subject of the Recent Mobs and Riots in the City of Baltimore* (Annapolis, 1813), p. 169.

15. *Interesting Papers Relative to the Recent Riots at Baltimore* (Philadelphia, 1812), p. 81.

16. *Baltimore Evening Post*, Oct. 19, 1808; *Federal Gazette*, Oct. 28, 1808; *American*, Oct. 22, 1808; Constitution and Bye Laws, Oct. 17, 1808.

17. *American*, Oct. 20, 1808; *Whig*, Oct. 21, Dec. 5, 1808.

18. *Whig*, Nov. 26, 1808.

19. *Ibid.*, Jan. 25, 28, 30, 1809; Constitution and Bye Laws, Jan. 23, 1809.

20. *American*, Nov. 14, 16, 1808.

21. *Ibid.*, Nov. 14, 22, 1808.

22. *Ibid.*, Aug. 29, 1811; *Federal Gazette*, Aug. 22, 25, 1809; vols. 1–10, Indentures, Orphans Court, Baltimore County Register of Wills, MHR.

23. Constitution and Bye Laws, July 17, 1809; *Federal Gazette*, Aug. 22, 25, 1809.

24. *American*, Sept. 26, 29, Oct. 9, Nov. 28, 1810.

25. *Ibid.*, June 20, Dec. 13, 1810, Jan. 1, 1811.

26. *Ibid.*, Dec. 17, 18, 1810, Oct. 18, 1811.

27. *Ibid.*, Jan. 1, 1811; vols. 1–10, Indentures.

11

THE CRISIS OF REPUBLICAN POLITICS

On June 27, 1807, the British warship *Leopard* attacked the U.S. frigate *Chesapeake* as it sailed out of Norfolk, Virginia. From that date until Madison declared war on Great Britain five years later, Baltimore politics lunged from one international crisis to another. As in the 1790s, political activity moved into the streets. After 1807 a politics of plebeian protest emerged: vast open-air demonstrations of loyalty to the republic, July 4th celebrations honoring the militant republicanism of the Revolutionary generation, political riots against alleged enemies of the republic. Republicans were able to focus on the international scene while minimizing conflicts among themselves, as they had from 1794 to 1798. But one thing had changed: the mechanic leadership that had figured so prominently in the Republican party of the 1790s was inactive. Not once after 1807 did the mechanics hold a general meeting, which had become almost commonplace in the 1790s.

Nowhere was this breakdown of leadership clearer than in the political riots. In contrast to the Ramsdell-Senton riot of 1794, prominent master craftsmen took no leading role in the Martin riot of 1807. Five years later, when Baltimore experienced a second and far more serious disturbance, none of the traditional sources of crowd leadership asserted itself, which permitted new social elements to emerge that included militant journeymen. In short, the growing inability of the city's authorities to contain street politics within the bounds set during the 1790s underlined tensions that had been gathering in the mechanic community for over a decade. The collapse of the Mechanical Society, the localization of mechanic political power, the growing conservatism among some master craftsmen, the rise of a new generation of republican mechanics, and the emergence of a journeymen movement—these ingredients combined to produce what was in 1812 the bloodiest riot in American history.

The *Chesapeake* affair shocked all America. Royal officers had boarded the ship, removed four sailors suspected of desertion, and left the crippled vessel to limp back to port. Several American seamen had been killed. Almost immediately Baltimore was buzzing with news of the attack. Two days later a town meeting estimated at between 3,000 and 10,000 condemned the "daring outrage" and pledged to support whatever retaliatory measures the president should choose to pursue. In early July Mathew Brown of the *Gazette* wrote that "the town has been full to overflowing, and the citizens not a little agitated, with rumors and reports." The big rumor was that the British had declared war. According to Brown, it had "nearly put a stop (momentarily we are confident) to mercantile transactions."[1]

The *Cheseapeake* affair conjured up bad memories of the British attack on American shipping in early 1794, and it produced the same tense atmosphere as people readied themselves for war. The first step was to mobilize the militia. But as past experience had demonstrated, calling up the troops was a highly charged political act. By allowing mechanics to organize their own companies and elect their own leadership, it encouraged them to become vocal politically. Both the radical Whig Club of 1777 and the republican Mechanical Society of 1793 had had strong ties to the Mechanical Volunteers. Thus it was no surprise that mechanics inundated the militia units in the wake of the *Chesapeake* incident. Of the 212 militia officers whose names appear in the *American* in 1807 and 1808, 41 percent were mechanics and 30 percent merchants. These figures revealed a major social overhaul in the militia leadership. In 1794 and 1795 mechanics had made up only 22 percent of the thirty-seven militia officers identified in the *Daily Intelligencer*, merchants 57 percent. The mechanics not only stepped into company command as captains, lieutenants, sergeants, and ensigns; they also received regimental appointments. The Baltimore Battalion, it will be recalled, consisted of four regiments: the 5th, 6th, 27th, and 39th. In 1794 and 1795 the four lieutenant colonels commanding the regiments were merchants. By 1805 the mechanics secured a foothold when

Joseph Biays replaced John O'Donnell of the 6th. Biays had been one of the Point's top shipbuilders in the 1790s, although after the turn of the century he was calling himself a merchant. Two years later the mechanics received unambiguous representation when James Mosher, bricklayer, took over command of the 39th.[2]

Mechanic and merchant officers tended to avoid each other's company. Seventeen of the sixty-nine companies appearing in the *American* chose largely mechanic officers. These units made up only 25 percent of the total but accounted for 61 percent of the mechanic officers and 88 percent of the mechanic captains. Only one mechanic, silversmith Standish Berry, commanded a unit whose lower-ranking officers were merchants. Some of these mechanic units traced their origins to the crisis of the 1790s and earlier. The Mechanical Volunteer Company, founded in 1775, turned out. So did the First Baltimore Light Infantry Corps, which had paraded with the Volunteers in 1793. Its original captain, carpenter John Mackenheimer, received a promotion to major in the 5th. He left the captaincy to cooper John Shrim, his lieutenant. Another old corps was the Baltimore Friendship Volunteer Company, which in 1798 had joined the Mechanical Volunteers in saluting General Samuel Smith, then campaigning for re-election to Congress. Rope maker John Chalmers was still in command. Some of the units broadcast their constituency by adopting the word "mechanic" in their titles. In the 1790s only the Mechanical Volunteers had done so. A decade and a half later the Baltimore Battalion included the Baltimore Mechanical Blues, Baltimore Republican Mechanical Volunteers, Baltimore Mechanical Junior Pikemen, and Fell's Point Mechanical Volunteers, in addition to the original Baltimore Mechanical Volunteers. Although these units welcomed nonmechanic members, they rarely failed to elect mechanic officers.

The case of the Mechanical Volunteers shows how the workingmen maintained themselves in power. In the summer of 1807 the Mechanical Volunteers needed reorganization badly. On July 2 the "remaining part of the MECHANICAL VOLUNTEERS" declared in the papers that they wished to meet "all patriotic Mechanics who are desirous of forming a Volunteer Corps at this eventful crisis." Within eight months the company had put its affairs in order and issued a second notice. "Gentlemen who are not mechanics," the announcement read, "and have a desire to join this association, can now have an opportunity of becoming members." The mechanics were enlisting nonmechanics, but note the timing of the call: it came after the company had elected officers.[3]

Particular trades now wanted their own units. The carpenters, who belonged to one of the city's oldest craft associations, considered forming a separate company. They had even picked a name—the Baltimore Carpenter Volunteers—but later abandoned the plan. Rather than creating a new unit, the carpenters decided to revitalize the old Baltimore United Blues. They kept the Blues' old captain, sailmaker Jacob Grafflin, who had commanded since the 1790s, but elected carpenters to the lower-ranking positions. The "Tanners and Curriers of Baltimore" also discussed organizing on their own; whether they carried out their plans is unknown. On July 18 the newspapers announced the formation of the Baltimore Republican Draymen Volunteers. The draymen had been active politically over the past several years, parading conspicuously on Independence Day and earning the praise of the Republican press. But unlike the skilled workers, the draymen did not elect a captain from among their own numbers. Lacking the organizational elan of the carpenters and the economic power of the tanners, the draymen deferred to their employers and chose merchant George Howard as captain. Shipbuilders were prominent in the Fell's Point units. Eight of the sixty-nine companies incorporated the words "Fell's Point" or "Deptford Hundred" into their titles. Mechanics supplied fourteen of the nineteen known officers and all of the captains. Half of the mechanic officers were shipbuilders like Dixon Brown, who inherited the command of the venerable Fell's Point Volunteer Corps from shipwright David Stodder.[4]

The mobilization of the militia always carried the potential for crowd violence. In 1776 and 1777 militia officers had been largely responsible for the riotous activities of the Whig Club. They were no less conspicuous in the Ramsdell-Senton riots of 1794. In both cases the disturbances came amid frenzied efforts to organize, equip, and train the raw troops. In both they provided mechanics with an opportunity to assume leadership that other groups either would not or could not take up. From this perspective shipbuilder David Stodder, the central figure in the 1794 rioting, was re-enacting a role played by Whig spinning wheel maker David Poe seventeen years earlier. In the wake of the *Chesapeake* affair Baltimoreans learned that the links between militia and crowd were as strong as ever. In 1807 Aaron Burr was charged with inciting treasonable activity in the west. He stood trial at Norfolk, Virginia, with Chief Justice John Marshall presiding. The Baltimore press covered the case closely because Luther Martin and Robert Goodloe Harper, two of the city's top lawyers and Federalists, were leading the defense. The Federalists said that President Jefferson was waging a personal vendetta against his enemy Burr. The Republicans, rallying to the support of the president, called for a guilty verdict. The trial went through the summer. By fall it was over—Burr went free.[5]

In late October Luther Martin made what he considered a triumphal return to Baltimore. With him came the notorious Burr and one of the alleged co-conspirators, Harman Blennerhassett. Never one to duck a fight, Martin published a letter in the Federalist press on November 2 that he knew would infuriate Republicans. He praised Marshall for protecting the Constitution against a vindictive president who was determined to destroy a foe at whatever cost. Martin was particularly pleased with his own performance. "We have proved," he boasted, "that in America there are lawyers who cannot be intimidated by fear of presidential vengeance, nor by the phrenzy of a deceived, misguided people, from securing even to those destined to be the victims of power, those rights for the enjoyment of which the constitution is and ought to be their sacred honor and inviolate pledge." Martin asked his fellow townspeople to withhold their judgment on the case until receiving a transcript of the trial.

True to form, the militia took the first steps to silence the Federalist lawyer. On the same day that the letter appeared, Captain Leonard Frailey marched his Patriot Volunteers to Martin's home on Charles Street "with charged bayonets playing the rogue's march." The next morning, November 3, the *Whig* printed the following:

AN EARNEST PROPOSAL

It is proposed to the young men of Baltimore, of *all* descriptions, whether it would not evince more strongly our attachment to the *best government on earth*—and at the same time confer a mark of distinction on our '*illustrious strangers*,' by treating them *this very* DAY, with a suit of *tar* and *feathers*, each. Such means, or ones *more rigid* must be taken to intimidate traitors. *What think you?* Luther Martin, I think—is also a very WORTHY man.

By noon a handbill was making its way through town, informing the citizens that at three o'clock in the afternoon the effigies of the "traitors" would be "*Marshalled* for execution by the hangman on *Gallows-Hill*, in consequence of the sentence pronounced against them by the unanimous voice of every honest man in the community." Meanwhile people were busily making effigies of Martin, Marshall, Burr, and Blennerhassett. Each wore a placard specifying his crime.[6]

Events were moving quickly, too quickly for Mayor Thorowgood Smith. After the handbill appeared, the mayor called several prominent citizens into his office, including Walter Dorsey, the chief judge of the Baltimore County Criminal Court. Both Smith and Dorsey were Federalists. Neither of them sympathized with what looked to become a massive Republican demonstration. They decided to "call on the militia and prepare for the worst." Between two and three o'clock that afternoon Mayor Smith assembled his fifteen constables, told them a riot was possibly in the making, and asked if he could depend on them. Getting assurances from the militia posed a trickier problem. Captain Frailey's harassment of Martin had been ominous. Smith and Dorsey confronted General John Stricker, the commanding officer of the Baltimore Battalion: could they count on the militia's support? The Republican Stricker answered with a qualified yes. He sent messages to captains James Biays of the Fell's Point Troop of Light Dragoons, Samuel Hollingsworth of the First Baltimore Troop of Horse, and Joshua Barney of the First Baltimore Hussars, ordering them to assemble the cavalry. They were to await further instructions. Barney and Hollingsworth obeyed. "But Captain Biays," it was later reported, "assuring the officer who called upon him with those instructions that no mischief would be done by the people, declined ordering out his troop, with which determination the officer was satisfied."[7]

By this time the parade of the effigies was underway. It began at the Point and headed toward Old Town, ultimately across Baltimore to Federal Hill. The marchers had displayed the effigies in a pair of carts, located in the middle of the procession. They moved from the Point to Old Town unopposed. But when the parade reached the bridge crossing Jones' Falls into the city, it confronted two constables who ordered the crowd to disperse, warning them that cavalry units had been stationed uptown. Those at the front of the line answered that they were in violation of no law, but merely expressing their "detestation of traitors and enemies of their country." The crowd pushed past the police and into Baltimore.

During this exchange Captain Biays was in the parade. When he heard about the cavalry, he hurried to find Hollingsworth and Barney. He hoped, as he later explained, to convince his fellow captains that the crowd was peaceful. Biays was still looking for the troops when he received a message from the mayor requesting his presence at the corner of South and Market streets, where the parade would soon pass. Biays found the mayor jittery and reluctant to unleash the militia. Smith calculated that Captain Biays, whose popularity must have risen after his refusal to mobilize his unit, could defuse the situation. Would he, the mayor asked, meet the parade now coming down Market Street and lead it peacefully through town? Biays said he would try. By this time the crowd had reached them. Biays stepped into the street, stopped the procession, issued a plea for orderly behavior, and called for a round of "huzzaas" as a sign of agreement. So far everything was going smoothly. With Captain Biays now in the lead, the procession resumed its march.[8]

It had not gone four or five blocks before a new crisis developed. The parade now stood at the intersection of Market and Charles streets; just down the block was Martin's house. Captain Biays later said that he continued the march past Charles Street with the front half of the procession in tow. But unknown to him the rear of the column behind the effigies turned toward Martin's house. Mayor Smith and Judge Dorsey had already planted themselves at the gates to the house, but neither man could restore order. The crowd gathered around the house, raised a few mocking cheers, and started throwing rocks. The situation was dangerous because several dozen armed men had occupied Martin's home and threatened to fire on the people outside. By now Captain Biays had doubled back to Charles Street. After a few tense moments he persuaded the crowd to resume its march. It continued up Market Street and around the basin to Federal Hill. There in a great bonfire the effigies were destroyed.[9]

The trouble was not over yet. The next day, November 5, Judge Dorsey issued arrest warrants for Biays and seven others who had allegedly instigated the rioting. On November 7 a constable served Biays with the warrant. The captain declared that he would go to jail before posting security. Mayor Smith faced the prospect of another confrontation. After unsuccessfully entreating Biays to enter security and even offering to stand as his bail, Mayor Smith went in search of Judge Dorsey who, he hoped, might prove more conciliatory. Three days later Captain Biays was still waiting for the mayor's decision. But Smith was powerless. He had already come under withering attack for mobilizing the militia. On November 5 the city's Republicans assembled and censured all city officials responsible for calling up the cavalry. Two days later at a Republican-sponsored town meeting the magistrates were condemned for "an assumption of power hostile to our constitution." The officials' rash behavior, the Republicans claimed, had demonstrated the deficiencies in the unreformed city charter. Thus the meeting appointed a committee to draft a petition for charter amendments which, as we have seen, were adopted a few months later. Presiding over the meeting was none other than Captain Biays, whom the Republicans thanked for "his distinguished conduct in the chair"—a slap at Dorsey.

Bad tempers died slowly. On November 9 Captain Joseph C. O'Reilly, one of the eight named in Dorsey's warrants, paraded his troops through the city. It was rumored that the militia intended to burn Dorsey's effigy before his home. Over a hundred citizens reportedly turned out to repel the feared assault and dispersed only when a company officer denied the rumor. In January, 1808, a number of citizens petitioned the assembly for the removal of Judge Dorsey. A committee considered the question but concluded that the judge was innocent of the "high judicial misdemeanors" that would alone justify removal. Four months later Walter Dorsey resigned as chief judge of the Baltimore County Criminal Court.[10]

The Martin riot conformed closely to the patterns set by the Ramsdell-Senton riot of 1794. Both occurred five months after the British navy committed what almost all Americans considered unprovoked aggression. Both occurred while the militia was mobilizing. Both began at Fell's Point, a well-known plebeian section of the city. In both riots militia officers took leading roles. In both the most prominent figure was a shipbuilder. In both a Federalist judge found himself the target of popular outrage. In both, legal authorities had to retreat before the will of the townspeople. Both riots resulted from seemingly insignificant gestures—a recalcitrant ship captain hoisting the American colors reversed, a conservative lawyer printing a letter critical of the Republican administration. But these acts carried great symbolic import because they happened when the republic itself seemed endangered. In tarring and feathering Ramsdell and Senton and in burning Martin's effigy, people were stating their determination to defend the republic against all its enemies. At least one citizen, "Sicilias," saw such a connection between the two riots:

> Are there not crimes for which law can assign no penalty, and yet ought not to go unchastised. When one who had pirated on our merchants' property abroad under a commission from those who hate us [Senton], and came to insult those he had injured at home. When another hung the national colours reversed and degraded in the harbour and bosom of our city [Ramsdell], in front of the citizen militia paraded on an American anniversary, was there any punishment but the resentment of the people, for such audacious offences? and was it not well applied to repel them.

There was nothing hysterical, unthinking, or paranoid about this behavior. America was skirting the brink of war with Great Britain, the world's most powerful monarchy—no threat to republicanism seemed insignificant.[11]

But one thing had changed from 1794 to 1807: mechanic leadership. Six of the seven men whom Judge Samuel Chase accused of instigating the 1794 riots were mechanics, and half of them were officers of the Mechanical Society. By contrast, the eight men named by Judge Walter Dorsey included no more than one mechanic. Although the occupation of William Conklin does not appear in the city directories, he was likely a mechanic because he was a sergeant in the Fell's Point Mechanical Volunteers. The others were newspaper editor Baptiste Irvine, storekeepers Joseph C. O'Reilly and Arthur Hill, grocer Samuel D. LeGrand, tavernkeeper George Peterson, and china store owner Joel M. Munson.[12]

That left James Biays, a transitional figure, a man who personified the changes that both mechanic and crowd leadership was undergoing. Biays began as a shipbuilder, one of Baltimore's biggest. In 1788 when the town's ship joiners organized to march in celebration of the ratification of the Constitution, they asked Biays to lead them. Ten years later the city's mechanics held what was reported to be the largest meeting in their history: Biays was in the chair. As a militia captain he consistently acknowledged the mechanics in the company's July 4th toasts. Typical was one offered in 1801: "The Mechanics of Baltimore.—Plenty of work; long bills; prompt pay; and unanimity in support of republicanism." Although James never served as an officer in the Mechanical Society, his brother Joseph did. James was also a Republican party stalwart and neighborhood spokesman. In 1798 he was one of General Samuel Smith's most outspoken supporters; the Federalists called him a Republican "FIRE-BRAND." Two years later his company gave a toast testifying their loyalty to Smith while poking fun at Robert Goodloe Harper: "Our worthy statesman, Gen. SAMUEL SMITH.—May he continue the *trumpeter*, but never become the HARPER of Patriotism." In 1801 Biays chaired a meeting of Fell's Point Republicans celebrating Jefferson's election to the presidency.

In addition to his republicanism, Biays's commitment to the Point was well known. In 1799 the citizens of the Point appointed Biays to a committee considering the establishment of a Fell's Point bank. Eleven years later he was elected to the board of directors of the Marine Bank of Baltimore, based at the Point. While James never served in the city council as his brother did, Ward 8 elected him as elector of the mayor and Second Branch in 1802. The militia bolstered Biays's popularity. As early as 1794 he was secretary of the Deptford Fuzileers. Four years later he had risen to captain of the Fell's Point Troop of Light Dragoons. By 1807 he was also serving as captain of the Fell's Point Juvenile Pikemen, a corps of teenagers too young to enlist in the regular militia.[13]

The mechanics, the Republican party, Fell's Point, and the militia were the bases of Biays's popularity. But during these years his identity was undergoing a change; James Biays was slipping from the world of mechanics into the world of merchants. From 1799 until 1804 he called himself a "ship joiner" in the city directories. He was one of Baltimore's most prosperous tradesmen. In 1804 Biays's tax assessment placed him in the top 6 percent of the city's property holders. In 1800 he owned ten slaves, in 1810 twenty. At some imperceptible point Biays crossed the threshold separating the successful shipbuilder who happened to invest in commerce from the merchant first and foremost, one of whose interests was shipbuilding. In the 1804 city directory Biays was still in the transition, listing himself as a "merchant and ship builder." Three years later he shed the mechanic identity and thereafter appeared as "merchant." Those years brought Biays great wealth. By 1815 he ranked in the top .5 percent of Baltimore's property holders.[14]

The Martin riot, in sum, reflected the disunity that had been growing in the mechanic community since 1800. Mechanics had played no active role in the disturbance. We can only speculate about why the mechanics withdrew from street politics. But central to any explanation must be the fact that the institutional structure within which mechanics could assert community leadership had collapsed with the dissolution of the Mechanical Society seven years before. There was still Ward 7, the heart of the mechanic population and the center of their political power. But Ward 7 seems to have remained aloof during the disturbance, at least that part of Old Town that belonged to the ward. None of the eight men charged by Judge Dorsey lived in Old Town. Both the Republican press by implication and Federalist papers explicitly claimed that Fell's Point—Ward 8—was the main recruiting ground for those who participated in the events. The *Gazette* reported: "The people of Baltimore took no part in the frolic." Thus the emergence of Captian James Biays as a crowd leader reflected not so much his strong following among mechanics as his popularity at the Point.[15]

The Martin riot initiated two years of regular street demonstrations. In December, 1807, Congress passed the Embargo Act prohibiting American exports. The effects were felt immediately in Baltimore, particularly along the docks at Fell's Point. Suddenly sailors were out of work. According to "W. H.," who belonged to the "Sons of Neptune," all major cities except Baltimore had provided relief for their inactive seamen. On February 3, 1808, "a number of sailors" assembled at the Point and marched to the office of the mayor "in regular order, with colors flying." They presented him with a petition signed by 259 sailors, asking for assistance in their "distressed situation." Mayor Smith received the petitioners "with his accustomed civility" and promised to do what he could.[16]

In the fall the embargo was still setting the tone of street politics. On September 30, 1808, the Republicans held a huge meeting at the flour mill of General Stricker on Jones' Falls. The Federalists were making a bid for a congressional seat, supporting candidate William H. Winder; the Republicans wanted to drum up support for their nominees, Alexander McKim and Nicholas R. Moore. The Republicans invited the inhabitants of the city and county to the meeting where they might hear the various candidates speak. According to the *Whig*, nearly 4,000 citizens turned out to hear the political aspirants and enjoy the barbecue. McKim addressed the crowd; Winder failed to appear. The keynote speaker was Senator Samuel Smith, who was waxing at his republican best that Friday afternoon. The Federalists, he declared, had stumbled from one catastrophe to another while in power. Wasn't their legacy the Alien and Sedition acts, a crushing national debt, and unpopular excise taxes that provoked agrarian insurrection? By contrast, the Republicans had lowered the debt and protected the constitutional freedoms that the Federalists had trampled. Smith defended the Embargo Act and condemned the British orders in council that required American ships to pay "TRIBUTE" on imported goods.

Then came the climax of the speech. "But gentlemen," the senator exclaimed, "I hold in my hand incontestible proofs of the exaction of tribute under these orders in council." What Smith held were the ship papers of the brig *Sophia* that had entered the harbor the day before, carrying a cargo from Rotterdam including six pipes of gin. On July 10 the *Sophia* had been boarded by the commander of a British gun brig and forced to land at Harwich, England. There the *Sophia's* captain paid a tax of eight pence per gallon on the gin. "What *American*," Smith asked, "will submit to this?—Is there a man in all this vast assemblage who would stoop to pay tribute to England?" The *Whig* reported the answer: "No! No! from all quarters!" After the senator's dramatic flourish "about 2,000 active republicans" marched into the city "with the American standard and martial music." Following the banner "No Winder—no Tribute—Moore & McKim, and American Independence," the parade gave three cheers as it passed McKim's house and dispersed.[17]

The Republicans were not finished with the gin. On October 2 the *American* printed the following notice:

NO TRIBUTE

SPIRIT OF 1776

The six pipes of Gin, arrived in the brig Sophia, capt. Carnan, on which *tribute* has been paid to Great Britain, will be consumed by fire on Tuesday evening on Gallows Hill.

The next day a parade gathered at the Point. First came the trumpeter, followed by over a thousand "horsemen." Next was the ensignia honoring the farmers of Baltimore County: "God Speed the Plow." An assemblage of more than 300 sailors marched behind, carrying the banner: "A Proof that All American seamen are not gone to Halifax." Assemblyman Tobias E. Stansbury of Baltimore County, plow in hand, followed in a "triumphal car" festooned in "boughs of poplar and evergreen, as emblems of rural life and *civic* triumph." Then came the schooner *Democratic Republican*, commanded by Captain Timothy Gardner. On board were the newly elected Republicans: Congressmen McKim and Moore and assemblymen Theodoric Bland and Robert Steuart. The townspeople by the "thousand" brought up the rear. After circling the Point and crossing into Baltimore, the parade broke up for dinner. Later that evening the townspeople reassembled at Gallows Hill. The *Whig* described the ceremony:

The immense crowd was formed into a great circle by marshalls on horse-back, the *tributary* gin in the centre, over which was erected *a gallows* with this inscription over it:—

'BRITISH ORDERS IN COUNCIL.'

About eight o'clock the *Car* and *schooner*, with their crew and convoy of sailors and citizens, bearing torches arrived—the fatal faggots were lighted—and applied—the GIN was blazed to Heaven—the vast concourse repeatedly huzzaed—as a hogshead burst, or the gallows with 'British orders,' &c. was consumed, and fell; while a salute of seventeen shots was fired from a couple of six pounders on the hill.

The demonstration was tightly organized. Baptiste Irvine estimated that more than 7,000 townspeople had participated in the evening's ceremonies.[18]

During the next four months as the Embargo Act came under increasing attack, Baltimore's Republicans continued to assert their support of the measure in large-scale demonstrations. On January 30, 1809, they called a meeting "for the purpose of expressing their sentiments of the measures of government." A stage had been constructed at Market Space downtown for the speakers, over which flew the national flag. By mid-morning the grounds were filling up. "The windows of the adjacent houses," according to one report, "were lined with spectators." At about eleven o'clock "*the Patriots from Fell's Point*, the pride and ornament of Baltimore," marched into Market Space to join the hundreds already there. Led by James Biays, the hero of the Martin riot, the parade included a "brisk band" playing "Yankee Doodle" and "Hail Columbia." At the head of the procession was a "car" carrying a flag, which the *Whig* described as follows: "The *British Lion* appeared crouching in terror and agony, Clutching a *feeble* bird [the French cock], whom he champed in his bloody and treacherous jaws, the American eagle pouncing upon him, and darting his talons into his skull—forming a picture, very truly styled 'Justice.' Over all was the motto—'*Liberty or Death.*'"

The meeting was chaired by the newly elected Republican mayor, Edward Johnson. A committee framed resolutions and James A. Buchanan, a prominent Republican and Baltimore's first mayor, delivered a speech praising the embargo. The committee

blamed "the stagnation of our commerce" on the "anti-neutral edicts" of Great Britain and France, and reaffirmed Baltimore's faith
in the embargo, "the wisest measure, which, under existing circumstances, could be opposed to those edicts." The committeemen took a few shots at the leading opponents of the act, although
they later disclaimed any intention to malign local Federalists.
Both the *American* and *Whig* reported an attendance of 5,000.[19]

With this recent history of out-of-doors political demonstrations, it was natural that in 1809 the Republicans should consider
a mass Independence Day parade. Only once before had Baltimore's mechanics marched by trade: the May, 1788, parade celebrating the ratification of the federal Constitution. The Republicans intended to re-enact that event and reaffirm the patriotic
fervor that accompanied it. A week before Independence Day the
newspapers published the "Order of the Procession Observed by
the citizens of Baltimore on the 1st of May, 1788—the same will
be adhered to, as far as circumstances will permit, on the ensuing
anniversary of American independence." In numbers and in their
preparations the mechanics overwhelmed the parade. The *Ameri-*
can claimed that nearly 2,000 mechanics had marched along with
450 merchants and traders, 400 farmers, 350 sea captains and sailors, 72 draymen, 50 pilots, and 30 constables. But because the
paper gave estimates for only twenty-four of the thirty-three
crafts participating, the mechanics were actually more numerous.
Perhaps closer to 3,000 marched. The three largest trades—carpentry, shoemaking, and masonry—accounted for 800 marchers
alone. As in 1788 the workingmen displayed symbols of nationalism and craft indentity. The stone cutters designed the most elaborate exhibit, a "Temple of Minerva." Over the temple was a banner showing a chevron and compass, emblems of the trade, along
with various tools stone cutters used. A soaring eagle at the top of
the flag declared: "*Under my wings the arts shall flourish.*"[20]

But the preparations for the parade revealed the divisions
that had beset the mechanic community since 1788. In the weeks
before the celebration the various crafts placed announcements of
meetings in the city newspapers. Most of these statements said
simply that craftsmen would assemble on a certain date to make
arrangements for the parade. Some of them stated that both employers and workingmen would meet and march together. The

call for a meeting of bricklayers came not from the employers but from the "Journeyman Bricklayers beneficial Society." Whether the journeymen bricklayers cooperated with their employers is unknown; their "Society" is never heard from again. The cabinet makers appointed a committee of six to make preparations; three represented the "employers" and three the "Journeymen." The master and journeymen shoemakers assembled at the Pantheon Hotel at the Point. They called on their fellow mechanics to make their contributions at any of seven stores belonging to prominent shoemakers. The secretary of the meeting was journeyman A. Sergeant.[21]

The street politics that had started after the *Chesapeake* affair reached its culmination in 1812. For a half-decade the townspeople had grown accustomed to seeing mass political demonstrations; thus far they had remained within fairly well-defined boundaries, never especially violent and always Republican-led. There was no reason to suspect the events of 1812 to be different. On June 18 the United States declared war on Great Britain in retaliation against grievances that had been accumulating for almost twenty years. Alexander C. Hanson, Federalist editor of the Baltimore *Federal Republican*, attacked the decision. "We are avowedly hostile to the presidency of James Madison," he wrote two days after the declaration of war, "and we never will breath under the dominion direct or derivative of Bonaparte, let it be acknowledged when it may." Hanson had been a constant irritant to Baltimore's Republicans since establishing his paper in 1807. Even before the appearance of his editorial, some townsmen wanted to silence the paper permanently. On June 19 several hundred people reportedly gathered at Myer's Garden at Fell's Point. They decided to make an example of Hanson's partner, Jacob Wagner, by clothing him in a terrapin shell (a symbol of Maryland), a sheep skin and pair of horns (symbols of the cuckold). Three days later on June 22 the office of the *Federal Republican* was besieged. Thirty or forty men tore down the building while three to four hundred watched. Mayor Johnson tried to stop the destruction, telling the crowd that all rioters would be punished. His pleas were futile. He later claimed that "by one person I was threatened, by all I was told that my person was safe unless I attempted to interfere with them; that they would complete the destruction in spite of me, or any thing I could do." The mayor went home.[22]

The fall of the Federalist press unleashed a wave of attacks on persons suspected of toryism. A crowd searched for Wagner at his Charles Street home. They also sought a certain Hutchins who had allegedly said: "Damnation to the memory of Washington, and all who espouse his cause." With between 800 and 1,000 people gathered at Hutchins's house, Mayor Johnson succeeded in distracting the attention of the crowd while their prey crawled out the back window and escaped. The crowd also targeted Charles Smith, who was said to have remarked "that the streets of Quebec would be paved with the bones of those troops who should march from the United States to attack Canada." Smith left town. An English mechanic named Prior, whose shop sign read "from London," was also forced to flee. Meanwhile, a group dismantled several ships at the Point, which had allegedly carried provisions to allies of Great Britain. Mr. Mactier, the owner, continued to receive anonymous notes ordering him to leave town. A rumor circulated that somebody living in the house of free black James Briscoe had declared that "if all the blacks were of his opinion, they would soon put down the whites." A crowd destroyed Briscoe's house.[23]

Hanson left Baltimore to establish a new press in Georgetown, but he continued to mail his paper to Baltimore subscribers, which inflamed passions in town. In late June and July Hanson began writing to prominent Federalists across the state in an attempt to enlist their support for his planned return to Baltimore. He won over about three dozen men from many of Maryland's leading families. On Saturday, July 25, Hanson slipped into Baltimore and occupied a house on Charles Street. The next day his Federalist comrades began to converge on the house with enough guns, powder, and shot to repulse a prolonged siege. Hanson brought issues of the *Federal Republican*, dated July 27 and carrying the Charles Street address on the title page. The issue contained an editorial that condemned the city officials for their silent complicity in the riots. On Monday morning the papers were out.

If Hanson and his friends were attempting to provoke a confrontation, which they surely were, the city's Republicans did not disappoint them. By evening a crowd had gathered around the Charles Street house. For several hours the two sides hurled insults back and forth. Then they began throwing rocks. The Federalists fired a round of warning shots over the heads of those in the streets, causing people to scatter for cover. When it was discovered that no one had been hurt, the crowd regrouped and intensified its efforts to dislodge the Federalists from their stronghold. A group led by physician Thadeus Gale stormed the door. He was shot dead entering the house. Another Federalist bullet killed John Williams, a stone cutter, who was standing across the street. The crowd now began to arm itself in self-defense. One man found cover behind a tree and fired shots into the third-story window, apparently wounding Federalist Ephraim Gaither. Several of Hanson's friends, their courage faltering, attempted to escape and were captured. One was beaten badly. Suddenly a cannon appeared at the scene, wheeled into position before the house.[24]

The city authorities now acted. They were overwhelmingly Republicans with little sympathy for the Federalists trapped inside the house. Those Federalists had already killed two men, one apparently an innocent by-stander. Many of the Republican officials were veterans from the Martin riot five years earlier. They could remember the protest that resulted from the mobilization of the militia. Before the firing of the warning shots, several alarmed citizens sought out General John Stricker and pleaded with him to call out the troops. He was noncommittal, insisting that two magistrates sign a warrant entitling him to mobilize his men. By the time the signatures had been obtained, Gale and Williams were dead. Around midnight General Stricker ordered Major Joshua Barney, another figure from the Martin riot, to station his cavalry unit at the corner of Baltimore and Charles streets in preparation for action. Only a handful of troops responded to Barney's call. After waiting several hours, General Stricker ordered Barney and his men to move down Charles Street toward the besieged house. Already the city authorities, after considerable haggling, had persuaded the Federalists to surrender. The reasoning was simple: the only safe place in town for the Federalists was the city jail. The militia formed a cordon around the two dozen Federalists still in the house and, accompanied by the mayor, marched to the city jail amid jeers and brickbats.[25]

On Tuesday morning, July 28, the Federalists seemed safe inside their prison cells. As a precautionary measure General Stricker ordered up the 5th Regiment to safeguard the prison along with two artillery units and two cavalry corps. Thirty men reported for duty, although the 5th Regiment alone could claim between 800 and 1,000 troops. Most of the men who turned out were Federalists. General Stricker decided to disband the troops. In his opinion there were not enough of them to resist a riot and their political sympathies promised only to exacerbate the hostilities.

The dismissal of the troops left the prison unguarded. In the evening several groups began to converge around the jail door. There was soon talk of storming the prison. Mayor Johnson, who had anticipated trouble, tried to dissuade the men in the prison area from carrying out their intentions. He failed. Apparently with the collusion of the jailer the prison doors opened. Dozens of men poured into the jail. It was easy to identify most of the elite Federalists amid the plebeian inmates, and they were seized as they attempted to escape. Nine were beaten senseless and tossed into a heap apparently dead. Among the wounded was John Hall, who later testified that the rioters formed a ring around the beaten Federalists and joined hands to sing: "We'll feather and tar ev'ry d—d British tory, And that is the way for American glory." General James M. Lingan, the aged hero of the Revolution, died of wounds inflicted during the beating as he begged for mercy. John Thompson was captured fleeing from the jail. He was tarred and feathered, stabbed with dirks and knives, and set on fire.[26]

During the next week an uneasy calm set over the city. But it ended on August 3 when the relentless Hanson published another issue of the *Federal Republican* in Georgetown and sent it through the mail to Baltimore. Crowds were soon in the streets threatening to attack the U.S. post office. The city's magistrates again resorted to the militia but with greater success this time. Mayor Johnson assured the troops that they were defending property of the U.S. government, not Hanson's paper. On the evening of August 4 the cavalry charged into several groups gathered around the post office and dispersed them. For the rest of the week the militia guarded strategic locations leading to the post office. The rioting was over.[27]

At the time the Baltimore riots were viewed as a great break from the past. Most outsiders and many townspeople as well condemned Baltimore as the "Mobtown" of America, a reputation it kept during the nineteenth century. Without doubt the disturbances of the summer of 1812 were bloodier than anything Americans could remember. The city's authorities had been paralyzed for weeks. Historians have also interpreted the riot as a major turning point, revealing the irreconcilable differences that had arisen between the Republican and Federalist parties of Maryland and reflecting the collapse of an "Anglo-American mob tradition" in which limited violence was aimed at a few well-defined targets.

These perspectives are useful for understanding the riot. But what has perhaps been overlooked is that the "Great Baltimore riot" witnessed the emergence of new social elements in the street politics that had been gaining momentum since 1807. The main figures in the 1812 disturbances were small mechanics. At its July, 1812, session the Baltimore County Criminal Court indicted fifty-two men for rioting, thirty of whom can be identified in the city directories. Twenty were mechanics, seven traders, and three professionals. The twenty-two whose occupations are unknown probably came from the lowest segments of society least likely to establish permanent residences and be listed in the directories. As for the three professionals, none belonged to the community's elite. Physician Jacob Small apparently lived in Baltimore for a short time. Editor Thomas Wilson ran the short-lived *Baltimore Sun*. Apothecary Philip Lewis could claim no taxable property in 1815. The twenty mechanics contrasted sharply with past mechanic crowd leaders. None had served in the Mechanical Society, Mechanical Fire Company, or Mechanics' Bank. None was a militia officer. Except for a brief entry onto the court dockets, they left little trace in the historical records.[28]

Perhaps the most remarkable of the merchants were three journeymen shoemakers: George Wooleslager, Abraham Wright, and James Darling. Wooleslager was accused of helping to demolish the *Federal Republican* office. Wright faced the charge of murdering General Lingan. Darling was accused of vandalizing the Charles Street house on the morning after the riot. This was not the first time these journeymen had crossed the law. In October, 1808, Wooleslager was among the seven men indicted for the tarring and feathering of Robert Beatty. Less than a year later Wright and Darling numbered among the thirty-eight members of the Union Society of Journeymen Cordwainers whom the criminal court indicted for conspiracy. In short, Wooleslager, Wright, and Darling were not just journeymen—they were militant journeymen.[29]

Wooleslager was especially active. After the riots the state assembly compiled depositions of Baltimoreans who had witnessed the events, which were published in a 347-page book. In all the accounts only one deponent singled out a specific individual for participating in the planning and organizing of the riot. When asked whether the attack on Hanson's office had been pre-arranged, Alexander Briscoe answered that he had "heard George Wooleslager say some time before (say eight or ten days) the office in Gay-street was pulled down, that there was a committee appointed who were trying to obtain signatures to pull down the office, and that there were one hundred and odd already subscribed."

Briscoe may have jumped at the chance to implicate Wooleslager. A substantial shoemaker, he could have had little sympathy with a militantly republican journeyman. Wooleslager seemed to be everywhere during the rioting. On June 22 he was one of thirty or forty men who helped pull down Hanson's office. A month later the city watch arrested Wooleslager apparently in connection with the attack on the Charles Street house. He spent the night in the watch house. On the afternoon of July 28 Wooleslager was released from custody and appeared in Gay Street where the militia was gathering to protect the city jail. In the evening he led a group of men to the jail yard and called for the blood of the Federalists. The next morning he was still lingering around the jail. In the testimonies taken by the assembly Wooleslager was the only person identified as organizing the August 4 attack on the post office.[30]

Mayor Edward Johnson left a vivid account of Wooleslager. On July 28 the mayor had stationed himself in the prison yard to prevent the attack he feared was imminent. As he was patroling the grounds and calming tempers, Wooleslager jumped over the jail wall and rushed for the prison doors with thirty or forty men behind him. The mayor testified that Wooleslager "with the strongest voice I ever heard, said, where are those murdering scoundrels who have come from Montgomery and slaughtered our citizens in cold blood! in that gaol my boys; we must have them out; blood cries for blood!" The mayor stepped before the roaring shoemaker and told him that he had the duty to protect the Federalist prisoners. Wooleslager raged at how the night watch had jailed him the day before: "The damn'd orangemen took me up and kept me all night, and I will go to the Point and take satisfaction." The mayor assured Wooleslager that if the watch force had committed any misconduct, he would see that they were reprimanded.[31]

Conciliated by the mayor's promise, Wooleslager underwent a sudden change of heart. "Mr. Mayor, you talk very reasonably," he said, "and we will support, well, my boys, we will support the Mayor, three cheers for the Mayor." In the company of his new ally the mayor walked over to another group of men gathered suspiciously at the jail door. He heard someone say that he could batter down the door with a log. Warning the group against such action, Mayor Johnson suddenly found himself surrounded by angry citizens. One of them, "more violent than the rest," exclaimed: "You damn'd scoundrel don't we feed you, and is it not your duty to head and lead us on to take vengeance for the murders committed. . . ." Wooleslager stepped between the mayor and his accusers and declared "we will protect the Mayor." In the meantime some persons had obtained an axe and began chopping down the jail doors. "I observed to George Wooleslager," the mayor later claimed, "it is not yet too late, support me, and we may prevent the horrid scene." At the urging of the mayor Wooleslager pushed his way through the crowd to the jail door. But now he had second thoughts. He turned to the mayor "and placing his two hands on me, observed that we were only risking our lives without any prospect of success." Captain James Biays, who appeared at the doorstep, persuaded the mayor to leave. The old Republican firebrand and crowd leader realized that neither he nor the mayor could control the political violence at the jail door. Through the entire episode before the jail Mayor Johnson claimed he suspected Wooleslager of colluding with the crowd.[32]

From 1807 to 1812 Baltimore witnessed a revival of the street politics of the 1790s. An essential ingredient in the new political scenario was the mobilization of the militia, which followed the British attack on the *Chesapeake* in June, 1807. Mechanics rushed to form units and elect officers, gaining greater prominence in the Baltimore Battalion than ever before. Six months later the volatile situation exploded over the issue of Aaron Burr and Luther Martin. Having successfully defended Burr on charges of treason, the Federalist Martin attacked the Jefferson administration in the city newspapers. The protest parade that followed demonstrated that street politics was as alive as ever but that in one respect it had changed since the 1790s: the prominent master mechanics who had been crowd leaders a decade before were conspicuously absent. After 1808 the townspeople continued to participate in vast political demonstrations out of doors in support of the Republican administrations's tough commercial measures against Great Britain.

Finally, in 1812 Alexander C. Hanson, the rabidly conservative editor of the Baltimore *Federal Republican*, condemned the declaration of war on Great Britain and accused the president of being a dupe of Napoleon. In June his printing office was destroyed. A month later the disturbance escalated into a full-scale confrontation between armed Federalists and the crowd. For weeks the city authorities were powerless to stop the violence that left three men dead: two members of the crowd and a Federalist. During the rioting new social elements emerged that had never been seen in crowd actions before, most notably militant journeymen. Thus the journeymen, who had since 1805 been organizing, striking, and gaining political notoriety through their tarring and feathering of Robert Beatty, now stepped forward as crowd leaders. The tradition of street politics was just as strong from 1807 to 1812 as it had been in the 1790s, but the social groups who carried it forward had changed.

NOTES

1. *American* (Baltimore), June 29, 30, 1807; *Federal Gazette* (Baltimore), July 6, 1807.

2. The data on militia officers are derived from notices for company meetings that frequently included the names of the captain, lieutenant, sergeant, ensign, and secretary. The officers were identified in the *Baltimore Daily Intelligencer*, Dec. 1793, through Sept., 1794, and the *American*, Apr. through Nov., 1807.

3. *American*, May 3, 1800, July 2, 15, Aug. 11, 1807, Mar. 4, 1808; *Baltimore Daily Intelligencer*, Aug. 19, 1794.

4. *American*, May 3, 1800, July 9, 11, 16, 18, 20, 24, Aug. 12, 1807; *Baltimore Daily Intelligencer*, Aug. 19, 1794.

5. *Dictionary of American Biography*, s.v. "Luther Martin"; Frank A. Cassell, "The Structure of Baltimore's Politics in the Age of Jefferson, 1795–1812," in Aubrey C. Land, Lois Green Carr, and Edward C. Papenfuse, eds., *Law, Society, and Politics in Early Maryland: Proceedings of the First Conference on Maryland History, June 14–15, 1974* (Baltimore, 1977), pp. 289–90.

6. Most of the documents relevant to the riot were collected by the committee appointed after the disturbance and published in the *American*, Nov. 19, 1807.

7. *Ibid.*; *Federal Gazette*, Nov. 4, 1807.

8. *American*, Nov, 19, 1807.

9. *Ibid.*

10. *Ibid.*, Nov. 7, 9, 19, 1807, Jan. 21, Apr. 7, 1808; *Federal Gazette*, Nov. 10, 1807; *Baltimore Evening Post*, Nov. 10, 1807.

11. *American*, Nov. 20, 1807.

12. *Ibid.*, Nov. 19, 1807.

13. *Maryland Journal* (Baltimore), May 6, 1788; *American*, Oct. 18, 1799, Feb. 26, Mar. 26, 1801, June 30, Aug. 13, Nov. 9, 1807; *Federal Gazette*, Sept. 27, 1798; *Baltimore Daily Intelligencer*, Mar. 12, 1794.

14. Second Census of the United States, 1800, Baltimore City; Third Census of the United States, 1810, Baltimore City; Alphabetical Lists of Assessed Persons, 1804, Baltimore County Commissioners, MHR; Baltimore Assessment Record Book, MS, 55, MHS. See also city directories from 1796 through 1820.

15. *Federal Gazette*, Nov. 4, 1807.

16. *American*, Feb. 4, 6, 1808.

17. *Ibid.*, Sept. 28, Oct. 1, 1808; *Whig* (Baltimore), Oct. 1, 3, 1808.

18. *American*, Oct. 3, 1808; *Whig*, Oct. 5, 6, 1808.

19. *Federal Gazette*, Jan. 21, Feb. 6, 1809; *American*, Jan. 31, 1809; *Whig*, Jan. 31, 1809.

20. *American*, July 5, 1809.

21. *Ibid.*, June 19, 22, 23, 1809.

22. *Federal Republican* (Baltimore), June 20, 1812; *Report of the Committee of Grievances and Courts of Justice of the House of Delegates of Maryland*

on the Subject of the Recent Mob and Riots in the City of Baltimore (Annapolis, 1813), pp. 22, 138, 160–61, 174. For recent studies of the 1812 riot, see Frank A. Cassell, "The Great Baltimore Riot of 1812," *Maryland Historical Magazine*, 70 (Fall, 1975): 241–59; Donald R. Hickey, "The Darker Side of Democracy: The Baltimore Riots of 1812," *Maryland Historian*, 7 (1976): 1–20; Paul A. Gilje, "The Baltimore Riots of 1812 and the Breakdown of the Anglo-American Mob Tradition," *Journal of Social History*, 13 (Summer, 1980): 547–64.

23. *Report of the Committee*, pp. 22–23, 42, 50, 63, 66, 120, 149, 161–62.

24. *Ibid.*, pp. 26–27, 43, 64, 98. For Hanson's correspondence, see *Facts and Documents Relative to the Late Attack on Liberty of the Press in Baltimore* (Philadelphia, 1812).

25. *Report of the Committee*, pp. 274–75, 164–66.

26. *Ibid.*, pp. 168–70; *Facts and Documents*, p. 59.

27. *Report of the Committee*; pp. 28, 153–57, 171–72.

28. July, 1812, Session, Criminal Dockets of the Court of Oyer and Terminer, Baltimore City Criminal Court, MHR; *Fry's Baltimore Directory, for 1812* (Baltimore, 1812).

29. July, 1809, Session, Criminal Dockets; *Interesting Papers Relative to the Recent Riots at Baltimore* (Philadelphia, 1812), p. 81.

30. *Report of the Committee*, pp. 58, 76, 91, 111, 126–27, 169, 179, 226; vols. 1–10, Indentures, Orphans Court, Baltimore County Register of Wills, MHR.

31. *Report of the Committee*, p. 169.

32. *Ibid.*, pp. 169, 170.

12

MECHANICS AND METHODISM

The rise of Baltimore's Methodist church encapsulates the major changes that the mechanic community underwent in the late eighteenth and early nineteenth centuries. From its beginnings in the 1760s the Methodist church attracted the white "middling classes," mechanics in particular, and blacks who found no place in the older congregations. One reason was that it offered a new democratized doctrine of salvation that appealed to whites and blacks alike. Another was that it opened positions of leadership to mechanics who had little chance of rising in the Episcopal, Presbyterian, or German churches. The last reason was that Methodism espoused a creed of industry, discipline, and thrift that attracted skilled workingmen striving to separate themselves from a lower-class subculture where drinking and gambling were prevalent.

At the same time, however, the church revealed the tensions arising within the mechanic community. Consider the cases of three trades that established strong ties to the Methodist church. In the shoemaking craft, masters, not journeymen, joined the church. Masters were drawn to Methodism for its profession of sobriety, hard work, and diligence and its condemnation of such social discord as striking and labor militancy. Among shipbuilders the small craftsmen converted to the church rather than the big ones. The small shipbuilders found in Methodism an implicit rejection of the paternalistic system at the yards where a few powerful masters, with large slave work forces, exerted great economic and social influence. At the iron works outside the city, on the other hand, Methodism bolstered the paternalistic relations between masters and workmen. Thus Methodism evolved as not one church but many.

Baltimore was a cauldron of religious diversity. The Episcopal church had strong roots there, especially among the wealthy and powerful. Establishing their first church in 1763, Presbyterians multiplied rapidly as Scotch-Irish immigrants flooded into Baltimore from Pennsylvania. The German Lutheran and Reformed churches had sizable congregations that maintained close ties to their fellow churchmen in western Maryland. Roman Catholics had their own church, which drew financial and emotional support from southern Maryland. By the 1770s evangelical denominations like the Baptists were active in Baltimore, and later Mennonites and Quakers also established congregations. But without doubt the church that prospered most in Baltimore was the Methodist. A map of 1801 shows eleven denominations maintaining churches and meeting houses in the city: Roman Catholic, Episcopal, Mennonite, Presbyterian, German Calvinist, German Lutheran, German Reformed, Christ Church, Baptist, Quaker, and Methodist. None of the denominations had more than one meeting house, with the exceptions of the Roman Catholic and Methodist. The Methodists had the most: one on Light Street in Baltimore, another on Green Street in Old Town, and the last on Fleet Street in Fell's Point.[1]

The Methodist church grew rapidly, despite early obstacles. The first preachers in the 1760s faced a difficult dilemma. By criticizing the mother church's lack of evangelical fervor, they had angered the established Episcopal authorities. On the other hand, they aroused the suspicions of patriots for their continued loyalty to the mother church and their hedging on the question of independence. Still, by 1773 nearly half of the 1,160 American Methodists who were reported to the general conference lived in Maryland. A year later the conference appointed four of its eighteen ministers to the Baltimore circuit alone. The church received a boost in 1784 when Francis Asbury and other church leaders severed ties with the Church of England and established the American Episcopal Methodist Church. Asbury was elected first bishop. The conference, not surprisingly, took place at Baltimore. Thus in the church's formative period, when Asbury and his associates were striving to create an ecclesiastical hierarchy and mass following, Baltimore served as the informal headquarters of the Methodist church.[2]

In Baltimore the greatest surge of membership came at the turn of the century. In the 1790s and early 1800s a "Great Revival" swept across the South. Giant camp meetings occurred in Kentucky and elsewhere, creating the impression that the evangelical movement was largely a backcountry phenomenon. But the ferment was no less intense in cities like Baltimore. Reverend Ezekiel Cooper was assigned to the Baltimore circuit at the beginning of the revival. In April, 1789, he wrote in his journal:

> We had a watch night in Town where the power of God came down among the people & a great number were converted. There was such an out-cry that the town was put in a great surprize the like they had never seen nor heard before. The cry I judge could have been heard a mile. There had been several shouts in Town but none to equal this. There would be 30 & 40 all on their knees at once crying for mercy.

Cooper estimated that in the past seven months 300 converts had entered the church, 100 in February alone.

In 1800 Baltimore underwent a second major revival. Sarah Beasman, whose father had been one of Baltimore County's earliest converts, exclaimed that "the Lord was pleased to pour out his spirit, and a great revival of religion, took place, and hundreds, if not thousands, were converted to God, so that Baltimore—town, and county, was rejoicing in the God of our salvation." Even the Reverend Joseph G. J. Bend, rector of St. Paul's Episcopal Church in Baltimore and something of a Methodist baiter, had to admit: "The late stir of the Methodists has been general. I am told, that the extravaganza wanted very little of the grade, which it reached in the year 1790 in Baltimore." Membership continued to climb in the early nineteenth century. In the period 1800 to 1815 the number of Methodists in Baltimore City and County rose 265 percent, from roughly 1,500 to 6,600, while the city's population increased only 120 percent. By 1815 perhaps one Baltimorean out of fourteen was a Methodist.[3]

The Methodists enjoyed special advantages in Baltimore and Maryland. The Episcopal and German churches, which resisted the evangelical style of the Methodists, were relatively weak in Maryland. For this reason Baltimore, which attracted a heterogenous population, became a center of religious schism in the early nineteenth century. Methodists were able to recruit new converts from the disaffected of the older churches. In 1814 the Reverend Philip William Otterbein, a friend of Bishop Asbury, led his Baltimore congregation out of the German Reformed church to form the United Brethren in Christ. Two years later the Reverend George Dashiell, rector of Anglican St. Paul's, broke from the Episcopal church and established the Evangelical Episcopal church. In this setting of religious strife Methodists could lure away large numbers of churchgoers who desired an evangelical religion that their own ministers failed to provide. Why the Presbyterians failed to participate on a widespread basis in Baltimore's revivals is unclear. Elsewhere they became enthusiastic revivalists. Perhaps the reason was that Baltimore's Presbyterian church had been dominated by the Scotch-Irish merchant elite since the Revolutionary era. Socially, the Presbyterian was the established church of Baltimore. It is not surprising that the wealthy families who supplied the church's leadership were cool toward a religious awakening that might threaten their own authority.[4]

Methodism appealed strongly to blacks. In 1800 they made up 34 percent of Baltimore's congregations, in 1807 37 percent, and in 1815 47 percent. Most of the blacks were probably free because the Methodist church opposed the institution of slavery and discouraged slaveholders, in the first decades at least, from joining. In the 1780s the church leaders went so far as to consider expelling slaveowners. If the church did admit slaves and permit them to attend services and meetings, it must have been with the consent of their masters. The Methodists were sensitive to the charge of fomenting unrest among the black population. Enrolling a slave against the will of his or her master would have aroused just the resentment the Methodists were trying to allay.

If the opinions of Maryland planter Tench Tilghman are any indication, few masters could have welcomed the prospect of their slaves' conversion. "You know the fact," he wrote to Episcopal Bishop James Kemp of Maryland in 1815, "that the best disposed of our servants are attracted to the Methodist churches and they will make a difficulty of uniting with us on that account." Two years later Kemp received a proposal that would establish an Episcopal school for free blacks to offset what he saw as the harmful effects of Methodism. "Methodism," he wrote, "has keyed their passions too high for the '*peaceable* fruits of righteousness' & they have (many of them) possessed religion with very little knowledge of *christianity.*"

The Methodists supervised the black membership closely. Blacks met in weekly classes separately from whites, and women separately from men. Without exception the class leaders were white. Although women conducted a few of the classes of black females, men were usually in charge. The church prided itself on the discipline it maintained among its black members. In 1796 the Maryland Society for Promoting the Abolition of Slavery, a Baltimore-based organization influenced by the Methodists, reported to the American Convention of Antislavery Societies in Philadelphia that

> a large majority of them [free blacks] appear religiously disposed as is manifested by their attachment to places of Worship—numbers of them Zealously attending the same, particularly amongst the Society of Methodists—which Society have liberally appropriated a part of one of their Meeting houses, for their religious Instructions, some of their Number attending with them for that purpose, & to see that good order & decorum is preserved in their Meetings, which appears for the most part to be reputedly conducted.[5]

The white Methodists, who in 1815 constituted slightly over half of the total membership in Baltimore, represented what was often called the "middling classes." It is possible to identify the occupations of white males in the city directories, although we know no more about the white women than about the blacks (see Table 18). Mechanics constituted the largest single group among white male Methodists. They made up slightly under half of the congregation at Baltimore and over half at Fell's Point. If we add the small-time traders and nonprofessionals to this group, the "middling classes" accounted for about three-fifths of the white males at Baltimore and up to nine-tenths at the Point. Thus the typical white male Methodist may have been a master shoemaker who operated his own shop and employed a few apprentices and journeymen, a ship carpenter who worked at one of the yards at the Point, a ship captain who resided in Baltimore when not at sea, or a grocer who owned a small business in town. The Methodist church failed to attract many individuals from the most

TABLE 18

OCCUPATIONS OF WHITE MALE METHODISTS: 1800, 1815

	Baltimore Town		Fell's Point	
Occupation	1800 (N=99)	1815 (N=193)	1800 (N=24)	1815 (N=57)
Mechanic	46%	48%	54%	60%
Merchant	25	22	4	—
Trader	11	8	4	12
Laborer	8	7	17	5
Professional	5	10	8	9
Nonprofessional	5	5	13	14
Total	100%	100%	100%	100%

SOURCES: City Station, Class Records, 1799–1803, 1813–19, Lovely Lane Methodist Episcopal Historical Society, Baltimore; *New Baltimore Directory and Annual Register; for 1800 and 1801* (Baltimore, n.d. [1800]); *Baltimore Directory and Register, for 1814–15* (Baltimore, 1814).

prestigious groups. Merchants were a minority in the Baltimore church and practically nonexistent at the Point. Indeed, not a single merchant belonged to the Point's congregation in 1815. The professionals were also few in number. Nor did the church enlist many among the least privileged white group, the common laborers, although the figures are not entirely trustworthy. The city directory tended to omit common laborers, which makes it impossible to identify many who appeared in the Methodist membership lists.

The success of Methodism among free blacks and the white middling classes, mechanics especially, stemmed from the democratization of the doctrine of salvation. The church offered the hope of forgiveness and sanctity to social groups who had felt either unwanted or unworthy in the older denominations. The Reverend Freeborn Garrettson, who was one of the first Maryland-born circuit riders and who occasionally preached in Baltimore, summarized this chief tenet of Methodism: "Believe in the Lord Jesus Christ, and you shall be saved. You shall feel your sins forgiven. The guilt, power, and love of sin shall be removed, and your soul shall be happy in God."

The Methodists condemned the doctrine of predestination, which they claimed the other churches continued to uphold. That doctrine, they said, was fundamentally elitist. Who but the privileged and propertied, the Methodists asked, could believe that an all-merciful God would select a handful of individuals for salvation and cast the rest into hell? Bishop Asbury maintained that the idea of predestination freed men from moral responsibility for their sins; their fate had already been decided, which encouraged a fatalism with "the most pernicious and destructive consequences in human society." The Methodists maintained that this Calvinism had become entrenched in the Church of England and prevented it from undertaking the task of converting the multitudes: why bother, since they had probably been damned anyway? In turn the officials of the Episcopal church attacked the Methodists for popularizing and degrading the doctrine of salvation. One Anglican minister from Maryland's Eastern Shore said "the Methodists carried matters too far, that a man could not know his sins were forgiven: all we might expect in this life was a hope springing from an upright life." But while the Anglicans decried the Methodists' ideas on salvation, they could not deny their popularity. In 1815 Bishop Kemp admitted that the Methodists' appeal sprang from *"the certainty of salvation held out to all who would become their members."*[6]

Not surprisingly, the Methodists supported the party most committed to the democratization of politics: the Republicans. In 1798 Episcopal Reverend Mr. Bend, a conservative Federalist himself, wrote: "I have been fully convinced, for sometime, of the Jacobinic principles of the Methodists; nor is this fact wonderful. They are for the most part, persons of the lower class in life, & distinguished by that ignorance upon which the Jacobin chiefs work so successfully." Bend seems to have been infuriated by the actions of John Chalmers, a Methodist class leader and ropemaker from the Point. Chalmers had recently helped organize a Methodist militia company named the Friendship Volunteers, and was an active supporter of Republican Congressman Samuel Smith during his 1798 re-election campaign.

Another prominent individual who personified the links between mechanics, Methodists, and Republicans was Adam Fonerden. He was president of the Mechanical Company, an officer in the Baltimore Association of Tradesmen and Manufacturers, president of the Mechanical Society, and a supporter of

Congressman Smith. He was also a Methodist class leader and preacher. Indeed, the first meeting of the Mechanical Society where Fonerden was chosen president took place in a Methodist meeting house. Fonerden was the only political figure among the Methodists whose aspirations went beyond the city council. Perhaps there were not more Republican leaders among the Methodists because the religion was too controversial. When in 1806 Fonerden declared his candidacy for the state legislature, his prominence in the Methodist church immediately raised questions. "A Voter" demanded that Fonerden clarify his status in the church:

> ARE you in connection with the people called Methodists, or are you not?
> Do you, or do you not, preach occasionally in the places of public worship or elsewhere?
> Are your services as a preacher sanctioned by that religious denomination, or are they not?

"A Voter" did not ask the same questions about the religious affiliation of other candidates. Fonerden lost the election.[7]

A second reason why Baltimore's mechanics, in particular, joined the Methodist church was that it offered them a unique opportunity to assume positions of prominence and prestige. Bishop Asbury and the other church fathers had to create an ecclesiastical government virtually from nothing. They invested great authority in the upper levels of the hierarchy—bishops, elders, general conferences—but they also allowed considerable autonomy at the local level. Indeed, the Methodist church evolved into an army of lay officers. In 1805 Asbury described his idea of a model church order: "My continual cry to the Presiding Elders is order, order, good order. All things must be arranged Temporally, and Spiritually like a well disciplined army." In this elaborate chain of command the shoemaker, ship carpenter, ship captain, and grocer could aspire to posts of authority. In the older churches, on the other hand, these same men would have been effectively barred from power. The Methodist church, then, opened avenues of social mobility to mechanics and others in the middling classes. With the proper balance of piety and ambition a

Methodist craftsman could hope to become a class leader, local preacher, exhorter, deacon, or elder.[8]

The most accessible office was that of class leader. Appointed by the traveling preachers and church elders, the class leaders were the lynchpins of the Methodist machinery. The classes were small, no more than twenty or thirty members. It was therefore possible for class leaders to know their students individually, to watch their spiritual progress, to exert considerable influence over their behavior inside the church and out. The classes met once a week after Sunday services, and the frequent contact further enhanced the authority of the class leaders. The Methodists were careful to ensure the continuity of the classes. A new group of converts were divided among already existing classes. To have reorganized the class structure continually as new individuals joined the church would have disrupted the relationships the class leaders had cultivated with their students.

As the correspondence of Bishop Asbury suggests, the class leaders assumed greater prominence as the church grew. In 1788 Asbury wrote to Cooper and urged him to preach directly to individual churchmen. "If possible visit house to house," the bishop exhorted, "and that regularly once a fortnight for no other purpose than to speak to each in the family about their souls, that they may be ready for your help." Asbury was telling Cooper to circumvent the class leaders. In 1791 he conceded that the ministers could not realistically shoulder such a burden. In a letter to the Reverend Nelson Reed, presiding elder of the Baltimore circuit, Asbury instructed the ministers to delegate authority to the local officials: "Examine your preachers at every two months, like a conference, of their growth in grace and walk with God, and be very particular to know how the classes' meetings are, and establish bands." In 1796 Asbury went even further in relinquishing power to the class leaders. He informed John Hagerty, a former itinerant preacher who had settled in Baltimore, to have the classes meet twice a week rather than once.[9]

Most of the class leaders were mechanics. At Baltimore they constituted slightly over half of the leaders and at the Point well over two-thirds. Moreover, the mechanics tightened their hold on the local leadership. In 1800 they provided 45 percent of the class leaders of the Baltimore congregation. During the next fifteen years forty-six new leaders were appointed as the old ones moved, retired, or died. Of this group, 57 percent were mechanics. At the same time the contribution of the merchants declined. In 1800 they made up 39 percent of the class leaders, but by 1815 they had dropped to 20 percent. In addition to the 112 male class leaders, seven women also received the appointment. All of them taught at Fell's Point. At least four and possibly six of these women were related to Methodist mechanics, either by blood or marriage. Thus, rather than representing an autonomous female group within the church, the women leaders enhanced the mechanics' influence.

The large majority of mechanic class leaders were small-scale operators. No more than four of the sixty-four mechanic officers could be considered manufacturers engaged in large-scale production. Adam Fonerden owned a comb manufactory, Frederick Shaeffer a brush manufactory, Benjamin Berry and John Hignatt brickmaking kilns. While the mechanic class leaders were typical handicraftsmen generally, they were also prosperous ones. In 1815 they were assessed at an average of $1,247, while the ordinary property-holding mechanic in the city was worth $666. The mechanic leaders of the Baltimore congregation were the richest, assessed at $1,699; the class leaders of Fell's Point had only $456 in taxable property. But even at the Point the mechanic class leaders were better off than their mechanic neighbors, whose mean wealth holding was $387.[10]

The Methodist church also attracted mechanics because it espoused the social values of industry, sobriety, and discipline that formed the heart of the skilled workingman's self-perception. Imagine a master mechanic who had undergone an apprenticeship of seven years, lived frugally as a journeyman and banked his savings, and by the age of thirty had opened his own shop, married, and started a family. He had seen fellow journeymen and apprentices, not so lucky or resolute, fall behind. He had seen them become permanent wage earners without hope of getting an "independency," seeking what consolation they could find in the tippling houses and grog shops. He had seen them slip into a lower-class subculture whose values were antithetical to his own. Such a man would cling to the habits of industriousness and thrift fostered during his youth not only because they had served him well in the past but also because they were psychological defenses against the ever-present insecurity of his livelihood. The master mechanic who had become prosperous enough to provide his family the "common comforts of life" could not ignore the possibility of unforeseen calamity wiping out a lifetime of work. We need only recall the fate of master tailor James Cox to appreciate this danger. The official *Discipline* of the Methodist church spoke to the psychological needs of this man. It condemned intemperate drinking, swearing, ostentatious dressing, gambling, fighting, and discord. To more than one observer the Methodists looked like latter-day Puritans with long faces and dark gloomy clothing. But to the mechanic who embraced the Methodist social creed, these were outward badges showing others and reminding himself of his distinctiveness.[11]

The lower-class subculture that the Methodist mechanics rejected has left little trace in the historical record. When we catch a glimpse of it, it is usually in the courts. In the late eighteenth and early nineteenth centuries Baltimore's magistrates began scrutinizing the places where the lower classes, blacks and whites, congregated. The most troublesome spots were the drinking houses. They were literally everywhere. In 1809 the Baltimore County Criminal Court granted 157 licenses to "Retailers of Spiritous Liquors" and another 350 to ordinary keepers who sold liquor in small quantities. In addition, Baltimore had an unknown number of illegal tippling houses that had not obtained licenses and often catered to apprentices, servants, laborers, mechanics, slaves, and free blacks. Perhaps M. L. Weems best expressed the magistrates' distrust of these places in his 1812 pamphlet, *God's Revenge against Gambling*: "those sinks of sin, where whiskey is sold by the half pint, and where the worthless and idle meet to drink, and swear, and hatch mischief."

The Baltimore city council was continually trying to curb illegal activity in the drinking houses. The ordinances related to gambling piled up until 1803, when the council issued a comprehensive measure to "restrain gaming," one of the most alarming activities encouraged by the taverns. If an individual was apprehended in a simple game of cards at a licensed ordinary, the council fined him $10. Some of the taverns operated illegal betting tables: faro was the most popular game. Anyone caught playing at such a table received a $15 fine while the tavern owner paid $20. The most dangerous betting, in the eyes of the council, took place in the unlicensed tippling houses because the police had difficulty patroling them. A game of cards at an illegal establishment carried a fine of $20, twice the penalty for gambling inside a licensed ordinary.[12]

The council's efforts to clean up the public houses did not satisfy everyone. At the July, 1816, session of the Baltimore County Criminal Court the grand jury issued a wholesale denunciation of the "tippling shops," expressing the hope that "a stop will be put to them." "The Vast increase of tippling Shops," the jury said, is "an evil destructive to the morals of the poorer class of people. These tippling shops alike the rendezvous of the worthless white and slave are the fruitful source of Crimes and quarrels. The Sabbath day is violated by the most disorderly and riotous conduct and it would be difficult to say what Crimes and offences do not originate in these Houses."

The grand jury was asking for the impossible. The police force was not strong enough to monitor the tippling houses. The watchmen were underpaid and overworked. In 1796 the watch force protested the city council's proposal to reduce their numbers from thirty-two to twenty-six. "The watchman," they declared, "must clean & repair his lamps the day before the watch; he is up all night walking; the next day he is so tired as to be good for nothing." Moreover, they were paid only 1s. 8d. a night. To police the public houses, the sheriffs had to resort to informers. But that strategy often proved to be self-defeating. In 1804 Andrew Price, a boarding house proprietor, protested to the city council that the informer Benjamin Chartellier had enticed him into a game of whist and then betrayed him to the authorities. Another petitioner, who had been fined for playing billiards at a Fell's Point establishment, said the informers were "men that have been fined themselves for playing & Betting."[13]

The drinking houses seemed to produce every type of undesirable activity. At each of its sessions the criminal court heard cases like that of Joshua Mills, who had operated a tavern at High Street in Old Town. Mills had received a license as an ordinary keeper but in 1808 the court discovered he kept a faro table. He served drinks at the front of the tavern while Henry Labruere and Matthew Henderson dealt cards in the back. It seems that Labruere was a sought-after card man, for in 1809 the court charged him with keeping a faro table for Frederick W. Hank. The drinking houses brought together whites and blacks, servants and slaves, which alarmed the city magistrates. In 1810 Benjamin H. Head came before the court because he persisted in serving liquor at his house without a license. More seriously, he had sold grog to "apprentices and Slaves." William Riley had also sold liquor and allowed "negro Slaves to collect in large numbers at his House on the Sabbath day." The public houses were often tied to prostitution. Women usually ran the "bawdy houses," but occasionally a man was in charge. Prostitution also violated the conventions governing race relations; in 1810 Susannah Mills, for example, was charged with "keeping a number of females for the purpose of prostitution" and "entertaining Slaves on the Sabbath."[14]

The tippling houses offered "the worthless white and slave" something they could not get elsewhere: entertainment and social camaraderie. By the early 1800s a common laborer made $1 a day, the poor journeymen shoemakers and tailors $8 or $9 a week, and the carpenters $2 a day. Most respectable entertainment went beyond their pocket books. During the theater season a seat in the pit cost 75¢ and a box seat $1. The circus frequently passed through town, as did rope dancing acts, puppet shows, and horsemanship displays. That they were all costly is suggested by the license fee charged by the city council: $8 a performance for circuses or equestrian shows, $10 a week for rope dancing and puppet shows, $5 a night for musical parties.

About the cheapest entertainment available was the traveling tavern show. In 1799, for example, a tavern at Fell's Point distributed handbills advertising that the "Italian Scaramouch" would "dance a jig, and during the time of his dancing will transform himself into ten different shapes, in the presence of the audience!!!" The same bill included "Mr. Macabee, the Tumbling Sailor, who will dance a hornpipe equal, if not superior to any dancing master on the continent." The Scaramouch-Macabee show cost 25¢ a ticket. The one sport that reportedly attracted many followers among the lower classes was cock fighting. Not surprisingly, the city council in 1807 prohibited all "match or main of cocks" within the town limits on pain of a $20 fine. The council was not alone in its opposition to such popular entertainment. In 1812 more than 300 citizens, many of whom were Methodists, petitioned the city council against theater performances as "highly injurious to Religion, the morals, and consequently, to the civil prosperity of society."[15]

The Methodist creed of discipline and diligence was not embraced by all mechanics. In the shoemaking and shipbuilding trades the church reflected the divisions within the mechanic community. The Methodist shoemakers were master mechanics. They were the elite of their trade. They personified the successful craftsman who had established a manufactory, employed large numbers of apprentices, and periodically battled their journeymen over wages. In 1800 the clothing trades as a whole accounted for 44 percent of the 59 Methodist mechanics identified in the membership lists, in 1815 32 percent of 127 (see Table 19). During the same period they made up 36 percent of the 65 mechanic class leaders. These figures are disproportionately large. In the city directories of 1796 and 1815 the clothing trades were only 28 percent of the artisan population. The average Methodist clothier was financially well-to-do with an assessment in 1815 at $1,460. Among the clothiers, shoemakers had the greatest success at attaining the rank of class leader. From 1800 to 1815 thirteen master shoemakers were appointed to the office, 20 percent of all mechanic class leaders. They included some of the largest apprentice holders in the city. William Duncan, for example, was a Methodist class leader and the largest apprentice holder among the nearly 400 master shoemakers who from 1794 to 1815 acquired an indenture at the Baltimore County Orphans Court. Another class leader was James Ives, the third largest apprentice holder.[16]

The master shoemakers saw in Methodism the social ideology they were struggling to impose on their workmen. The shoemaking trade, as we have seen, experienced a surge of labor strife in 1794 and continual unrest after 1806. The Methodist church condemned the social discord that journeymen committed through their strikes and boycotts. The church said to the journeyman that only through hard work, thrift, and industriousness could he expect to obtain economic self-sufficiency. In 1810 forty-six shoe-

TABLE 19
OCCUPATIONS OF METHODIST MECHANICS: 1800, 1815

| | Baltimore Town | | Fell's Point | |
Occupation	1800	1815	1800	1815
Clothing	23	32	3	9
Construction	11	24	1	6
Wood	5	10	1	0
Stone/Clay	3	3	0	0
Shipbuilding	1	5	6	14
Food	1	4	1	1
Leather	1	5	1	0
Luxury	1	2	0	0
Metal	0	8	0	3
Other	0	0	1	1
Total	46	93	13	34

SOURCES: See Table 18.

makers organized the United Master Shoemakers to combat the Union Philanthropic Society of Journeymen Cordwainers. This employers' organization pioneered in strike-breaking tactics that included blacklisting all members of the journeymen society and importing scab workmen from outside the city. Seven of the thirteen master shoemakers who served as Methodist class leaders from 1800 to 1815 belonged to the United Master Shoemakers. The number would have been greater but some of the remaining six class leaders had undoubtedly moved from Baltimore by the time the employers' organization was formed.

Put differently, Methodist class leaders supplied over one-eighth of the membership of Baltimore's single most militant employers' association. The journeymen shoemakers understandably refused to join a church where their employers exerted such great authority. Only one of the sixty-two known members of the Union Society of Journeymen Cordwainers, which functioned from 1806 through 1809, entered the Methodist church. In 1804 journeyman James Darling converted. He soon had second thoughts, though, for his name does not reappear on subsequent membership lists. Darling's decision to leave the church may have resulted from his increasing activity in the journeymen movement. In 1808 the Baltimore County Criminal Court indicted him and several others for tarring and feathering Robert Beatty. A year later Darling was again indicted along with other members of the Union Society for conspiracy in the strike against master shoemakers James Sloan and Angello Atkinson. In 1812 he was one of several journeymen shoemakers to stand trial for participating in the *Federal Republican* rioting.[17]

Methodism meant something radically different in the shipbuilding trade. Rather than drawing large employers who dominated their craft, as it did in shoemaking, Methodism embodied the aspirations of skilled employees. In 1800 six of the thirteen mechanics identified in the Fell's Point congregation were shipbuilders and in 1815 fourteen of thirty-four, an average of 43 percent for both years. Seven shipbuilders were class leaders. They were not wealthy men. Only Benjamin Hardesty, who in 1815 was assessed at $2,357, ranked in the top tenth of Baltimore's wealth holders. The other class leaders who had accumulated enough property to qualify for assessment fell below the city's average shipbuilder, who was worth $1,500. The Methodist shipbuilders were the carpenters, riggers, caulkers, and sailmakers who worked at the yards and sail lofts. They were employed by the giants of the trade, James Biays, David Stodder, John Steele, William Price, Joseph Despeaux. Not one of these substantial contractors joined the Methodist church.

The cultural split in the shipbuilding trade emerged clearly over the issue of slavery. The master shipwrights were the largest slaveholders in Baltimore, employing their bondsmen as caulkers and hiring them out to their fellow tradesmen. More than anything else, slaveholding separated the large contractors from their white workingmen. The Methodist church attacked slavery and the social dependence it produced, and thus hurled a direct challenge against the economic and social pre-eminence of the top shipwrights. Not surprisingly, the nonslaveholding shipbuilder responded to this ideal. Of the seven shipbuilder class leaders, only Hardesty was a slaveholder. But he only owned one slave in 1800 and two in 1820. He did not rank with Duncan who by the latter date had twenty-four, Biays with twenty, or Stodder with seventeen.[18]

Baltimore's Methodists fought actively against slavery, although modifying their tactics over the years. They had originally threatened to excommunicate all slaveholders. This measure proved unfeasible. By the 1790s the church was simply urging the membership to manumit their slaves. In 1789 a group of Baltimoreans organized the Maryland Society for Promoting the Abolition of Slavery, one of a number of antislavery associations loosely coordinated out of Philadelphia. The Methodists did not dominate the society but supplied many of its leaders and members. Two years after its formation the Maryland assembly, bespeaking the anxieties of a slaveholding planter gentry, reported that the society consisted "principally of Quakers, Methodists, and emigrants from Ireland since the revolution." For several years Adam Fonerden was the society's president. By 1797 the Maryland society had grown to 231 members, behind only Philadelphia with 591 and New York with 250. A year later it disbanded. The political climate had grown increasing hostile. Not only had many townspeople attacked the society for meddling in their domestic affairs, but the courts rebuffed the society by rejecting its freedom suits.

Baltimore's mechanics had been a powerful force in the antislavery organization. In 1796, according to a membership list submitted to the American Convention for Promoting the Abolition of Slavery, mechanics constituted a third of the society's members who lived in Baltimore. Perhaps David Rice best captured the spirit of the mechanics' opposition to slavery. His *Slavery Inconsistent with Justice and Good Policy*, published in 1792, circulated widely in Baltimore and elsewhere. It forcefully depicted how slavery debased all labor, whether black or white. Rice summarized the attitude of a typical white southerner toward work: "To labour, is *to slave*; to work, is *to work like a Negro*; and this is disgraceful; it levels us with the meanest of species; it fits hard upon the habit of mind of arrogance." Rice described how the slaveholder, being constantly surrounded by obedient bondsmen, would come to expect servility in all workingmen: "If I have been long accustomed to think a black man was made for me, I may easily take it into my head to think so of a white man." Rice might have been addressing the dilemmas of Baltimore's small shipbuilders as they attempted to assert their own cultural independence from the top master contractors.[19]

Another type of Methodism developed at the iron works of

Baltimore County. Northampton iron work, a good example, was located ten miles north of town. It had been founded by the prominent Ridgely family in the 1760s. The vast majority of the Northampton work force were unskilled laborers, digging the iron ore, transporting it to the furnaces, cutting wood for the forges. There were also a few skilled workmen—moulders, wheelwrights, carpenters. In the late eighteenth century most of the iron workers were indentured or convict servants from England and Ireland. But with the decline in the indentured servant trade after the 1780s, slaves replaced the Anglo-American workers. Northampton resembled a large plantation where workers were isolated and under the continual scrutiny of the iron master and his representatives. They enjoyed little of the independence or collective identity of the city's mechanics.[20]

The area surrounding Northampton witnessed intense Methodist revivalism. As early as 1769 the Reverend Joseph Pilmore, who toured the colonies at the request of John Wesley, reported finding at Gunpowder Neck near Northampton "dreadfully *Wilde and Enthusiastic*" men who claimed the gift of tongues. Pilmore scorned this "wildness, shouting, and confusion." In the early nineteenth century Methodist preachers could always count on a faithful following in the Northampton area. In September, 1803, September, 1804, October, 1807, September, 1808, and August, 1809, Methodists held enormous camp meetings within a few miles of the iron work. The newspapers claimed that the 1804 revival drew 12,000 persons and in 1809, 10,000.

Impressed by the devotion of the Methodists at Northampton, Harry Dorsey Gough, a prominent churchman and planter who lived in Baltimore County, constructed a chapel in the woodlands near the iron works. The iron masters of Baltimore County also converted to the church. In his travels through Maryland Bishop Asbury sought out the county's wealthiest families and tried to win them over to Methodism. He had a close relationship with the Gough family, who resided eight miles from Baltimore City. According to the Reverend Henry Smith, a Methodist preacher familiar with the area, the mansion of the Gough family "was the largest dwelling house I had ever seen." Harry Dorsey Gough, the lord of the manor, was married to Prudence Ridgely, the sister of Captain Charles Ridgely, who owned Northampton until his death in 1790. Bishop Asbury became a confidant of Rebecca Ridgely, the captain's wife. Rebecca, in turn, was the daughter of Caleb Dorsey, who owned an ironwork at Elk Ridge, eight miles from the city. The Goughs, Ridgelys, and Dorseys were some of the Methodist church's most prominent converts.[21]

In 1775 Bishop Asbury could not conceal his excitement at the prospect of converting the powerful Captain Charles Ridgely: "Preaching on Friday at William Lynch's, the wealthy Mr. Charles Ridgely was present. And who can tell but the Lord may reach his heart!" Captain Ridgely never converted to Methodism and may actually have been nettled by the wild preaching, but he did support the church on his estate. Perhaps he wished to mollify his Methodist wife. On the other hand, he may have seen that the church provided stability on the estate by gathering together workers and masters. The Ridgely estate became a favorite retreat for Methodist circuit riders. It was the site of many "watch nights" and "love feasts." During the 1789–90 revival, over a hundred of Baltimore's finest citizens mounted their horses and climbed into their carriages to join a procession to Northampton, where they spent the night in prayer and celebration. The next morning the cavalcade assembled again for the return trip. Captain Ridgely gave Robert Strawbridge, Maryland's first Methodist preacher, a farm. He also built a stone chapel for his workers and neighbors. In March, 1789, the captain donated a stove "for the use of the Methodist Congregation at the Stone Meeting House." Ridgely also brought young William Duke, one of Asbury's favorite pupils, into his home where he received instruction from the family tutor.[22]

Rebecca Ridgely wrote about her own conversion experience. Since childhood, according to her account, she had grappled with a spiritual malaise. Rebecca apparently inherited her high-strung temperament from her Quaker mother, who had always warned her about superficial signs of sanctity. The mother refused to baptize Rebecca or any of her other children. Rebecca attended Anglican services after marrying but did not find them satisfying. She also went to a few Quaker meetings, which left her morose. Finally, in 1774 Rebecca joined a Methodist gathering and there experienced the spiritual awakening she had been seeking for years. Her conversion followed a common pattern. It started with a sudden awareness of her own sinfulness and ended with a revelation of God's mercy. Rebecca wrote that her ecstatic behavior was not completely condoned: "O How I fell on my knees and pray'd to the Lord to Call me once more and how I would Run, it was then a Shame to kneel before the people." After her conversion Rebecca was the ever-present representative of the iron master's family at local church services and class meetings. Bishop Asbury continued to prod her to attend services on the estate even after she turned deaf. That he exercised great persuasive powers over Rebecca is suggested by the large sums of money she gave him. The bishop confided to Rebecca, "I am under personal obligations to you, and some others, as my Benefactoress. It cannot be supposed that 150 Dollars per year is sufficient my highest claim from the 7 Conferences being 24 Dollars each, to buy me clothing, horses, and carrage, and to pay all my expences in Travelling 5000 miles a year." "If I had not here and there," Asbury wrote appreciatively, "a friend like Mamma Ridgely."[23]

When Northampton's Methodists assembled for worship, their services revealed the paternalism that suffused class relations at the iron work. They met in class meetings, love feasts, prayer meetings, band meetings, church services, camp meetings, and watch nights. Only one first-hand account of a Northampton Methodist meeting survives, but it vividly portrays the domination of the masters. At the end of his career as an itinerant preacher the Reverend Henry Smith recalled a class meeting he had attended in 1807 on the Ridgely estate. According to Smith, the class was composed of "a people most of whom lived in what was called Gen. Ridgely's wood-cuttings. They were mostly poor people." Here was where the Ridgelys obtained wood for the furnaces. In the middle of the meeting Harry Dorsey Gough appeared with his family. He arrived "on horseback, and his family in a coach drawn by four splendid white horses." A better scenario for inspiring the awe of the workers would be hard to imagine. At the end of the meeting Smith stepped back as Gough and his wife "took these poor people by the hand, with great cordiality, and rejoiced with and over them."

To Smith the scene showed "perfect equality in the house of God." His mind turned to a passage in the Scriptures that seemed fitting: "Mind not high things, but condescend to men of lower estate; Let the brother of low degree rejoice in that he is exalted; but the rich in that he is made low." But the preacher noticed that the "poor people" failed to draw the appropriate lesson from the Goughs' presence. "But these dear people," he wrote, "were so humble as to think that they were not in every respect Mr. and Mrs. Gough's equals, or fit companions in life. Their education, their circumstances, their callings and habits, all impressed this lesson of humility." In assembling the patrician Ridgelys and Goughs with the iron workers of Northampton, the Methodist church helped to perpetuate the "lesson of humility."[24]

The rise of the Methodist church represented the most spectacular development on Baltimore's religious scene. It was linked directly to the growing aspirations and heightened confidence of the mechanics. Because the new church offered a democratized vision of salvation, opened unprecedented opportunities for exercising ecclesiastical authority, and provided an alternative to the lower-class subculture of the city, many mechanics as well as blacks flocked to convert. But Methodism did not appeal to all mechanics equally. In the shoemaking trade it exposed the division between employers, who were attracted by the church's emphasis on discipline and industry, and their militant journeymen employees. In the shipbuilding trade it revealed the split between the small employees, who saw in Methodism a rejection of the paternalistic system at the yards, and the big slaveholding contractors. In the iron-making industry of Baltimore County the Methodist church assumed yet another form, bolstering the authority of the iron masters and reinforcing the dependency of the workingmen. Perhaps the key to the success of Methodism was its very adaptability, its ability to accommodate itself to local needs and circumstances.

NOTES

1. Map available at MHS.
2. Gordon Pratt Baker, ed., *Those Incredible Methodists: A History of the Baltimore Conference of the United Methodist Church* (Baltimore, 1972), pp. 31, 41, 69.
3. Ezekiel Cooper Journal, vol. 1, sec. 5, pp. 38, 51, 62, Ezekiel Cooper

Papers, Garret Theological Seminary, Evanston, Ill.; Sarah Beasman Journal, Misc. MS., p. 10, Lovely Lane Methodist Episcopal Historical Society, Baltimore; Joseph G. J. Bend to William Duke, Sept. 22, 1800, Maryland Diocesan Archives, MHS; *Minutes Taken at the Several Conferences of the Methodist-Episcopal Church, in America, for the Year 1800* (Philadelphia, 1800); *Minutes Taken at the Several Conferences of the Methodist-Episcopal Church, in America, for the Year 1815* (Philadelphia, 1815).

4. A. W. Drury, *The Life of Reverend Philip William Otterbein, Founder of the Church of the United Brethren in Christ* (Dayton, Ohio, 1913), p. 100; James Kemp to Bishop Claggett, Jan., 1813, Maryland Diocesan Archives; William Reynolds, *A Brief History of the First Presbyterian Church of Baltimore* (Baltimore, 1913), p. 122.

5. Tench Tilghman to Bishop Kemp, Nov. 26, 1815; George Weller to Bishop Kemp, ca. Sept., 1817, Maryland Diocesan Archives; Report of Maryland to Convention, American Convention of 1796, Pennsylvania Abolition Society Papers, Pennsylvania Historical Society.

6. Freeborn Garrettson, *The Experiences and Travels of Mr. Freeborn Garrettson, Minister of the Methodist Episcopal Church in North America* (Philadelphia, 1791), p. 22; Elmer T. Clark, J. Manning Potts, and Jacob S. Payton, eds., *The Journals and Letters of Francis Asbury* (London, 1958), 1:244; James Kemp to William Duke, Sept. 19, 1815, Maryland Diocesan Archives.

7. Joseph G. J. Bend to William Duke, Nov. 3, 1798, Maryland Diocesan Archives; *Baltimore Telegraphe*, July 9, 1798; *Federal Gazette* (Baltimore), Aug. 7, 8, 1798; *American* (Baltimore), Oct. 2, 1806.

8. Quoted in Charles A. Johnson, "The Frontier Camp Meeting: Contemporary and Historical Appraisals, 1805–1840," *Mississippi Valley Historical Review*, 37 (June, 1950):100.

9. Asbury, *Journals*, 1:66, 139, 100.

10. Baltimore Assessment Record Book, MS. 55, MHS; *Baltimore Directory and Register, for 1814–15* (Baltimore, 1814). To estimate the property holdings of the mechanics of Fell's Point, I combined Wards 7 and 8 in the assessment lists.

11. *The Doctrines and Discipline of the Methodist Episcopal Church in America* (Philadelphia, 1801).

12. M. L. Weems, *God's Revenge against Gambling Exemplified in the Miserable Lives and Untimely Deaths of a Number of Persons of Both Sexes*, 4th ed. (Philadelphia, 1822), pp. 12–13; *Ordinances of the Corporation of the City of Baltimore 1803–1812* (Baltimore, 1876), pp. 131–35.

13. Criminal Calendar, July, 1816, Session, Criminal Dockets and Minutes of the Court of Oyer and Terminer, Baltimore City Criminal Court, MHR; City Council, Petitions, 1796, fo. 11, 1804, fo. 210, 1805, fo. 211, Baltimore City Archives.

14. State v. Joshua Mills, July, 1808, Session, Dockets; State v. Benjamin H. Head, Jan., 1810, Session, Dockets; State v. Susanna Mills, Mar. 1810, Session, Dockets; State v. William Riley, Mar. 1808 Session, Dockets; State v. Henry Labruere, July, 1809, Session, Dockets.

15. City Council, Petitions, fo. 455; City Council, Ordinances, 1807, fo. 280, Baltimore City Archives; *American*, June 15, 1812.

16. Vols. 1–10, Indentures, Orphans Court, Baltimore County Register of Wills, MHR.

17. *American*, June 1, 1811; Constitution and Bye Laws of the Union Society of Journeymen Cordwainers of the City and Precincts of Baltimore, Baltimore County Commissioners, MHR; July, 1809, Session, Dockets.

18. Second Census of the United States, 1800, Baltimore City; Fourth Census of the United States, 1820, Baltimore City.

19. *At a Meeting of "the Maryland Society for promoting the Abolition of Slavery, and the Relief of free Negroes, and others, unlawfully held in Bondage," held at Baltimore, the 4th of February, 1792* (Baltimore, 1792); *Minutes of the Proceedings of a Convention of Delegates from the Abolition Societies Established in different Parts of the United States at Philadelphia, on May 3, 1797* (Philadelphia, 1797); *Constitution of the Maryland Society, for Promoting the Abolition of Slavery, &c., September 8, 1789* (Baltimore, 1789); Report of Maryland to Convention, American Convention of 1797, Pennsylvania Abolition Society Papers, Pennsylvania Historical Society; David Rice, *Slavery Inconsistent with Justice and Good Policy* (Lexington, Ky., 1792), pp. 18–19.

20. For fuller treatment, see my "The Pre-Industrial Iron Worker: Northampton Iron Works, 1780–1820," *Labor History*, 20 (Winter, 1979):89–110.

21. *American*, Sept. 26, 1804, Sept. 17, 1807, Sept. 21, 1808, Aug. 12, 1809; Frederick E. Maser and Howard T. Magg, eds., *The Journal of Joseph Pilmore, Methodist Itinerant* (Philadelphia, 1969), p. 138; Henry Smith, *Recollections and Reflections of an Old Itinerant* (New York, 1848), p. 197; Col. J. Thomas Scarf, *The Chronicles of Baltimore; Being a Complete History of "Baltimore Town" and Baltimore City from the Earliest Period to the Present Time* (Baltimore, 1874), p. 79.

22. Asbury, *Journals*, 1:151; Ezekiel Cooper Journal, vol. 1, sec. 5, p. 69; Mar. 31, 1789, Day Book 1788–89, B-14, Northampton Furnace, MS. 691, MHS; Baker, ed., *Those Incredible Methodists*, p. 34.

23. Account of Rebecca Ridgely, Feb. 2, 1786–Feb. 19, 1795, Ridgely Papers, MS. 692, MHS; Asbury to Rebecca Ridgely, Mar. 10, 1807, Ridgely Pue Papers, MS. 693, MHS.

24. Smith, *Recollections*, p. 195.

CONCLUSION

This book does not fall neatly into any one field. It has ranged over territory usually divided among labor, political, and intellectual historians. I have deliberately ignored the boundaries. Now I wish to consider the historiographical significance of this study.

From 1763 to 1812 Baltimore's mechanics articulated a new collective identity similar to the consciousness Alfred Young has found in other northern cities. According to Young, this consciousness operated on four levels. "Craft consciousness" united workmen around the traditions and loyalties of their trades. In Baltimore we see it in the Carpenters' Society, Typographical Society, and Union Society of Journeymen Cordwainers; in mass parades where workmen marched by craft; in the language of printers who referred to the thirteen states as "columns" supporting the republic, shoemakers who prayed for a "lasting" union, and butchers who brandished the "ax" before America's foes. "Mechanic interest consciousness" cut across craft boundaries on issues where all craftsmen had a stake. We see it in the movement for a protective tariff, the drive for the federal Constitution, and the establishment of the Mechanics' Bank. "Producers consciousness" reflected the mechanics' belief in the dignity of labor. We see it in Baltimore in banners proudly displaying the tools of the trades; in frequent expressions of contempt for the "idleness, extravagance, and effiminancy" of the commercial classes; and in protests of journeymen against employers who would degrade their skills. "Citizenship consciousness" fueled the mechanics' struggle for political equality and independence. We see it in the quest for a republican city charter, outcries against political intimidation by employers, and efforts to elect workmen to office. These levels of consciousness fused into what Professor Young has called "mechanic" or "artisan republicanism."[1]

The rise of artisan republicanism in Baltimore places three developments in a new perspective: the origins of the labor movement, the development of party politics, and the emergence of republican ideology.

The experience of Baltimore's workingmen raises doubts about the conceptual framework of John R. Commons and the "Wisconsin school" of labor historians. Although Commons's major works are more than sixty years old, they still dominate the writing of American labor history.[2] Only within the past two decades has a "new" labor history challenged the Commons approach.[3] A product of the Progressive era, Commons believed that skilled workers should organize along the lines of Samuel Gompers's American Federation of Labor. They should limit their demands to better pay and working conditions, avoid independent political activity, and entrust disinterested social engineers like himself to handle intractable disputes between labor and management. For Commons, American labor history was the success story of bread-and-butter trade unionism, purged of political activism. Politics, he argued, hindered workingmen from building strong and durable unions that could win concrete victories in the marketplace. During economic depression, politics held the greatest appeal, as workingmen watched their unions collapse and sought political panaceas. Then "middle-class intellectuals" could entangle workers in their visionary political schemes. Since trade associations did not become widespread until after 1827, Commons dismissed the first two centuries of American labor history as the "dormant period." Workers had no history, or very little, before the "awakening" in the Jacksonian era.

Commons could not see beyond what Herbert G. Gutman has termed "a narrow 'economic' analysis." In assessing the legacy of his interpretation Gutman writes: "its methods encouraged labor historians to spin a cocoon around American workers, isolating them from their own particular subcultures and from the larger national culture."[4] By treating workers solely as trade unionists, Commons could focus on "wage" consciousness while ignoring evidence of a broader "class" consciousness. His assumptions were fundamentally conservative.

In Baltimore the Commons approach misses on at least four points of analysis. First, it was the same political activity he decried as thwarting trade unionism, spearheaded by the Association of Tradesmen and Manufacturers and continued by the Mechanical Society, that led to the establishment of the earliest craft societies. The founders of the association called for the first city-wide meetings of the trades in Baltimore's history, while the society popularized the notion of benefit funds—the bedrock of all trade associations. Second, Baltimore exhibits no "repeating cycle of politics and trade unionism, political struggle and economic struggle, political organization and economic organization," as Commons claimed.[5] Political and unionist activity rose and fell together. The two outbursts of journeymen militancy in 1794 and after 1805 coincided with intense political struggle, the first over the city charter and Jay's Treaty, and the second over the Mechanics' Bank and charter reform.

A third point of divergence from the Commons thesis is that political activism did not culminate in economically bad times. The years around 1794 and 1805 witnessed rapid price inflation and a growing demand for labor, conditions that Commons argued militated against political activism. Workers turned to politics in hope and confidence, not desperation. Finally, the political leadership of the mechanics consisted not of middle-class intellectuals but rather of genuine master craftsmen like tailor James Cox, shipwright David Stodder, and stone cutter Robert Steuart. The leaders of the "political" organizations also led the first craft societies. Far from being irreconcilable, politics and unionism reinforced one another.

Nor can the Commons interpretation adequately explain the origins of trade unionism in Baltimore. He depicts journeymen unionists as inexperienced and disorganized, their societies fitful and futile, their strikes doomed to failure. No such bleak picture emerges from Baltimore. There, journeymen strikers exhibited notable discipline in keeping workmen out of the shops, sophisticated strategies in resisting their employers, and collective solidarity even in the face of hostile courts. In some trades journeymen had only recently organized; in others they had no formal organization at all. Yet they won their demands more often than not. Seemingly overnight journeymen devised all the modern weapons in labor's arsenal. Commons acknowledged this precocious development but never attempted to explain it, for that

would have taken him outside his narrowly defined trade unionism. The case of Baltimore suggests that journeymen were well
organized and successful because they, along with other mechanics, had been mobilizing for decades. Their participation in militia units, mechanic associations, crowd actions, and political
parties had accustomed them to acting in unison. And the articu-
lation of mechanic republicanism provided the ideological foundation for collective behavior. By tearing trade unionism from its
cultural and political context, Commons robbed it of meaning.

Many political historians have also failed to appreciate the
significance of mechanic republicans. The movement for the federal Constitution, the creation of the Republican party, the frag-
mentation of party politics after 1800—all reflected the politicization of Baltimore's mechanics. By focusing narrowly on national
political figures or the voting patterns of legislatures, recent historians have often obscured such local agents of change. For an
older generation of Progressive historians, on the other hand,
politics was made in the streets no less than in the assembly
halls.[6] Carl Becker argued that the Revolution triggered a struggle for "who should rule at home," as New York's mechanics battled the established merchant authorities.[7] Young has followed
that struggle into the 1790s: "if not strictly a class conflict," he
writes, "within it were the elements of a clash between 'the privileged and unprivileged' involving the mechanics as Becker suggested."[8] Baltimore was no different. There, mechanics also
fought over "who should rule at home" and in the process helped
shape a new republican political order.

The aspirations of mechanics molded the Republican party.
First, mechanics supplied Republican votes. The returns for the
1798 congressional election demonstrated that Samuel Smith attracted most of his support from the mechanic community, while
his opponent relied on merchants, lawyers, and some workingmen in the maritime trades. From 1800 to 1812 the most stead-
fastly Republican neighborhood was Ward 7, the heart of the mechanic population. By contrast, the downtown merchant wards
often went Federalist. Second, the mechanics contributed organization to the Republican party. After 1795 Smith built his local
following largely on the Mechanical Society, which supported him
through the Jay's Treaty controversy and the XYZ affair. As a

brigadier general of the state militia, he also transformed the units into a political "engine." The most politically active militia corps were led by mechanics, as the 1798 contest illustrated. The only nonmechanic organization that might be viewed as a branch of the Republican party was the Republican Society, consisting entirely of merchants and lawyers. But it dissolved in 1795, leaving Smith even more dependent on the Mechanical Society and mechanic militia units.

The mechanics also provided Republican party leaders. In the 1798 election the most conspicuous of Smith's political lieutenants were a cadre of mechanic militia officers including shipwright James Biays and ropemaker John Chalmers, many of whom had served under the general four years earlier in the march against the whiskey rebels. As Smith's opponents bewailed, the mechanic captains and lieutenants were party stalwarts who got their men to the polls. In sum, the case of Baltimore contradicts the prevailing view, expressed by one scholar, that political parties "began in the 1790's from the top down," "created" by "[e]lite politicians."[9] Nor can it support the conclusion of another recent historian that during the first party system the process of community decision-making in Baltimore was dominated by a "merchant oligarchy."[10]

Artisan republicanism also explains the collapse of Republican unity after 1800. During the 1790s mechanics forged a political coalition with Samuel Smith and merchants who had family, ethnic, religious, and business ties to him. But that coalition was fragile—it could not contain the mechanics' growing independence. As the 1804 election of Federalist Andrew Ellicott demonstrated, mechanics were prepared to bolt their party to support another candidate committed to their interests. They were not just Republicans; they were "independent" Republicans. After 1805 mechanics staged a successful revolt within the party. For three years they defied the established party leadership and returned Robert Steuart to the assembly, while activists like editor William Pechin tried desperately to hold the mechanics in line. One able historian of early Baltimore politics has argued that Republican disunity resulted in part from the "failure of Republicans to establish more formal party institutions."[11] But this gives "institutions" a magical power of cohesion they do not possess. Republicans like Pechin tried to devise such institutions but his schemes foundered on the mechanics' independence.

Mechanic republicanism illuminates the development of republican ideology generally. For many Progressive historians of the Revolution, ideology was "propaganda" masking economic interests. Within recent decades revisionists, in particular Bernard Bailyn, have demolished this reductionist view and restored ideology to a central place in the independence struggle.[12] Bailyn locates the source of Revolutionary ideology in an English Commonwealth tradition, which, he argues, passed to colonial Whigs intact. The Commonwealth ideas congealed into a politically moderate republican consensus. But here Bailyn goes beyond his evidence. We are left wondering whether all classes subscribed to a body of ideas extracted from a few hundred pamphlets that did not circulate widely. What about other sources of popular radicalism, the ones that crystalized in Thomas Paine's best-selling *Common Sense?*[13]

In Baltimore mechanics had their own republicanism. And it was not moderate—it was radical. Mechanic republicanism took a largely political form and appeared in the battle for a city charter. That local contest pitted a radical republicanism voiced chiefly by mechanics against a conservative republicanism drawing greatest support from merchants and lawyers. The issues were clear and fundamental: mechanics stood for unicameralism versus bicameralism, low versus high property qualifications for office holding, short versus long terms in office, ballot versus voice voting, direct versus indirect elections, biracial versus white suffrage. We need to know more about the sources of such popular republicanism. But we know enough in Baltimore to reject the notion of a single moderate republicanism. Historians should therefore shift their focus from republicanism to republicanisms: the republicanism of the yeoman, merchant, mechanic, as well as laborer. Ideology emerges not in a social void but within the class structure of society, and in turn interacts with it. Treating it as an independent force liberated from its economic and social context is ahistorical and reductionist. We merely substitute ideological determinism for the Progressives' economic determinism.

Crowd action also sheds light on popular ideology. The Baltimore crowd underwent a radical change in the early national period. First, consider its leadership. In 1794 a prominent master shipwright was the central figure; in 1807 a merchant-shipwright took command but lacked the authority and confidence of his predecessor; in 1808 journeymen shoemakers were the principal actors; in 1812 none of the traditional sources of leadership were apparent. Second, consider violence. In 1794 two men were tarred and feathered; in 1807 a house of armed men was nearly besieged; in 1808 one man received the "tory coat"; in 1812 three men were killed, dozens wounded, and several houses demolished. Finally, consider the targets. In 1794 the culprit was a foreign shipmaster who had insulted the American flag; in 1807 the targets were three Americans who had insulted Jefferson; in 1808 an anti-Republican British mechanic raised the furor; in 1812 the list of enemies was extended to several dozen Maryland Federalists. In short, the Baltimore crowd had become divorced from its customary moderate leadership, increasingly violent toward people and property, and more inclined to attack native enemies to the republic.

By the *Federal Republican* riot of 1812 the crowd had developed into a vehicle expressing lower-class political sentiments. The rough republicanism of 1812 differed from both the mechanic and merchant versions. It drew upon an intense Anglophobia, as when several dozen men joined hands and danced around the bodies of unconscious Federalists while singing:

> We'll feather and tar every d——d British tory,
> And that is the way for American glory.

It embodied animosities for the planter gentry of southern Maryland, as when one individual called for the blood of the "murdering scoundrels from Montgomery" County. It was expressed in traditional popular rituals, like the tar, feathers, and cuckold horns prepared for one Federalist. And it was tinged with racism, which resulted in widespread threats to the free black community and the destruction of one black man's home. The Baltimore crowd did not represent a "primitive" political form that died out as electoral politics gained legitimacy. On the contrary, the very success of party politics may have invigorated crowd action while redefining it in class terms. For as the middling classes learned to express their sentiments at the polls, those below continued to speak in the streets as well. The leaders of 1812 included militant journeymen, whose commitment to republican values remained unshaken but who rejected the big master employers who had traditionally articulated those values. Republicanism had passed to a new generation of workingmen.

"Class" is a term most American historians avoid. R. H. Tawney once commented on a similar reticence regarding the word "capitalism": "Verbal controversies are profitless; if an author discovers a more suitable term, by all means let him use it. He is unlikely, however, to make much of the history of Europe during the last three centuries, if in addition to eschewing the word, he ignores the fact."[14] The same may be said for class and the history of Baltimore. Mechanics forged a collective consciousness that surpassed the narrow "wage" and "job" consciousness historians have emphasized. That consciousness arose from struggle, not the make-believe clash of one monolithic class against another but the complex shiftings of coalitions and alliances. The struggle did not simply pit mechanics against merchants; it occurred within the mechanic community as well. By 1812 many of the master craftsmen who had championed mechanic republicanism abandoned it, but the tradition was preserved by lesser-known workingmen. Mechanic republicanism remained a legacy for the future.

NOTES

1. Young, "'By Hammer and Hand All Arts Do Stand': An Interpretation of Mechanics in the Era of the American Revolution" (unpublished paper, Organization of American Historians, San Francisco, Apr. 1980).

2. John R. Commons, et al., *History of Labour in the United States*, 4 vols. (New York, 1918–35). For a valuable critique of Commons, see Alan Dawley, *Class and Community: The Industrial Revolution in Lynn* (Cambridge, Mass., 1976), pp. 180–84.

3. For an important statement of the new labor history, see Herbert G. Gutman, *Work, Culture, and Society in Industrializing America: Essays in American Working-Class and Social History* (New York, 1977). See also Robert H. Zeiger, "Workers and Scholars: Recent Trends in American Labor Historiography," *Labor History*, 13 (1972):245–66; Thomas A. Kruger, "American Labor Historiography, Old and New," *Journal of Social History*, 4 (1971):277–85.

4. Gutman, *Work, Culture, and Society*, p. 10.

5. Commons, *History of Labour*, 1:5.

6. See esp. Carl Lotus Becker, *The History of Political Parties in the Province of New York, 1760–1776* (Madison, Wis., 1909); Arthur Schlesinger, *The Colonial Merchant and the American Revolution, 1763–1776* (New York, 1918).

7. Becker, *Political Parties*, p. 22.

8. Alfred Young, "The Mechanics and the Jeffersonians: New York, 1785–1801," *Labor History*, 5 (1964):276. See also Howard B. Rock, *Artisans of the New Republic: The Tradesmen of New York City in the Age of Jefferson* (New York, 1979).

9. Richard D. Brown, *Modernization: The Transformation of American Life 1600–1865* (New York, 1976), p. 108.

10. Whitman H. Ridgway, *Community Leadership in Maryland, 1790–1840: A Comparative Analysis of Power in Society* (Chapel Hill, N.C., 1979), p. 71.

11. Frank A. Cassell, "The Structure of Baltimore's Politics in the Age of Jefferson, 1795–1812," in Aubrey C. Land, Lois Green Carr, and Edward C. Papenfuse, eds., *Law, Society, and Politics in Early Maryland* (Baltimore, 1977), p. 285.

12. Bailyn, *The Ideological Origins of the American Revolution* (Cambridge, Mass., 1967), and his more strident restatement, "The Central Themes of the American Revolution: An Interpretation," in Stephen G. Kurtz and James H. Hutson, eds., *Essays in the American Revolution* (New York, 1973), pp. 3–31.

13. See Eric Foner, *Tom Paine and Revolutionary America* (New York, 1976), and Alfred F. Young, ed., *The American Revolution: Explorations in the History of American Radicalism* (DeKalb, Ill., 1976), afterword.

14. R. H. Tawney, *Religion and the Rise of Capitalism* (New York, 1947), preface to the 1937 edition, p. 4.

INDEX

McElderry, Thomas, 160, 161
McHenry, James: as candidate of
  Association of Tradesmen and
  Manufacturers, 87–88; in 1787
  assembly election, 89–90; in 1788
  convention election, 91–92; in
  1788 assembly election, 94–99;
  mentioned, 100, 155, 159
Mackenheimer, John, 147, 162, 174,
  202, 203, 204, 207, 230
McKim, Alexander, 135, 136, 137,
  139, 140, 175, 188, 239, 240
McMechen, David: in 1787 assem-
  bly election, 89–90; in 1788 con-
  vention election, 91–92; in 1788
  assembly election, 94–99; men-
  tioned, 72, 86, 87, 88, 136, 137,
  181
McMechin, Alexander, 36
Madison, James, 159, 223, 228, 243
Manufacturer: definition of, 111
Marine Bank of Baltimore, 237
Marshall, John, 205, 232, 233
Martin, James, 119, 187
Martin, Luther: in shoemakers'
  trial, 223; in 1807 riot, 232–39;
  mentioned, 158, 205, 250
Maryland Constitution, 125–26
Maryland Insurance Company, 126
Maryland Journal, 70
Maryland Society for Promoting the
  Abolition of Slavery, 257, 269
Massachusetts: tariff of, 86
Master Tailors' Society, 212
Mattison, Aaron, 62
Mechanical Company: and mer-
  chant-mechanic coalition, 11;
  functions of, 54; formation of, 54;
  significance of title, 55; composition of, 55–56; merchant membership of, 56; and Stamp Act
  protest, 57; elects a mechanic
  president, 60, 61; mentioned, 53,
  62, 65, 66, 75, 76, 77, 81, 84, 93,
  98, 113, 171, 259
Mechanical Fire Company, 55, 62,
  75, 113, 171, 180, 247
Mechanical Society: formation of,
  109; functions of, 109–11; leadership of, 111–13; opposes 1793
  charter proposal, 128; dominates

United Committees, 129; supports unicameralism, 132–33;
  unites with Republican Society,
  136–37; and Neutrality Proclamation, 144–45; and militia in
  1973–94, 146–47; opposes Jay's
  Treaty, 154; opposes merchants'
  instructions, 155–57; supports
  Samuel Smith, 155–58; dissolution of, 172–73; mentioned, 102,
  118, 119, 121, 143, 149, 162, 166,
  171, 180, 181, 189, 192, 197, 202,
  207, 208, 228, 229, 236, 237, 238,
  247, 259, 279
Mechanical Volunteer Company:
  composition of, 61; formation of,
  61; officers of, 62; and James Cox,
  66; reorganization of, 146; mentioned, 53, 76, 77, 81, 84, 93, 98,
  113, 160, 161, 171, 229, 230
Mechanics: crafts of, 14; wealth distribution of, 15–16; at Old Town,
  21; definition of, 55; as president
  of Mechanical Company, 60–61;
  in Whig Club, 65; William Goddard's attacks on, 71; in 1788 parade, 93; ideology of, 93–94; in
  1788 assembly election, 95–96;
  unite with merchants, 136–37;
  and French Revolution, 144; in
  1793–94 militia, 146–48; in 1798
  militia demonstrations, 161;
  dominate Ward 7, 174; support
  Robert Steuart, 179–87; in bank
  constitutions, 194, 195, 196, 197;
  and charter reform, 201–2, 207;
  in 1807–8 militia, 229–31; and
  crowd leadership in 1807, 239–
  40; in 1809 parade, 242; in 1812
  riot, 247; as Methodist class leaders, 261–62; and republicanism,
  276
Mechanics' Bank: constitutions of,
  192–95; debate over, 195–98;
  officers of, 198–201; mentioned,
  112, 180, 207, 208, 247, 276, 278
Mennonites, 254
Merchants: dominate independence
  movement, 58–59; abandon nonimportation, 59; in Whig Club,
  66, 68–69; support 1793 charter